Just Exchange

Civilized societies promote cooperation, and few institutions do so more effectively than the law of contract. Contract law is thus an indispensable feature of modern liberal society and serves as a foundation for modern economic systems. Moreover, contract issues inform the worldwide debate over privatization, globalization and neo-liberalism: issues that ultimately begin when two people enter into a contract.

Now, for the first time, there is a comprehensive, eminently readable book designed to focus thinking in this area. This book bridges the gap between law and economics by confronting normative values that economists too often deem the preserve of moral philosophers. Contract theorists, on the other hand, are seldom in sympathy with economic efficiency norms. Since free bargaining continues to be regarded with suspicion by legal scholars who are hostile to private ordering, the proper scope of free bargaining remains in dispute. Combined with a recent renewed interest in this field, these academic tensions mean that the time is right for a reconsideration of contract law.

Drawing on scholarship from diverse fields and using illuminating and erudite examples, *Just Exchange* is entertaining as well as informative. Of interest to economists, lawyers, public policy makers and those interested in contract theory, this volume is a valuable overview of a vital intersection between legal studies and economics.

F.H. Buckley is Associate Dean and Foundation Professor at George Mason School of Law in Arlington, Virginia and Executive Director of the George Mason Law and Economics Center in Arlington, Virginia.

The Economics of Legal Relationships
Edited by Nick Mercuro
Michigan State University

Just Exchange
A theory of contract

F.H. Buckley

Routledge
Taylor & Francis Group

LONDON AND NEW YORK

First published 2005
by Routledge
2 Park Square, Milton Park, Abingdon, Oxon OX14 4RN

Simultaneously published in the USA and Canada
by Routledge
270 Madison Ave, New York, NY 10016

Routledge is an imprint of the Taylor & Francis Group

© 2005 F.H. Buckley

Typeset in Sabon by
Florence Production Ltd, Stoodleigh, Devon
Printed and bound in Great Britain by
TJ International Ltd, Padstow, Cornwall

British Library Cataloguing in Publication Data
A catalogue record for this book is available
from the British Library

Library of Congress Cataloging in Publication Data
A catalog record for this book has been requested

ISBN 0–415–70026–4 (hbk)
ISBN 0–415–70027–2 (pbk)

For Esther and Sarah

Contents

Illustrations

Figures

Tables

Preface

Civilized societies promote cooperation, and few institutions do so more effectively than the law of contract. Enforceable contracts permit the New Man, the foreigner, the outsider to overcome the barriers of a closed society that exclude him from participation in its commercial and political life. Through the right to contract he can make his way, without membership in a favored party, religion, tribe or gender. Contract law is thus an indispensable feature of modern liberal societies. Nor could a modern economy exist without legal remedies for breach of contract. Yet free bargaining continues to be regarded with suspicion by legal scholars who are hostile to private ordering. To be sure, some bargaining restrictions are desirable on any conception of private ordering, and many of these were worked out by common-law judges in the nineteenth century at the high tide of free contracting. However, the proper scope of free bargaining remains in dispute, and this invites a reconsideration of contract law.

Contract law is best understood from the perspective of law-and-economics, which is the touchstone of private law scholarship, a key that appears to unlock every door. What law-and-economics leaves out, however, is a normative understanding of contract law that explains why its rules should be designed to serve efficiency norms. Economists see their discipline as a positive one in which words such as "ought" do not belong, and most law-and-economics scholars eschew normative questions. The economist can tell us how incentives work but leaves it for moral philosophers to explain why we should employ them. For their part, philosophers are sometimes more than a little ambivalent about the value of private contracting. What has resulted is a bifurcated world, with grand theories assigned to philosophers and small details given over to economists. We are left with two cultures: a self-consciously "high" one of philosophy and its cognates of academic feminism and political theory, which is skeptical about promissory institutions; and a more modest one of economic incentives and narrow legal rules. This is not what economists call a stable equilibrium.

The economist's abandonment of the philosophical high ground has weakened legal scholarship. It lays the economic approach open to the objection that its normative implications are suspect at a more compelling, philosophical level. It also makes the study of contract law a good deal more confusing for the law student, who must inevitably ask why contracts should be enforced and whether it much matters how a case turns out.

My project is at the border of philosophy and economics. Scholars in the two disciplines pay too little attention to each other's work, and this has weakened both disciplines. Contract rules are best understood through the prism of economics; but many of the problems that law students encounter in their first year of law school are philosophical in nature. How can public law be distinguished from private law? When should people be permitted to choose for themselves, and when should the law impose an outcome? When should a judge substitute his opinion about the fairness of a contract for that of the parties? These are the perennial questions of law, and are posed again and again during a student's legal education, in Contracts and in many other courses as well.

When we make promises or form contracts we invoke an institution already present in our language or law. To understand contract law is, then, to understand how we might be governed by an institution. Similarly, the project of defending a regime of contract law requires an examination of the benefits and costs of the institution. In Part I, I argue that this implies a consequential moral theory that looks to the consequences of adopting an institution, and that only the law-and-economics account of contract law can do this. Rival accounts of contract law are unpersuasive because they fail to take account of its status as an institution. In Part II (Chapters 5–9) I consider arguments at the overlap of economics and philosophy for restricting free bargaining. Fetters on bargaining rights can serve efficiency goals, and are best understood from an economic perspective.

The law-and-economics account of contract law rests on a Humean foundation. Two hundred years before the seminal articles in law-and-economics, David Hume recognized that promising could only be understood as a convention or institution, and that promissory institutions crucially supply the trust that is essential when two or more people join hands to exploit an opportunity. To say that promising and contract law are institutions is to say that they must be evaluated on the basis of their consequences, and this implicates a consequentialist moral theory. The question is what purposes these institutions might serve: are they beneficial and do the benefits exceed any costs they might impose?

The most prominent form of consequentialism is a utilitarianism that promotes political institutions and legal rules that maximize human happiness. Because the economist's goal of maximizing welfare is so similar, the overlap between the (normative) economist and the utilitarian is close. Indeed, both disciplines are joined at the hip, since their nineteenth-century progenitors were often the very same people, notably Jeremy Bentham and John Stuart Mill.[1]

Utilitarian moral theories have attracted trenchant criticism, and this in part explains the reluctance of law-and-economics scholars to enquire too closely into the normative foundations of their discipline. I shall not review these objections, as I think them adequately answered by utilitarian theorists such as Richard Hare and Derek Parfit.[2] The least attractive feature of modern legal scholarship is the compulsion to reinvent the wheel, to assume (like Flaubert's Bouvard and Pécuchet) that the scholar's goal is to incorporate every piece of past learning. I will examine fundamental questions of contract theory, and leave it at that.

When I began this book I conceived of it as an intelligent person's guide to contract theory. I wished to discuss the foundational issues that contract law teachers would raise (usually without answering) in their classes. I did not want to assume a prior knowledge of economics, and therefore explain some basic concepts with which law-and-economics scholars are already familiar.

As I wrote the book, however, I realized that the problems of contract theory are some of the most profound questions of our day, or any day. I recalled that I was a student of Raymond Klibansky; who, in turn, was a student of Ferdinand Tönnies; who was a protégé of Friedrich Engels; so that only three generations separate the reader from the co-author of *The Communist Manifesto*. And from Engel's time (and before) to today, every major political thinker has had to wrestle with the morality of contract law and the contractarian view of society. These are the issues that inform the debate over privatization, globalization and neo-liberalism, issues on which great political battles are fought, issues that begin when two people wish to enter into a contract.

Several ideas in this book were first expressed in some of my articles. The basic argument in Chapters 1–4 was first made in "Paradox Lost," *Minn. L. Rev.* 72: 775 (1988). The analysis of substantive fairness in Chapter 8 was developed in "Three Theories of Substantive Fairness," *Hofstra L. Rev.* 19: 33 (1991). And some of the objections to free bargaining in Chapter 9 first saw light in "Culture and Liberty," *Quinnipiac Law Rev.* 19: 665 (2000).

I have not by any means tried to resolve every question about the economics of contract law, or even every question about paternalism, perfectionism and other restrictions on bargaining freedom. I discuss incommensurabilty and relative preferences only in passing. Students who wish to pursue some of these problems further might profitably consult two excellent books: Richard A. Epstein's *Skepticism and Freedom* (Chicago: University of Chicago Press, 2003), and Michael Trebilcock's *The Limits of Freedom of Contract* (Cambridge, MA: Harvard University Press, 1993). In addition, I have consciously omitted most overtly political questions, such as how free bargaining might be limited by antitrust and regulatory laws, or by any of the other ways in which the administrative state derogates from *laissez-faire* principles.

Nevertheless, I do have a point of view. I think free bargaining an indispensable tool in creating wealth and fostering liberal, democratic values. This is not to say that free contracting is a necessary feature of every society, and it is easy enough to imagine a private law system shorn of enforceable promises. One has only to turn the clock back to the sixteenth century, before *Slade*'s case crafted a remedy for breach of promise out of the action on the case.[3] What is harder to imagine is a counterfactual world without contract law and its cognates of partnerships, corporations, secured lending and bankruptcy, as well as franchise, joint venture, licensing and dealership agreements, and all of the other forms of business relationships, a pre-modern world found almost nowhere in the world today. Legal theories that question the value of enforceable promises are as irresponsible as political theories that would return us to a medieval economy and polity.

This book was written with the assistance of the George Mason Law and Economics Center, to which I am grateful (the more so since I am its Executive Director). I am grateful too to the George Mason law library, particularly Deborah Keene and Rae Best; to Elodie Taylor, who helped with the diagrams and formatting; to Jeff Smith, who provided valued research assistance; and to Deans Mark Grady and Dan Polsby for their long support. For their useful comments on portions of this book, I am indebted to Francesco Parisi, Walter Berns and to participants at workshops at the faculty of law at the University of Aix-en-Provence, New York University Department of Economics, Paris II, St Vincent's College and the Canadian Law and Economics Association annual meeting. I owe a special obligation to Bertrand Lemennicier, who invited me to spend two terms at the Sorbonne as a visiting professor. I am extremely grateful to Terry Clague, Robert Langham and Mike Wendling at Routledge, and to Donna Gregory and Rachel Hutchings at Florence Production Ltd, for their most valuable assistance. Finally, Esther Goldberg read the book closely and gave invaluable editorial assistance, and for this I am more than grateful.

Part I

The enforcement of contracts

1 The promising game

A promise would not be intelligible before human conventions had established it.

David Hume

Contracts, and the promises from which they are formed, are institutions. By that, I mean that they could not exist but for a convention in our laws and language that gives them meaning. To understand contracting and promising, we must therefore begin by asking how an institution might give rise to obligations that bind its participants.

The rules of contract law are pragmatic, and respond to the real costs and benefits of joint production. As such, they are most easily grasped through the prism of economics. But to understand the institution of contract law, one must begin not with economics but with ontology.

Ontology is the study of being, of how the world is and how facts exist. For most of us, the idea that being might be a philosophical puzzle will seem very odd. Consider, for example, the simple statement:

(1) The man hit the ball over the fence.

There is nothing mysterious about this. We understand that man, ball and fence exist, in a certain relation, whether or not the observer is there to see them, and whether or not a language exists in which the act of hitting a ball may be described and understood. Suppose that, in a Tower of Babel moment, we lost the ability to communicate with each other, so that sentence (1) could not be understood in any language. Nevertheless, the man could still repeat the act of hitting the ball over the fence.

But now consider the deceptively similar statement:

(2) The Expos' right fielder hit a home run.

While (2) might seem to resemble (1), the two statements are radically different, for in (2) the act is described as a move in a game. Following

John Searle, I call (1) a *brute statement* and (2) an *institutional statement*.[1] In turn, the two kinds of statements refer to two kinds of facts: brute and institutional.

Institutional statements are parasitic upon brute ones (as are institutional facts upon brute ones). For every institutional statement there is a brute statement that makes the same claim about the way the world is. I once brought a Ugandan student to an Expos baseball game, and found myself reduced to describing the action through brute statements, since right fielders and home runs mean nothing to those who are unfamiliar with the institution of baseball. Nevertheless, for everything that happened on the field I could always tell my friend what had happened, without referring to the rules of the game. (When runners cross the plate the number on the board increases.) Through brute statements we can describe everything that happens in a game – except why any of it is of interest to us.

Institutional statements are meaningless absent a convention or institution that endows them with sense. All such statements are of the form:

x counts for y in a game Θ

where x is a brute fact, y an institutional fact, and Θ a game, convention or institution that transforms brute into institutional facts. Thus, the game of baseball transforms a ball hit over a fence into a home run.

Since institutional facts are ancillary to background brute facts, one might think them uncommon. But that would be wrong, for the structure of our everyday life is shot through with institutions and conventions. Consider the following statements, both of which are institutional:

(3) Stealing this book is illegal.
(4) This book costs $19.95.

Statement (3) assumes the existence of a state with a criminal code that imposes a penalty for theft, and with rules that specify who is bound by the laws of the state and how laws are made. It also assumes a legal institution of property, in which certain things are linked to certain people who possess rights over them. Further, it assumes that the bookseller possesses such property rights over the book; and if the bookseller is incorporated it assumes that the corporation is properly formed. Statement (4) makes the additional assumption that, under the laws of the particular state, there is such a thing as legal tender and that owners may set prices and sell things according to the state's law of sale of goods. Both statements assume several institutional facts.

It is sometimes difficult to distinguish between brute and institutional facts. Because institutional facts have a social reality and usually depend upon a convention among a group of people, a first cut might be to ask whether a Robinson Crusoe might encounter them on his desert island. Crusoe cannot play baseball since the game cannot be played alone. He can hit a ball, however, and this is a brute fact. Similarly, Crusoe can tell when he is awake and thinking about a particular thing, and consciousness is also a brute fact. Unlike the game of baseball, the fact that I am conscious does not depend on the existence of a convention. We might enter into a compact that I not feel anything when I pinch myself, but were I to test this I would encounter a brute fact.

However, the Crusoe standard does not provide a satisfactory criterion of brute and institutional facts. A solitary person might encounter an institutional fact, as Crusoe would if he played a game of solitaire, observing the rules he remembered before he was abandoned, or even inventing new ones. Moreover, the existence of other people is a brute and not an institutional fact, as is the fact that they are conscious (which philosophers call the "other minds" problem). Other people's consciousness is obviously a special kind of brute fact, and quite different from the existence of baseballs, which don't care about people. Nevertheless, both are brute facts. Otherwise a convention might establish that a certain class of people does not feel things as we do and that we might therefore do what we want with them. Turning a brute into an institutional fact in this way is often a prelude to barbarism, and is ruled out by both morality and ontology. The compact changes nothing and does not excuse misbehavior to the class.

There are differences between the two kinds of brute facts, for we do not talk about consciousness as we do about inanimate objects. To ask "Is he conscious?" in a hospital is to ask, for example, whether a patient can hear us. To ask "Is that a real ball?" is to pose a different set of questions, for example, "Is it made of papier-mâché?" or "Is it a holograph?" But once again the answer to these questions does not depend on a social convention about consciousness or balls.

If consciousness is a brute fact, so too are the intentions one might form with respect to things. All consciousness is consciousness about something – about how it looks, what it does, or what I mean to do with it. My intention to hit the ball tomorrow is a brute fact, as is the purpose I form to frighten some birds by throwing the ball at them (as baseball player Dave Winfield once did, more successfully than he had wished). The function that a ball serves for me (to bounce against a wall or to frighten birds) is also a brute fact that need not implicate the existence of a social convention.

The intentions I form with respect to other people might also be brute facts. I might decide to give you the ball, for example, and whether I have that intention or not is a brute fact. While others might sometimes find it difficult to gauge my intentions, I at least know them, and when questioned might either report them truthfully or lie about them. And when I lie about them, my intentions might sometimes be proven in court. In response to the medieval judge who said, "The devil himself knoweth not the mind of man,"[2] a more pragmatic nineteenth-century jurist responded that the state of a man's mind is as much a fact as the state of his digestion.[3] We might therefore show that a man intended to steal a book in spite of his protestations of innocence. ("Goodness! What was *that* doing in my pocket?")

If my intentions with respect to other people may be a matter of brute fact, so too are the intentions others might have about me. For example, I might form an intention in common with another to take a book from a store. I will take it from the shelf when no one is looking and he will put it in his bag. Were we to describe the taking as theft we would have strayed into the realm of institutional facts, but our joint intention to take the book is a brute fact even though both of our intentions are conditional upon the other's participation in the taking.

I have finessed a major problem: how might the two participants communicate their intentions to each other without a language in which to do so? And a language must implicate institutional facts, since it requires a convention in which meanings are assigned to words. Language is like a game in which the speech acts we hear as words and sentences "count" as meaningful utterances, just as hitting a ball over a fence counts as a home run.

For now, however, I suppose that the joint plans are simple and that the parties may cooperate without language. After all, my dog plays fetch with me, having learned that the game goes better when she returns with the ball and drops it at my feet. Similarly, evolutionary biologists describe how complex patterns of cooperation might arise between different species, as if by contract, without the use of any language.

I must also qualify the distinction I made between brute and institutional statements. Since a brute statement is expressed in a language, it assumes the existence of an institution. Nevertheless, there is still a difference between the two kinds of statements. A brute statement states a brute fact, and the truth or falsity of a brute fact does not depend on the existence of an institution. If I tell you that I have hit the ball, you cannot understand me without the institution of a common language. However, if you have seen me do it, you can understand that I have hit the ball without relying on an institution.

This analysis helpfully reveals a misunderstanding by John Searle. Searle argues that the kind of multi-party joint intentions or understandings that I have described are qualitatively different from an aggregation of individual intentions. At some point (just when is not clear) we pass from individual to "collective" rationality, from brute to institutional facts. Otherwise, says Searle, we would require an extraordinary number of joint intentions when more than a few people are involved. There might even be an infinite regress in which my beliefs are contingent on your beliefs, which are contingent on my beliefs about your beliefs, and so on. John Maynard Keynes' metaphor for the stock market is something like this. Since stock prices depend on the valuation others place on the stock, the aggregation of information on Wall Street is like a beauty contest in which the trick is to pick not who you think is the prettiest girl, but who you think others will think is the prettiest girl, and who they think you think is the prettiest; and some may play the game at the fourth or fifth level. To solve this difficulty, suggests Searle, we might posit a collective understanding about beauty or market prices.

This is clearly wrong. There is no collective mind that gives meaning to joint intentions or standards of beauty, or makes them understandable. The collective mind fallacy appears to stem from a misreading of F.A. Hayek's explanation of how market prices reflect far more information than that possessed by any individual trader or planner. The more complex and difficult the information, the greater the advantage of markets over individuals, who need to know very little market information for markets to work.[4] However, there is no super-rational group mind, nor a collective intention that is anything other than the sum of individual intentions. The market price quoted on the financial pages of a newspaper is simply derived from the trades of a large number of individual buyers and sellers. If we had to speak of some more general collective intention in the *n*-person case, we would also have to do so in the two-person case, and no two people could form a joint intention to take a book without a fuzzy collective intention to back them up.

What is behind the collective intention fallacy is the mistaken belief that joint activities would be impossible without a common understanding that is different from the parties' individual beliefs. But individual beliefs are all the parties need to coordinate joint activities. Before forming his plans, all that each need do is apply a discount factor against the possibility that the other party will get cold feet. Where I expect the joint project will fall apart, I might value it at a fraction of its worth as a sure thing. With more participants there is a difference in complexity but not in quality. The joint intentions of a group of people are brute facts, so long as no institution (such as language) is invoked. And if one is, we are in the realm of institutional facts, even if only one person plays the game.

How to create a game

The joint intentions and understandings that groups of people might form may become extremely complex, and the best example of this is the creation of a social convention or game. When parties play a game, they coordinate their behavior in a special way, by agreeing to be bound by a set of rules. Without rules there is no game.

We can imagine something like a game, in which the actions of the parties follow a regular pattern. For example, we might think of Abner

Doubleday (the reputed inventor of baseball) describing the game (as sportswriters often do) as a kind of dance. Alternatively, he might be thought to have offered predictions about how the parties would move. These would all be brute facts. But none of this would capture the idea of playing a game.

Playing a game means following rules. A group of 18 individuals who gather in one place with the private intentions of adhering to Doubleday's instructions do not play baseball unless they also agree to observe its rules. Otherwise we could not complain if a batter decided halfway through to seek four strikes from the pitcher. One cannot break the rules unless one is playing a game, and one is not playing a game unless something counts as breaking the rules.

When we speak of playing a game we move from brute to institutional fact. It is a brute fact that an individual intends to act in a certain way (in accordance with the instructions for baseball), and it is equally a brute fact when this intention is contingent on 17 other people having the same intention. But playing a game is more than this, for it requires an agreement that certain behavior is prescribed, that people are supposed to act in a certain way.

The difference may be expressed by invoking the canonical distinction between rules and regularities. Rules are normative, for they tell us what we ought to do. Regularities are non-normative. Kant might have taken a stroll at the same hour each day, so regularly that housewives set their clocks by him, but he was under no requirement to do so. There was no rule that bound him to take a walk. This is not to say that normative rules must have a specifically moral force. There is a requirement in baseball that runners must touch each base before proceeding to the next, but the runner is not morally compelled to do so. Nevertheless, failure to touch a base is more than irregular behavior. It is the breach of a rule.

Distinguishing between rules and regularities helps to dispel the confusion surrounding the collective rationality fallacy that we saw in the last section. Searle thought that a collective understanding that something serves as money is necessary before it can serve as a medium of exchange. This cannot be right, since the practice of accepting cigarettes as a form of currency in prisoner of war camps was a matter of brute and not institutional fact. There was no rule that cigarettes served as legal tender, but only a regularity which prisoners learned by observing how they traded. However, when a state adopts a currency as legal tender this is an institutional fact. Not merely have people accepted paper currency as money, but there is a rule backed by a state that they must do so.

Normativity is the glue that turns a collaborative effort into a game. Norms tell people how to behave, and all games do this, by specifying what can and what cannot be done within the rules of the game. Ludwig Wittgenstein thought that there is no special content to the idea of games, but only a series of family resemblances among similar games. There are games like hockey and soccer and baseball, which in one way or another may resemble each other, but nothing that is common to them all. Against this, Searle argues that a game consists of "a series of attempts to overcome certain obstacles that have been created for the purpose of trying to overcome them. Each side in the game tries to overcome the obstacles and prevent the other side from overcoming them."[5] But what about games without obstacles or teams, like solitaire? Nevertheless, there is something that all games have in common, if they are games, and that is a set of rules that specify how the game is to be played. Hitting a tennis ball against a wall is not a game because it has no rules and nothing counts as "not playing the game." However, when I introduce bounds and a requirement that I hit the ball before the second bounce, I have transformed mere play into a game.

Like games, all institutions specify a set of rules that tell us when an action conforms or does not conform to its norms. This is obviously so for the institution of language, with its rules for spelling and grammar. There is such a thing as correct English or French, even if the rules of a language might on occasion be so imprecise or poorly followed that they shade into regularities (for example, the shall–will distinction in English, which not one person in a hundred observes). When this happens, when a usage is a regularity and not a rule, it sheds its normative force and we are in the realm of brute and not institutional facts.

For some institutions the rules assume a moral force, for others not. For the institution that is the state, with its rules against treason and theft, the rules invoke deep moral duties; but for baseball and language games there is no moral lapse on a breach of the rules. The difference arises exogenously, from the moral significance of the institution when seen from the outside. Is the institution a valuable one that promotes good ends? If not, the institution cannot bootstrap up the moral significance of its rules by specifying that breach is immoral.

If normativity is a special feature of institutions, it does not follow that all norms assume a background institution. Some kinds of rules, called *regulative* rules, can be understood without reference to an institution. One example is the prohibition of murder, which has nothing to do with conventions about what counts as human life. That is why the debate over abortion is so vexed, and why efforts to solve the issue through a social convention about what counts as life are bound to fail. People might disagree about whether abortion is wrong, but for those who oppose it a law or social understanding that life begins only at birth changes nothing, and it shows a primitive moral sense to think otherwise. Similarly, we cannot expect those who believe that life begins at some later point to change their views with a convention that life begins at conception. People who say "murder is wrong but that is simply how we feel about things over here" show that they do not understand how moral discourse works.

Table 1.1 Institutional and non-institutional

	Institutional	Non-institutional
Facts	Institutional	Brute
Statements	Institutional	Brute
Rules	Institutional	Regulative

It is sometimes difficult to distinguish regulative from institutional rules. Take property rules, for example. Locke's defense of property rights in his *Second Treatise of Government* ascribed a regulative status to property rights as natural rights. Under this view, however, it is difficult to explain why property law protects some forms of ownership but not others. While Lockean rights would seem to apply to every species of thing, property rights in patents are recognized only for a limited period of time. And some kinds of intellectual assets, such as a web site, have no property protection at all. If you laboriously assemble a web site around the paintings of a famous long-dead artist, I can expropriate the pictures without your permission. So viewed, the difference is simply one of legal institutions and a matter of institutional and not regulative rules.

The seventeenth-century debate over the divine right of kings might also be seen as one over regulative and institutional rules. If kings have a natural or divinely sanctioned right to govern, as Robert Filmer thought, then our duty of allegiance to them would be regulative. These antique views did not survive the drubbing they took in Locke's *First Treatise*, and his *Second Treatise* went on to espouse an institutional theory of the state as the product of a social contract or convention.

Regulative rules are moral injunctions. Since they apply to everyone without regard to background institutions, they must be something more than merely customary or social rules, such as the rules of etiquette. This might explain why Filmer defended the absurd idea of a regulative divine right of kings with such passion: he must have thought that a merely institutional allegiance could too easily be erased, as had happened in the English Civil War. In walking away from an institution, one also walks from its institutional rules. A similar explanation might underlie the recent revival of interest in regulative natural laws. A non-natural set of institutional rules might be thought to provide an insufficient barrier to a moral relativism that permits one to pick and choose ethical rules.

Such efforts to bootstrap institutional into regulative rules are bound to fail. First, the difference between institutional and regulative rules depends on whether they assume a background convention, and cannot be made to turn on strategic concerns such as the desire to lever up a moral code. Moral relativism might indeed be troubling, but that cannot change the status of a rule from an institutional to a regulative one. Second, the moral force of an institutional rule might be as strong as that of a regulative rule. The prohibition of treason is institutional, as it assumes the existence of governmental institutions. Yet, treason is a far more serious moral problem than regulative rules against bopping strangers on the head with a pillow.

There are two differences between regulative and institutional rules. First, regulative rules may be understood without the need for a background institution. Second, regulative rules bind all of us, without regard to a relationship with any institution. By contrast, the rules of a particular institution bind only one who is linked to it in such a way as to make it *his* rule to follow. Otherwise the institution binds others, but not him. In *R. v. Joyce*,[6] for example, the accused ("Lord Haw-Haw") broadcast Nazi propaganda to England from Germany during the Second World War. When captured by the British in 1945 he was tried for treason and sentenced to death. On appeal, the House of Lords affirmed the sentence, even though Joyce's counsel had raised grave doubts that Joyce owed any allegiance to Great Britain. Joyce had been born in Ireland before its independence and fought for the Black and Tans. He subsequently emigrated to America where he became a naturalized citizen. His only act acknowledging any tie to Britain had been to apply for a British passport before the war. Nevertheless, the court held that this was enough to support a duty of allegiance to Britain and a sentence of treason in a British court, and Joyce was executed. While no one mourned his death, the link between Joyce and Britain was so tenuous that his execution resembled legalized murder. If Joyce was not subject to British institutions, British courts had no right to try and to hang him.

In exceptional cases, an institutional rule may trump a regulative one. Those who think capital punishment justified assert that the regulative prohibition of murder does not extend to the death penalty, when the institutional safeguards of criminal procedure are followed. This was also what Pascal had in mind when he wondered how it was that a charge of murder might depend on which side of the sea one lived: when Spaniards kill Spaniards it is murder; when Frenchmen kill Spaniards in wartime they do so in the exercise of a supervening institutional duty.[7] But because these cases are exceptional they are usually hemmed in with stringent procedural safeguards, such as presumptions of innocence and declarations of war. In any event, to say that a case is exceptional is to say that it provides little information about ordinary cases.

There is a special kind of institutional rule, called a *constitutive* rule, through which subsidiary games or institutions are created.[8] For example, the institution called the State of Virginia may, under a constitutive Corporations Code, create institutions called corporations, whose constitutive charters provide for Boards of Directors, whose constitutive resolutions may create executive committees; and so on. Logically, there is no limit to the number of subsidiary institutions that might be created in this way.

While constitutive rules create institutions, not every institution is created through a constitutive rule. Institutions might arise spontaneously, without the need for a rule-maker or a rule-making institution. Otherwise we would encounter an infinite regress in a search for the first rule-maker (unless, perhaps, one could find the kind of Unmoved Mover that divine right theorists sought). Many of our most fundamental institutions, such as language and markets, are simply too complex to have issued from a single directing mind. That was Frederic Bastiat's point, in satirizing dirigiste impulses. "What a miracle it is that Paris is fed," he said. All that food moving through the stalls at Les Halles, and no grand planner!

The twentieth century was not kind to expert planners, and today few people would subscribe to these views. Instead, the Hayekian insight that better information is produced by markets than by a single price-setter is now everywhere conceded. Similarly, the English language grows without the need for an English Academy to rule upon words, and the Internet is beyond the power of a single individual to plan. The contrary view was aptly characterized as the planner's "fatal conceit" by Hayek.[9]

It is, therefore, unnecessary to suppose that every institution stands in need of a supporting constitutive rule and a corresponding rule-maker. We need not explain how it is that the English language exists, or how we have come to associate a particular word with a particular thing or event. We need not have recourse to a social contract or a lawgiver like Sparta's Lycurgus to explain how a state and its laws come into existence. Our search for higher and higher constitutive rules must at last come to an end. Thus, the Virginia Corporations Code is an institution created by the constitutive rules of the State of Virginia, which as a sovereign state is not itself the creature of a more fundamental institution. The search for a principle of legitimacy must always stop somewhere, in the social acceptance of a deep institution, such as the State of Virginia or the institution of promising.

Because fundamental institutions require a degree of general acceptance before they can become social conventions, their existence at times is uncertain. This is particularly the case when one institution replaces another. There is usually no clear dividing line, and subsequent efforts to find one often look like special pleading. For example, on the Whig interpretation of the Glorious Revolution, King James II left England on some whim, and as the Crown was vacant Parliament offered it to William and Mary. What happened, of course, was that one king fled in the face of an invading army and a new king seized the crown. Blackstone embraced the Whig view of the events of 1688, but only as a legal fiction, for he candidly admitted that one cannot find a way to account for a revolution from within the confines of an existing legal regime. The revolution that sweeps away a prior regime logically sweeps away anything within the *Ancien Régime* that might justify it. In extreme cases, as on the collapse of communism, a revolution might be justified from without as a response to an oppressive regime; but it cannot be explained from within as a legally sanctioned constitutional reform. Changes in the most fundamental institutions must come through social acceptance, which alone accords legitimacy to them. And this is apt to be a slow process. Even in Blackstone's day, the young men of Oxford wore the white rose to symbolize their attachment to the Jacobite pretender.

Hume on promising

The distinction between brute and institutional facts is fundamental. Curiously, however, academic deconstructionists mistake brute facts for socially constructed institutional facts. And some contract theorists make the opposite mistake of confusing the institutional rules of contract law for regulative rules. This view of contract law cannot survive a study of Hume's analysis of promising as a convention.

Deconstructionism asserts that our understanding of the world is a social construct and derived from our language. While we experience the world directly through our senses, we understand it only through language. Our senses give us fleeting glimpses of the world; our language interprets these experiences and gives content to them. Each word leads to another word, in an endless circle, without ever coming to rest in reality or a determinate meaning. Every meaning is arbitrary, and for every interpretation there is an equal and opposite counter-interpretation. How we see the world, therefore, depends on our language, which, in turn, is embedded in power structures and ideologies.

Deconstructionism was wonderfully lampooned by physicist Alan Sokal. If physical reality is a social construct, the physicist must take a back seat to the political and literary theorist in explaining hard science, and this was just what a scholarly deconstructionist journal, *Social Text*, asserted. Sokal submitted a hilarious send-up of deconstructionism to the journal, full of obsequious bouquets for its editors and *ad hominem* attacks on their enemies.[10] He compared the axiom of choice in set theory to the pro-choice abortion rights movement; he appended four footnotes after a single, lonely comma; and he described the geometric term π, which one learns is a constant in third grade, as a variable. The wonderful thing about the parody was that Sokal invented nothing: he simply presented what the leading deconstructionists had asserted, and had the wit to see that it was ludicrous. Needless to say, the editors of *Social Text* were not amused when it all came out.

Some contract theorists of a Kantian stripe make the reverse error, taking an institutional as a regulative rule. They purport to explain promising on a theory of abstract natural right, while ignoring its conventional nature. But no one has yet provided a satisfactory reply to David Hume's analysis of promising as an institution. In his *Treatise on Human Nature*, Hume argued that promising and contract law could not be understood absent background institutions or created out of nothing where the institutions do not exist. "A promise wou'd not be intelligible," said Hume, "before human conventions had establish'd it."[11] Contract law rests upon a convention or institution and can never be turned into a system of regulative rules.[12]

Without a background institution of promising, said Hume, two would-be bargainers could not create it. To test this, let us examine a non-promissory society, the Pacific island of Tonga that lies east of Fiji and south of Samoa. Apparently there is nothing in the Tonganese language that means "promise."[13] There is something like "I intend to do X," but nothing like "I promise to do X." Tonganese society places great importance on the maintenance of personal relationships and on reciprocal acts of assistance. A Tonganese "promise" recognizes a bond of solidarity, with the expression of a willingness to assist in the future evidencing a present desire to preserve a relationship. But the future is uncertain, and if performance becomes difficult it may be omitted without moral sanction. "That was then," a Tonganese promisor might say. "Now is now."

The Tonganese concept of promising would seem a feature of most primitive societies. Sir Henry Maine reported that:

> no trustworthy primitive record can be read without perceiving that the habit of mind which induces us to make good a promise is as yet imperfectly developed, and that acts of flagrant perfidy are often mentioned without blame and sometimes described with approbation.[14]

The trickster, like the wily Ulysses, is often the hero of the piece. Over time, a convention that promise-breaking is a fault might develop as bargaining becomes more profitable. But until then our institution of promising is not to be found.

A society without promising might thus exist. More importantly, whether or not Tonganese "promises" differ from our own, we can imagine a society that lacks a word for promises. Through a thought-experiment, we might erase the word from our language and then pose Hume's question: how can promising be created when it does not already exist?

Hume asserted that one cannot create the institution of promising on one's own. Against this, "will" theorists have argued that a special mental act – the "act of will" – might ground the obligation to perform. But this would seem to come down to nothing more than a private resolution, possibly accompanied by teeth-clenching. Now, a person who forms such a resolution might intend to be bound, and might even perform out of what he perceives as a sense of duty. Hume's point, however, is that the resolution does not generate an *obligation* to perform. Thinking oneself bound is not the same thing as being bound to perform.

What the institution of promising crucially supplies is an obligation. Like other games, the promising-game is normative, and specifies what counts as a breach of the rules. Unlike brute statements of intention, promises create prima facie obligations, in the sense that the promisor ought to perform unless he can successfully plead an excuse (like mistake). With a statement of intention or resolution a person reserves the freedom to change his mind; but it is a contradiction to say "I promise to do X but am under no obligation to do so." Such a person is either not promising or does not understand what it means to promise.

Without a background convention, the promisor is driven within himself if he seeks to create a promise. As Hume noted, however, will theorists are unable to provide a phenomenological account of what it means to promise. There is no mental act that corresponds to promising, from which one can create a self-generated promise. I cannot say "I intend to do X," silently willing a duty to perform, and make an obligation stick. Nor can two parties mutually bind themselves through mutual statements of intention, accompanied by the most ferocious private acts of will, and turn this into a contract. Their resolutions, intentions and acts of will are all brute facts; but promising is an institution and the act of promising is an institutional fact which cannot be self-created.

A private act of will is neither a sufficient nor a necessary condition of promising. It is not a sufficient condition because a private mental act of "promising" is not binding without a public act that others may recognize. And it is not a necessary condition because (unless the promisor is unconscious or incapacitated) a promise unaccompanied by a particular mental act is still a promise. Under the "objective" theory of contract, the promisor's private reservations or equivocations do not excuse non-performance when a reasonable observer would have concluded that a promise had been made. By upholding the promise, the court "exercises its jurisdiction for the enforcement of the truth, and makes a man's acts square with his words."[15] Otherwise, the parties would drastically scale back their reliance upon promises, and the benefit of the institution would be lost. As J.L. Austin noted, "accuracy and morality alike are on the same side as the plain saying that *our word is our bond*."[16]

Does anything change when the interior act is vocalized? The promisor might say "I intend to do X and you get to blame me if I fail to perform." Similarly, where no institution of contracting exists, two parties might seek to make a contract through mutual statements of intention and willingness to be bound. Though institutions of promising and contracts are absent in their society, the idea of moral guilt does exist. Can the parties invoke a general sense of duty and attach it to their statements? Joseph Raz has argued they can,[17] but this seems wrong. Since contractual obligations are institutional, they cannot be self-generated by a brute intention or resolution. I cannot say that "I intend to visit New York and you can blame me if I don't," and thereby create an obligation to do so. You might possibly fault me for being weak-willed if I fail to carry through any of my resolutions, but what I will not have done is breached an obligation to you.

Were Raz correct, I should be able to attach the idea of personal guilt to an act without invoking the institution of promising. I should be able to say that "I don't promise to do X, but I intend to do so and you get to blame me if I don't." However, this is a self-contradictory statement. Promises, and only promises, create obligations.

The idea behind private resolutions, like those made on New Year's Day, is that there are moral requirements I owe to myself if I am to flourish and achieve a worthy goal in life. These are regulative requirements and have nothing to do with promising, unless the intention is crystallized by invoking the convention of promising. For example, I might promise my wife to spend more time with my family. But this is to make a promise to her, and before then no obligation exists. Nor can I make a private "promise" to myself that is anything other than a private resolution.

In exceptional circumstances, promises might serve as evidence of the existence of a regulative duty. For example, a man who is severely injured while saving another's life has a claim against him for his injury. At common law, the claim sounds in restitution or quasi-contract rather than contract. It arises because one party has been enriched and another impoverished and it would be unjust not to redress the balance. This implies a non-institutional regulative requirement, and need not rest on a promise. Nevertheless, the restitutionary claim is sometimes strengthened if the rescued man promised the salvor a reward. What the promise supplies is evidence that the salvor did effect a rescue. It also quantifies what a reasonable recovery might be.[18] In such cases, regulative duties overlap with promissory obligations.

A leading modern contract theorist, Patrick Atiyah, would have turned the exception into the rule. In *Promises, Morals, and Law,*[19] Atiyah argued that promises and contracts do not in themselves give rise to a moral obligation. At best, he said, they certify the existence of a prior duty and do not create a new liability where none existed before. When I promise to support a charity the promise does not create the obligation, according to Atiyah. Instead, the duty arises because the charity is worthy of support, with or without a promise. This assumes a world thick with background duties, where everything is tort or criminal law and nothing is contract law, and betrays a fundamental misunderstanding of promissory institutions. It takes promises to be content-dependent, with the obligation arising from the desirability of the thing promised. But it is just the opposite: promises are content-independent.[20] The obligation arises from the fact of promising and not from the content of the promise. Until I make a promise to do X, I am ordinarily free to do X or not-X, as I please. It is only in the exceptional case that I was already required to do (or forebear from doing) one of them, under a regulative rule. More troubling than the philosophical confusion is Atiyah's deeply illiberal vision of society. If there is nothing to promise about, there is nothing to choose. In such a world, that which is not mandatory is prohibited.

The principle of fidelity

We have seen that the act of promising or contracting is unintelligible absent a background institution that endows it with meaning. The rules of promising are institutional and can only be understood as part of a language-game. But something more than an institution is needed before its rules bind anyone. Unless it can be connected to people, an institution and its rules must be morally indifferent, like the games of planet Pluto.

Consider the analogy to political obligation. Suppose that Norway may be characterized as a perfectly just society. Even so, it does not follow that, as a Canadian, I have a duty of allegiance to Norway.[21] Similarly, a society may have a convention that wearing a hat has a particular moral significance. If, hatted, I visit the society, a resident might claim that the convention has been invoked. Nevertheless, I might legitimately object that the convention does not bind foreigners, without some further principle that visitors are somehow bound by its rules. Nor can the foreigner commit treason against Norway, any more than he can against Pluto.

An alien is not bound to obey the laws of a foreign state unless a duty of allegiance may be invoked. Now, if this is so for foreigners, it is also the case for natives. (When does one stop being a foreigner?) In the same way, no one is bound by a convention merely because he performed an act that generates obligations according to the convention. Instead, one must ask what it is about the convention that makes it *his* convention to follow. We need a *principle of fidelity* that yokes a person to an institution before its rules can be said to bind him.[22]

If we could dispense with the need for a principle of fidelity, we might derive a promissory obligation from the mere fact of promising. That is, we might derive a normative "ought" from an existential "is," as John Searle has argued[23]:

(1) Promising is an institution in our society;
(2) It is the case that John has promised to do X;
(3) Therefore John ought to perform X.

However, to say that promising is an institution in our society is not to say that we are bound by its rules. Before we can reach the conclusion in (3), we first need a principle of fidelity under which those who invoke the institution are bound by it. Only then does an obligation arise, as in the following syllogism:

(4) Everyone who promises ought to perform his promise;
(5) John has promised to do X;
(6) Therefore John ought to perform X.

Unlike statement (1), statement (4) is a rule of fidelity that binds promisors to the institution of promising. And unlike existential statement

(1), statement (4) is normative, so that the second syllogism derives a normative conclusion from a normative premise. Absent a principle of fidelity, Searle's attempt to derive an "ought" from an "is" (called the "naturalistic fallacy") in the first syllogism fails.[24]

Searle argued that the fact of promising is sufficient to create an obligation, when the institution's internal rules are invoked. But without an external principle of fidelity that links the institution to people, promisors owe no allegiance to the institution or any duty to abide by its rules. To see this, consider the case of dueling, another institution with its own elaborate rules. The institution was highly inefficient, to be sure, but on Searle's analysis that changes nothing. Accordingly, Searle would have us think that Abraham Lincoln was at fault when he accepted a challenge and elected to fight with broadswords at 50 paces. While his opponent glowered furiously, Lincoln sat on a log at a safe distance away and twirled his sword in the air. Not merely was this a breach of the rules, but the whole point was to draw ridicule upon them. Yet, as the institution was immoral and did not deserve our respect, Lincoln's conduct was anything but blameworthy.

To satisfy the requirement of fidelity, two things are required. First, the institution's internal rules must specify that a participant is bound to adhere to it. That is, he must be on its membership list. Second, the participant must be morally bound to adhere to the rules under a fidelity duty. In Lincoln's case, the first requirement was satisfied since the *Codo duello* directed him to participate in the duel. However, the second requirement failed since Lincoln was permitted to opt out of the institution. When participants have exit rights, the requirement of fidelity does not arise.

The example of dueling illustrates how another attempt to circumvent the principle of fidelity fails. Kant argued that the rule that one ought to obey one's promises was a postulate of pure reason, like the rule that one should never lie.[25] If people were permitted to lie, then no one would rely on a factual statement and the institution of truth-telling would disappear; and if people were permitted to promise and thereafter fail to perform, the institution of promising would disappear, as promisors could no longer be trusted. But as John Stuart Mill noted, all this shows is that institutions are weakened when parties are given unilateral exit rights.[26] It does not establish that the background institution is valuable, or that it matters whether it survives.

What Kant recognized is that moral rules are universalizable, in the sense that to say that John should do X is to say that everyone similarly situated should do X. But if normativity implies universalizability, it does not follow that universalizability implies normativity. To say that an injunction can be stated as a universal rule does not endow it with normative force, and dueling is an example of this.

Fidelity rules cannot be institutional rules, or else we would encounter an infinite regress. If some higher institution bound us to obey the rules of promissory conventions, how were we bound to that higher institution? Fidelity rules therefore resemble regulative rules, since the source of the duty does not depend on a convention. However, fidelity rules are not regulative either, since they cannot be understood without reference to a background institution. There are, therefore, three kinds of rules: institutional, regulative and fidelity rules which, in part, resemble the other two kinds of rules.

A lawyer might too easily imagine that the institutional and fidelity rules of a game are precise and unalterable. To see this, consider whether it is possible to play baseball without a center fielder. When I played center field in Little League I noticed that the right fielder played left and the left fielder played right – which was fine unless the ball went up the middle towards me. I am inclined to think that the game would have gone on had I failed to show up. Similarly, when the game is played with an extra designated hitter, ten men a side American-League style, it is still baseball. (It's just less interesting.) Before the rules can be altered, however, one must invoke a convention that *ex ante* rule changes are permissible if everyone agrees. That is, institutional rules may be altered by invoking the institutions of promise and contract. Even then, there comes a point when the change is so drastic that one can no longer be said to be playing the game. We might agree that the pitcher can run up to the mound from second base and must pitch straight-arm, but that wouldn't be baseball. It would be cricket.

Fidelity requirements resemble the membership rules of an institution, since both link the institution to its members. But fidelity requirements add a crucial non-institutional dimension. What links me to an institution must be something outside the institution.[27] Otherwise, an institution might bind a stranger simply by adding him to its membership rolls, and that cannot be right. I cannot be made to pay dues to a club if I have not agreed to become a member.

By promising, then, I satisfy both the membership rules of an institution as well as the fidelity requirements that link me to it. The institution regards me as a member, under its institutional rules; and it is right to do so, under just fidelity requirements. How this might work in the case of contract law is a subject we take up in Chapter 4.

The rules of an institution are like the domestic laws of a country, which bind a person if the principle of fidelity is satisfied. In this sense, fidelity rules resemble the law of jurisdiction in private international law. Before domestic laws bind one, what is needed is something different from domestic laws, which lawyers call private international law: *international* because it is not domestic; and *private* because it deals with the relations between individuals and a state, and not the transactions between sovereign states that are the stuff of public international law.

The core question of private international law is when an individual or matter is subject to the laws of a particular state. Do the criminal laws of the US apply to its citizens when they smoke marijuana on a foreign ship outside of US territorial waters? Are tourists bound to obey the domestic laws of the countries they visit? When a contract is formed in Newfoundland between a New York and an Ontario company and stipulates that English law is to govern on a dispute, which law should be applied?

Private international lawyers solve these kinds of problems by reference to the *connecting factors* that link a person or a contract to a state and its laws. In the contract dispute, for example, the question is whether the contract itself (through its choice-of-law clause) may specify which law is to govern the contract.[28] So, too, the fidelity rules of an institution specify the connecting factors that bind an individual to an institution and permit us to blame him when he breaches its rules.

In one respect, the analogy to private international law is inapt. While it applies to trans-border transactions, private international law is still part of the internal law of a state. There is a private international law of Virginia, of Ontario and of England, and they might differ markedly. In principle it is possible for Virginian legislators to extend the scope of its private international law as broadly as they want, though principles of prudence and comity might restrain them. This would be akin to an institution that purported to solve the principle of fidelity through its membership rules, and this is just what institutions cannot do. I cannot create an institution with two or three others and drag you in against your will by putting your name down on the membership rolls.

Fidelity requirements might, nevertheless, be likened to rules of private international law that commend themselves on principles of justice. The work of identifying such rules resembles the work of defending a vision of what private international law *ought* to look like, and this comes down to specifying when a subject ought to support a state, which has been the central problem of political philosophy since Thomas Hobbes. Left on their own, and working in a backwater of the common law, private international lawyers worked out the details of legal obligation that had eluded political philosophers.

Summary

A distinction may be made between two kinds of facts, depending upon whether they may be understood without reference to an institution. Brute facts, such as "the ball was hit over the fence," are meaningful quite apart from any background institution or convention. By contrast, institutional facts cannot be understood except as part of a game. In a game, a brute fact can be described in a wholly different manner, as a move in a game.

Two kinds of rules correspond to the two sets of facts. A regulative rule, such as the prohibition of murder, might be understood without reference to an institution, while an institutional rule makes sense only as the product of an institution. The infield fly rule is meaningless unless seen as part of a game. Similarly, contract law is an institution that cannot be understood without reference to a background institution of promising.

In order to account for promissory obligations it is necessary to introduce a third kind of rule. A fidelity rule, such as the citizenship laws of a country, links an individual to an institution so that he becomes bound by its rules. An institution might have membership rolls that purport to include me; yet I might still ask what makes it *my* institution so that I must attend to its rules. Like institutional rules, fidelity rules cannot be understood without reference to an institution; like regulative rules, they are not created by an institution.

A successful account of the foundations of contract law must therefore do three things:

1   It must be founded upon an analysis of promising as an institution or convention.
2   It must explain why fidelity duties are owed by promisors.
3   It must account for the basic rules of contract law and explain why some contracts are binding and others non-binding.

2 Rival theories of contract law

All is possible,
Who so list believe;
Trust therefore first, and after preve.
    Sir Thomas Wyatt, *Is It Possible?*

To persuade, a theory of contracts must do three things: it must recognize that promising is an institution; it must account for the promisor's fidelity duties; and it must explain the basic rules of contract law. Only one theory meets this challenge, the consequentialist explanation of contract law provided by law-and-economics that I discuss in the next chapter. It has generally been recognized that law-and-economics provides a compelling account of contract law; what is less well recognized is that only it does so, and that rival theories of contract law must be rejected.

There are three rival theories of contract law. Unlike the law-and-economics account of contracts, each denies the institutional nature of promising and seeks to ground promissory obligations on regulative rules. The first such explanation, called the *reliance theory*, sees contract-breaking as a tort in which promisees are harmed by their reliance upon the promisor. The second regulative account of promising is a *benefits theory* in which the promisor's retention of the benefit of a contract is wrongful unless he compensates the promisee by performing the promise. The third regulative explanation is the *will theory* we saw in Chapter 1, which asserts that we have an abstract right to contract that is independent of any convention. None of the three rival theories provides a satisfactory explanation of contract law.

Reliance theories

The reliance explanation of promising accords promisees a remedy for detrimental reliance against non-performing promisors. The duty can be stated as a regulative, non-institutional requirement that assimilates contractual to tortuous liability.

Whenever one party leads a second to rely upon him to the second's detriment, and the first party knows or ought to know that such reliance is a likely consequence of his action, then the first party is liable to compensate the second for his loss.[1]

This principle transcends promising, since the reliance might not have been occasioned by a promise. If I invite you to table and pull back your chair as you sit, so that you tumble on the floor and break a bone, I am responsible for the loss. The reliance might also follow upon a promise, where the promisee performs and the promisor holds back: the buyer pre-pays and the seller refuses to deliver; or the seller ships and the buyer refuses to pay. In such cases, the promise "is like a pit I have dug in the road, into which you fall."[2]

When narrowed to promising, the reliance duty becomes the principle of promissory estoppel found in section 90 of the Restatement (Second) of Contracts:

A promise which the promisor should reasonably expect to induce action or forbearance on the part of the promisee or a third person and which does induce such action or forbearance is binding if injustice can be avoided only by enforcement of the promise.

Having made such a promise, the promisor is barred (estopped, in law French) from denying that it binds him. Restatement § 90 liability will lie even though there is no contract because a necessary element of contractual recovery (such as consideration) is lacking.[3] That is, § 90 expands promissory liability beyond the law of contract. It does not subtract from but adds to the number of promises that are legally binding.

Under promissory estoppel, reasonable detrimental reliance is a *sufficient* criterion for legal recovery.[4] However, the reliance theory that I consider here makes the stronger claim that detrimental reliance is a *necessary* criterion for recovery. So viewed, detrimental reliance is more than a sword that expands promissory liability; it is also a shield that denies recovery in contract where reliance is absent. It subtracts from rather than adds to the stock of binding promises.

This is not how reliance claims have historically been understood. Promissory estoppel liability was thought to supplement contractual liability, not limit it. To show this, Grant Gilmore told how the doctrine of promissory estoppel came to be adopted in the Restatement of Contracts more than 70 years ago. Arthur Corbin had proposed relaxing the doctrine of consideration, under which promisees had to perform their part of the bargain or make a return promise before they could sue on the promisor's promise. Corbin thought this too restrictive and wanted the promisor to be bound even if there were no consideration from the promisee. However, this proposal was defeated and in its place Samuel Williston's more exclusionary test, which required consideration and excluded reliance-based remedies, was adopted.

> In Williston's view that should have been the end of the matter. Instead, Corbin returned to the attack. At the next meeting of the restatement group, he addressed them more or less in the following manner: gentlemen, you are engaged in restating the common law of contract. You have recently adopted a definition of consideration. I now submit to you a list of cases – hundreds, perhaps or thousands? – in which courts have imposed contractual liability under circumstances in which, according to your definition, there would be no consideration and therefore no liability. Gentlemen, what do you intend to do with these cases?[5]

What they did was adopt Restatement § 90, which codified the principle of reliance-based liability under the doctrine of promissory estoppel. The new provision was intended to increase, not decrease, the scope of promisor liability.

There are additional reasons why the attempt to turn detrimental reliance from a sufficient to a necessary condition of promissory liability is a nonstarter. Before an account of promising can commend itself, it must be able to explain why promissory institutions exist. Otherwise the institution might be abolished and one would have nothing to say about it. In contract law, for example, the freedom to contract is bounded by the doctrine of illegality, under which immoral or illegal contracts are unenforceable. Imagine, therefore, that the doctrine of illegality is permitted to expand to the limit, so that no contract is ever enforceable and bargaining freedom is entirely squeezed out. Private law shrinks down to nothing and the public law of non-consensual duty takes its place. Not a problem, says the reliance theorist.

A theory that casts a cold eye upon the demise of contract law cannot be said to provide a persuasive account of the institution. Since reliance theories cannot explain why a regime of private contracting should exist, they fail this test. Indeed, they suggest a reason for abolishing the institution. On reliance theories, promising is nothing more than an accident waiting to happen. No good comes of it, and every promise gives rise to a potential harm, since there is always a possibility of promisor breach and detrimental reliance by the promisee.

Reliance theories are also circular. Promissory institutions create reliance; reliance does not create the institution.[6] If promising did not exist (as in Tonga), we could not bootstrap up the institution through reliance claims based on a mere statement of intention to perform. Where there is no promising, there is no reliance upon a promise. Similarly, where contract law does not exist, the promisee cannot argue that he is entitled to a legal remedy for breach of contract. The promisee will have realized that, as the sanction for breach has been removed, the probability of performance is smaller. He will discount the gains from performance and reduce his reliance. Assume, for example, that the expected bargaining gain is 10. The probability of performance is 100 percent where contracts are legally binding and 50 percent in a non-contractual regime. In the latter case, the promisee will discount the gain by half and place a value of 5 on the promise. Half the time he will receive 10 and half the time he will receive 0. When he gets 10 he has no cause of action. But even when he gets 0 he has no claim for damages on reliance theories, since the expected value (probability times outcome) of his payout remains 5. Any award of damages would then amount to a windfall. There may be other reasons to create the institution of contract law, but detrimental reliance does not supply a reason to do so.

It gets worse. If we abandon the assumption that promises and contracts serve useful goals, it becomes difficult to assign responsibility for detrimental reliance losses to the promisor as opposed to the promisee. The promisor might cure the problem by performing or abstaining from promising; the promisee might cure the problem by abstaining from relying. Possibly we might sympathize with the promisee the first time around, but thereafter it is less clear. Fool me once, shame on you; fool me twice, shame on me. In non-contractual regimes, where no one would assume that promises are binding, the promisee has only himself to blame for his mistaken reliance.

People do not have free rein to impose reliance obligations on others. Otherwise a "reliance monster" could run up the tab through unreasonable acts of reliance. He might come to visit and, like *The Man Who Came to Dinner*, never leave. The prior question is always whether the reliance was reasonable, and this must depend on whether it is within the rules of the game prescribed by the background institution. Once again, the institution creates the reliance; reliance does not create the institution.

Reliance theories are, therefore, unable to account for the institutional nature of contract law or for the fidelity requirements that bind us to it. Nor are they able to explain the basic rules of contract law, such as how unrelied-upon promises are enforceable. If liability did not lie absent promisee reliance, promises would not be binding and contracts would not be enforceable before either party relied. However, this is wrong both in morals and in law. I cannot offer you a job and take back the offer the next day without committing a promissory and contractual breach. This is because purely executory contracts, where neither party has begun performance, are binding when made. Moreover, contract law does not limit recovery in damages to reliance losses. Promisees who expected to make profits of 10 on a contract, but who are only out of pocket by 2 through their reliance, can nevertheless recover the full expectation measure of 10.[7]

The limits on contractual recovery under reliance theories explain the vogue they enjoyed 30 years ago among legal academics who bore an animus against private ordering.[8] This was particularly true of the Critical Legal Scholars who objected to the libertarian principles they saw as implicit in the private law, and who celebrated *The Death of Contract*. That was the title of a 1974 book by Grant Gilmore, which argued that tort law (with its reliance interest) was supplanting contract liability (with its expectation interest). The same theme was echoed a few years later in Patrick Atiyah's *The Rise and Fall of Freedom of Contract*.[9] If reliance theories narrowed the scope of the private law, that was all to the good. Better still (for those who objected to market processes), a reliance requirement would have a particularly chilling effect upon commercial contractors. Because prices are more volatile in a commercial setting, business parties would have more incentive to throw up a contract if courts refused to enforce a contract before reliance has begun. Futures markets would disappear, and *inter absentes* contracts between parties who do not deal face-to-face would become riskier. When damages are limited to the reliance interest, sellers from Hong Kong would find that opportunistic American buyers would try to renegotiate the price once the goods were in transit. Long-term dealings that contemplate idiosyncratic investments would also invite chiseling after performance had begun. In all of these ways the incentive to embark on a business relationship would be weakened.

After the moral, economic and political failure of socialism, reliance theories no longer resonate. Within the legal academy, some of the credit for their decline goes to the defense of free contracting provided by scholars in the law-and-economics tradition which we will examine in the next chapter.

Benefits theories

Benefits explanations of promissory and contractual institutions fare no better. On such theories, one person is liable to account for benefits received from a second when it is unjust for the first to retain it. This principle, which underlies the law of restitution or unjust enrichment, permits recovery outside of contract. For example, faithless fiduciaries might be required to account to beneficiaries for benefits derived from an opportunity that belonged to the latter. Such recovery is quasi-contractual: it is as if the law implied a contractual bond under which retention of the benefit constituted a breach.

As we saw in Chapter 1, quasi-contractual liability might overlap with contractual relief when the person who receives the benefit promises to compensate the other party. In *Webb* v. *McGowan*, for example, an employee was severely injured in the act of saving his employer's life.[10] Immediately afterwards, the employer promised to look after the employee (who suffered a permanent disability from the accident). The estate of the employer failed to honor the promise, and restitutionary recovery corrected the injustice by treating the promise as binding.

Nevertheless, benefits theories cannot explain the basic rules of contract law. Restitutionary recovery merely requires the return of a benefit; it does not enforce the terms of a contract. Suppose that, in a contract of sale, the buyer performs but not the seller. Restitutionary relief would give the buyer his price back. It would not enforce the contract by giving the buyer his lost profits (or, exceptionally, by requiring the seller to deliver the goods). For that, what is needed is recovery in contract, which awards the promisee the expectation measure of damages.[11]

The benefits account of contract law fails in another way. Like reliance theories, benefits theories cannot explain why executory contracts are enforceable and why promises are binding when made. At the moment of contracting, when neither party has performed, no one has received a benefit and there is no basis for recovery on benefits theories. Nevertheless, executory promises are binding, both in morals and law. Thus, both benefits and reliance theories fail to account for one of the most fundamental features of promises and contracts. If this feature serves valuable goals, as I will show, then reliance and benefits theories must be rejected.

Once again, it is even worse. Not only are benefits theories unable to explain why executory contracts are binding but, like reliance theories, they suggest we would be better off abolishing them. Promissory institutions offer no advantages but only the possibility of restitutionary injury. Reliance and Benefits theories purport to explain contract law, but instead supply a reason to get rid of it. Some theories.

Will theories

The third explanation of contractual institutions sees promising as a fundamental right. Through contracts I assert my will; and a legal system which respects my right to do so, by removing barriers to the expression of the autonomy of the will, promotes libertarian principles. My freedom of choice has expanded in a most important area. One variant of the will theory, called the consent explanation of promising, locates the right to contract in our right to consent to the imposition of fetters on ourselves. By bargaining we consent to the rules of the contracting game, and legal enforcement of our contracts respects our free choice to do so.

In America, will explanations of contract law were first advanced by nineteenth-century judges who were influenced by transcendentalists such as Emerson.[12] In turn, the transcendentalists were deep into Hegel,[13] who located the basis of moral right in the autonomy of the will. By the will Hegel meant free will, and he identified two kinds of freedom. Subjective freedom is the intuitive sense that our choices are unconstrained by behavioral programing (or genetic codes). By contrast, objective freedom is a matter of intellectual deliberation in which the will purifies itself of all subjective impulses and through abstract self-contemplation invests itself with the universality and objectivity of moral right. The core moral category is the Hegelian will exercising its objective freedom, and this is prior even to concepts of rights. "It is only because right is the embodiment of the absolute concept or of self-conscious freedom that it is something sacrosanct."[14]

As manifestations of our will, said Hegel, property rights deserve respect. We have the right to "put our will into each and every thing" and thereby make it our own.[15] Indeed, property rights are the individual's "substantive end," as they mark the difference between persons who own and things that are owned. Contract rights are also asserted through an act of will, and for the same reason should be respected. In property acquisitions, I make a thing my own by infusing my will with it; in contractual sales I alienate a thing by withdrawing my will from it. Even in non-sale contracts, two wills are united in a common will – the common lawyer's "meeting of the minds."

The Hegelian account of contract law is unpersuasive. As we saw in Chapter 1, will theories cannot explain why promissory institutions ought to exist or provide the connecting factor that links us to them. Promissory obligations are institutional and not regulative. They do not arise through a brute mental fact of willing a moral duty. Without the institution, one might grit one's teeth and silently will (whatever that might mean) as much as one wants, without producing a promissory obligation or a binding contract.

Nevertheless, will theories rest on an attractive set of libertarian values, and for ideological reasons have enjoyed the support of a small but determined band of adherents. This was particularly true for an older generation of civilian jurists. "In its mystique," said René Savatier, "the autonomy of the will consecrates liberty for the parties to contract *as they wish* and *over everything which interests them*, since the Civil Code assimilates them to legislators."[16] As a thing of *mystique*, Savatier's free will had closer affinities to Charles Péguy's mystical nationalism and Henri Bergson's anti-mechanistic *élan vital* than it did to Hegel's rational free will. There is also a much more pronounced political content in Savatier's right to contract. For Hegel, there was no conflict between the realms of private law individual freedom and public law communitarian duty, since both were reconciled at the level of abstract rationality. For Savatier, however, the two realms are in conflict, and the contract theorist is necessarily on the side of personal liberty. Through contract law, the subject is emancipated from paternalistic public law fetters and becomes an independent self-legislator. In summing up this tradition, Hans Kelsen concluded that "one must finally admit that the political principle of autonomy in matters of contract rests on an individualist or libertarian conception of life."[17]

Even today, those most likely to subscribe to some version of the will theory are conservatives or libertarians such as Charles Fried and Randy Barnett. Because he sees promising as an institution, Fried rejects Hegel's will theory. However, Fried also rejects the utilitarian explanations of scholars in the law-and-economics tradition, and as an alternative proposes an "autonomy" theory of promising. "In order that I be as free as possible, that my will have the greatest possible range consistent with the similar will of others, it is necessary that there be a way in which I may commit myself."[18] This is not very different from Kelsen's "individualistic and libertarian conception of life," and Barnett's "consent" explanation of contracting would appear to rest on a similar political foundation.[19]

By subordinating the philosophical to the political, the will theorist makes the same mistake as the reliance theorist. On the left, scholars hostile to free bargaining, such as Patrick Atiyah, were attracted to reliance explanations that narrow the scope of contract rights and expand the realm of public duty. Granting recovery for unrelied-on promises, said Atiyah,

> rests upon a belief in the traditional values of free choice. Many still admire these values but they bring with them, inescapably, many other consequences which are today less admired. ... [T]he greater is the scope for the exercise of free choice, the stronger is the tendency for ... original inequalities to perpetuate themselves by maintaining or even increasing economic inequalities.[20]

On the right, free market scholars favor will theories that appear to limit public law restrictions on free bargaining. Both sides are wrong. Contract law theories cannot be adopted for strategic reasons, to advance a collateral political goal, however desirable it might seem. Promising and contract law can only be understood from an institutional perspective and, in mistaking an institutional as a brute fact, reliance and will theories are both flawed.

Even on its own terms, the will account of promising fails to offer a satisfactory account of how promissory institutions expand our freedom. To be sure, the institutions of promising and contract law give those who invoke them new powers. Their domain of alternatives has expanded, as it does whenever a new game is adopted, and there is one more thing they may do. Before they could not promise; now they can. Because they have more choices, there is a sense in which they are freer. This might be called positive liberty, in contrast to the negative liberty in which restraints on our options are relaxed.[21] When I sprout wings and can fly my positive liberty has expanded; when freed from jail my negative liberty is enhanced.

The kind of positive liberty I have in mind is a very technical kind of freedom, as that is not how we ordinarily speak of liberty. However, there is a more serious objection to the will account of promissory freedom. If the institution of promising increases our liberty by giving us more options, the same is true of baseball, since people could not hit home runs before the game was adopted. But if every new institution creates new alternatives, how can we say that one kind of autonomy is superior to another? Why is promissory autonomy to be preferred to baseball autonomy? From an abstract perspective, there is no way to weigh the two kinds of freedom. All we can do is look to the consequences of adopting each convention. Promissory societies without baseball are undoubtedly richer than non-promissory societies with baseball, but will theorists must forswear such utilitarian calculations since their abstract rights are independent of consequences and contingent facts. So what is left? There is no metric by which different sets of autonomy values can be measured and different institutions compared, except through their consequences.

Suppose that a society could vote on the introduction of new institutions, and that the Tonganese were presented with a choice between promising and baseball. As it happens, they would almost never promise but would quickly become fanatical baseball fans; and they know this. Looking at the consequences of the introduction of the two institutions, there is no question which one is superior, or how the Tonganese would vote. Would we then permit the will theorist, on some abstract principle, to object to the choice of baseball institutions? The Tonganese language might perhaps be inefficient; but it cannot be said to deprive anyone of fundamental promissory rights.

There is an infinity of games that might exist, far more than the meager stock now available to us. The failure to adopt any one of these games does not deprive us of any rights. Vows are an example. Roman law had a well-defined law of vows, but there is no parallel at modern common law. I cannot bind myself to perform a promise to God, and expect to see the promise enforced by a Roman aedile. Few of us would regard this restriction on choice as problematical. However, the will theorist must regard the failure to enforce vows as troubling, since his unilateral mental acts of will give rise to an obligation.

Moreover, the libertarian case for promissory institutions is ambiguous, for promising expands our freedom only by limiting it. *Ex ante*, at the time of contracting, we have more freedom for we can curtail future choices. But *ex post*, when the time for performance falls due, we have fewer choices, since failure to perform is a breach of contract. Which kind of freedom is superior? The freedom to constrain my choices in the future permits me to make a credible commitment to perform my promises, and invites a stronger degree of reliance from my promisee. But for this re-assurance the promisee might refuse to deal with me, with the result that the gains of joint cooperation would be lost. At the time of contracting, therefore, I will want to ensure that I will be bound when the time of performance rolls around. For Rousseau, however, the *ex post* freedom to change one's mind was superior to the *ex ante* freedom to bind oneself. The Rousseauian subject was "forced to be free," and not free to be forced. Similarly, some anarchists such as Murray Rothbard have objected to contractual enforcement because it represents a legal constraint of the future choices of the parties.[22] If forced to choose between the two kinds of freedom, scholars in the law-and-economics tradition would elect to adopt promissory institutions, as valuable bargain gains would be lost without the *ex ante* freedom to promise. But the will theorist, who rests his case upon abstract right, must be indifferent to the economic conse-quences of adopting or rejecting an institution, and would find the choice between *ex ante* and *ex post* freedom a vexed one.

Consent theorists such as Randy Barnett seek to sidestep the weak-nesses of will theories by focusing upon the promisor's consent to be bound. As an exercise of personal autonomy, it is claimed, one's consent deserves respect. What this adds to will theories is unclear, since it appears to rest on the same foundation of political libertarianism. Moreover, what-ever is novel in this approach is almost certainly wrong, since consent explanations of promissory institutions are circular, as Hume showed.[23] To see this, suppose that members of a non-promissory society try to create the institution through mutual consent, by specifying that a certain verbal formula signifies that an obligation has been undertaken. This might be: "Let me be bound to perform." Even then, it is still meaningful to ask whether this convention binds the participants. Without a prior conven-tion to uphold conventions, they are not bound. But what can this prior convention be, if it is not the institution of promising? The parties could only create such a prior private convention through a promise to adhere to its norms. If that promise was not binding, neither was their private convention. One cannot promise to obey promises unless the first promise is binding; and seeking a promise to perform that promise leads to an infinite regress. Bargaining is not created by a hypothetical bargain, or contracting by a social contract.

The circularity problem arises for contractual as well as promissory institutions. Where promissory institutions exist but contractual institu-tions do not, the parties cannot contract for the creation of contract law. They might through mutual promises bind themselves to abide by the rules of contract law. But there is no breach of contract if the promises are broken, and no liability at law. Contractual institutions cannot be created by contract, any more than promissory institutions can be created by promise, without circular reasoning.

This is not to say that consent cannot have moral consequences in a non-promissory society. Through their consent, the Tonganese might waive their rights or submit to the imposition of a cost. If the idea of property exists, they might consent to the alienation of some of their goods. Consent will even have moral consequences in the future: having consented to the property transfer, they cannot afterwards assert a right to get their goods back.

Nevertheless, the Tonganese cannot create promissory or contractual institutions by consent. Suppose, for example, that a Tongan is asked to participate in a cooperative scheme under which the parties are asked to share certain burdens in the expectation of joint rewards. Our Tongan expresses his consent to the scheme, and for a time passively receives its benefits. But when the time comes for him to perform he refuses to do so. Has he breached an obligation? John Rawls would argue that he has, and that he is bound to contribute his fair share.[24] But where promising does not exist, the Tongan is under no greater obligation than an American who says "I will consent to receive the benefits of the scheme but do not promise to contribute anything towards it myself." If the Tongan non-promisor is bound, so is the American non-promisor. But as he expressly denied that he was promising, the American is not bound. Neither, therefore, is the Tongan.

The final version of the will theory sees an analogy between promissory and property rights. If the obligation to perform can be thought of as being owned, then promising and contracting resemble property transfers. The benefit of my performance is reified and treated as a thing which, in promising, I sell to you. Hegel can be read as adopting this view of contracting. As we saw, he regarded ownership as a fundamental human right, and when he came to analyze contract law, the example of sales law was uppermost in his mind. Even a contract for services such as an employment contract might be seen, he thought, as an alienation of my productive capacity.[25]

The idea that contract law may be assimilated to property rights is an old one. At common law, a promise becomes a special kind of property (called a chose in action) when the promisee assigns it to a third party. Similarly, negotiable instruments law turns promises into property when a promisor's notes are endorsed by the promisee to a third party transferee. In the seventeenth century, Grotius generalized this into a defense of contract law: the right to contractual performance may constitute property, and the right to property embraces the right to alienate the bargained-for performance. Contractual promises have

> an effect similar to alienation of ownership. It is, in fact, an introduction either to the alienation of a thing or to the alienation of some portion of our freedom of action. To the former category belong promises to give; to the latter, promises to perform.[26]

When I contract I sell you the right to my performance. On this view of contracting, non-promissory regimes trench on property rights by restricting rights of alienation that are inherent in the concept of ownership.

The analogy to property is tempting. After all, balance sheets would look very different if accounts payable could not be reified and count as assets, and my retirement account would drastically shrink if I could not own the promises (bonds) of the firms in which I have invested. Moreover, the right to own the benefit of my promises can be seen as an aspect of self-ownership. Just as I own my body, I own services I can perform with it. And if I might own them, I might also sell them in a contract of services.

Nevertheless, property theories do not explain why promissory institutions ought to exist. Even if property rights were natural rights and did not depend on a background institution of property, they would not supply a reason why promissory institutions should exist. To assert that I have a natural right to promise, in a non-promissory society, would be to assert that someone owes me a duty to create promissory institutions. But just who that person might be in Tonga is a mystery. No one has a right to a verb.

Moreover, will theorists who subscribe to Kantian moral theories would find it objectionable to turn promissory obligations into property. Through promising, said Kant, I take possession of another's choice, in the sense that I have a right to his performance. But Kant was careful to distinguish between the real rights of property law and the personal rights of contract law. "By a contract I acquire something external." Not an external thing, however, nor even the benefit of his promise, but the promise itself:

> I have become *enriched* by acquiring an active obligation on the freedom and means of the other. – This *right* of mine is, however, only a right *against a person*, namely a right against a *specific* physical person ... ; it is not a *right to a thing*.[27]

The personal rights of contract law can be asserted only against the promisor, while the real rights of property law can be asserted against the world.

The distinction is protective of the promisor's liberty. Suppose that I bargain to sell you my services, and in breach of my contract sell them to a third party. If contract rights are personal you may sue me but not him; if contract rights are real you may sue both of us. Real remedies in people, said Kant, are incompatible with human rights. "So someone can be his own master but cannot be the owner *of himself* . . . still less can he dispose of others as he pleases."[28] He could only do so if they or their services were property, and before that could happen we would find ourselves treating people as ends. Kant insisted upon the point, because it was crucial to his understanding of ethics and the nature and dignity of man.

The principal difficulty with property explanations of promissory institutions, like other variants of the will theory, is that they rest on what I have described as positive liberty. They ask for expanded choice through the creation of an institution of reified promissory rights. But before we can show why an institution ought to exist, we must be able to show how life changes when we do so. We must examine the consequences of the introduction of promising and contract law. The economic analysis of contract law, which we examine in the next chapter, has a well-developed explanation of the benefits of promissory institutions. But will theorists do not have recourse to this kind of explanation, and their abstract defense of promising is unable to provide an answer to this challenge.

A final difficulty with will theories, in all their forms, is that they seem unable to explain the content of contract law. In one respect they are superior to reliance and benefits theories, since the Hegelian contract is binding when made, whether or not reliance or benefits claims will lie. But for other kinds of contract rules will theories are silent. They do not explain how a court might arrive at a set of implied terms when there is a gap in the express terms. For example, when the contract does not explicitly specify any warranties as to quality, and the goods are not supplied on an "as-is" basis, a court will imply a warranty that the goods be merchantable. Such warranties might serve efficiency goals, and be explained on an economic analysis of contract law. But since the parties did not come to an express agreement about the implied terms, they must be an enigma to the will theorist.[29]

Summary

In addition to law-and-economics theories, there are three rival explanations of promising and contract law: reliance, benefits and will theories. Reliance explanations would ground liability for the promisor's breach on the promisee's detrimental reliance. However, such theories cannot explain why the institution of promising should exist and suggest instead that we should ban promising altogether. Reliance theories also suffer from an inability to explain why the unrelied-on promise should be binding, and are therefore unable to account for a fundamental feature of contract law. Benefits theories give promises a restitutionary remedy when the faithless promisor retains the benefit of a contract and omits to perform, himself. Once again, this suggests a reason to ban the institution of contract law as a trap for the unwary. It also fails to explain why contracts are binding before anyone had begun to perform and no benefits have been conferred. Finally, will theories do not explain why promises and contracts are binding and are unable to account for basic contract law rules such as the law of implied terms.

For a satisfactory explanation of these problems, we must turn from reliance, benefits and will theories to the law-and-economics account of contract law.

3 The economic theory of contract law

> To breed an animal capable of promising – isn't that just the paradoxical task which nature has set herself with mankind, the peculiar problem of mankind?
>
> Nietzsche, *On the Genealogy of Morals*

We are now in a better position to evaluate the foundational questions of contract theory and to recognize wrong turns. It is very much a wrong turn to begin by asking why promises are binding. That is simply the way that the institution works; it is what it means to promise. As John Rawls noted, asking why that should be the case is like asking why batters do not get four strikes.[1]

Instead of asking why our promises and contracts are binding, the first question for contract theory is why such institutions are valuable. Why might members of a non-promissory society wish to adopt them, could they somehow be given the choice? Why is contract law a more valuable institution than, say, baseball? The answer is trust. What the institutions of promising and contract law crucially supply is the element of trust which makes promises credible and which permits promisees to rely on promisors. Without the trust created by contract law, opportunities for gain from joint projects would be lost and our society would be poorer.

An institutional perspective is necessarily a consequentialist one. We cannot evaluate the costs and benefits of adopting an institution without looking at the consequences of doing so. This is not to say that only narrow economic consequences count and that broader social considerations are ruled out of order. If the material benefits from contract law were somehow exceeded by the social costs of a coarser and more grasping society, the consequentialist would oppose its adoption, as would the economist. All consequences matter, even though problems of quantification make comparisons difficult. For now we assume that contractual regimes are benign and defer an examination of contract law's spillover effects until Chapter 9.

The need for trust

As we saw, Hume pioneered the institutional analysis of promising. In his analysis of bargaining, he was also one of the earliest economists, and several of Adam Smith's key insights may be traced back to him. In particular, the discovery that specialization of trade promotes economic growth should be attributed to Hume, who noted that "different men are by nature fitted for different employments, and attain to greater perfection in any one, when they confine themselves to it alone."[2] With economies of specialization the baker can restrict his business to bread-making; he can buy his flour from merchants and need not grow and mill his own grain. But he cannot do so unless he can trust the merchant to supply him with flour when he needs it. Without trust, the parties cannot rely on each other, and are driven back to producing all their own goods and foregoing the gains from specialization.

To illustrate the need for trust Hume took the example of two farmers who need to cooperate to exploit a bargain opportunity over future crops:

> Your corn is ripe today; mine will be so tomorrow. 'Tis profitable for us both, that I shou'd labour with you to-day, and that you shou'd aid me to-morrow. I have no kindness for you, and know you have as little for me. I will not, therefore, take any pains upon your account; and should I labour with you upon my own account, in expectation of a return, I know I shou'd be disappointed, and that I shou'd in vain depend upon your gratitude. Here then I leave you to labour alone; You treat me in the same manner. The seasons change; and both of us lose our harvests for want of mutual confidence and security.[3]

The opportunity for gain is before their eyes; yet the farmers cannot grasp it without the institution of contract law to solve the problem of trust.

Why would the parties pass up an opportunity for joint gains which would make them both better off? The answer is that what might make the parties jointly better off when they cooperate might not give each as much as he could have without cooperation. That is, what is collectively rational might be individually irrational. To see this, it is helpful to model the bargaining problem as a Prisoners' Dilemma game.

Table 3.1 The Promisor's Dilemma: how profitable joint opportunities may be lost because of individual incentives to defect

		Player Two	
		Cooperate	Defect
Player One	Cooperate	3, 3	−1, 4
	Defect	4, −1	0, 0

In the model, bargaining is seen as a two-person game, in which the outcome or payoff for each party is dependent not only on what he does but on what the other party does. The payoffs available to the parties are, therefore, represented as four possible outcomes in a 2×2 table (see Table 3.1). The first figure in each box indicates the payoff to Player One, and the second the payoff to Player Two, with the numbers arbitrarily selected to make a point about the gains from cooperation and the ways these might be lost through individual incentives to breach.

When both parties cooperate (the upper-left hand box), each promises and performs his promise and each receives a payoff of 3; when both defect (lower right), they fail to enter into a contract and receive 0 apiece. Where Player One cooperates and Player Two defects (upper right), or where Player One defects and Player Two cooperates (lower left), the cooperating party promises and performs and the defecting party promises and breaches. The seller delivers but is not paid; or the buyer pays but does not receive the goods.

Joint cooperation is the efficient (highest total payoff) solution, as the total gains of $(3 + 3 =)$ 6 exceed the total gains from any other strategy. With joint defection (0, 0), the parties wastefully pass up the bargaining gain. However, each party will prefer this to the situation where he performs and the other party defects. In that case, the performing party gets -1 (the "sucker's payoff") while the breaching party gets 4 (the "opportunist's payoff").

If joint cooperation is socially efficient, why would a party defect? The answer is that each party's private incentives are imperfectly aligned with their joint interests. Considered together (and summing both payoffs in each box), the two parties are best off when both cooperate; but considered individually, each is better off when he defects and gets the opportunist's payoff. In the upper-left box, Player One can increase his payoff from 3 to 4 by defecting; in the upper-right box, he can increase his payoff from -1 to 0 by defecting. Player Two can increase his payoffs in the same way through defection, moving from the upper-left to the upper-right box, or from the lower-left to the lower-right box. Whatever one party does, the other is always better off if he defects. For both parties, defection beats (dominates, in the language of game theory) cooperation in every state of the world. The logic of the game implies that the parties will both defect, ending up in the lower-right box where the contractual gains are lost.[4]

The nature of the game would change if the parties could enter into enforceable contracts with each other to cooperate, as this would change the payoff structure. For example, defectors might be required to pay damages equal to the amount of the other party's losses, which would remove the temptation to defect (see Table 3.2).

Table 3.2 is Table 3.1, with the difference that defectors are required to pay cooperator's damages of 3 for their lost profits. Here, the parties

Table 3.2 The Promisor's Dilemma after private contracting: where the defector is liable in damages for lost profits

		Player Two	
		Cooperate	Defect
Player One	Cooperate	3, 3	2, 1
	Defect	1, 2	0, 0

are always better off when they cooperate, and their private incentives are fully aligned with their joint interests. As such, neither will defect.

The Prisoner's Dilemma game illustrates how profitable joint opportunities may be lost when contracts are not enforced. When the buyer pays the price and the seller refuses to deliver, or when the seller delivers and the buyer refuses to pay, the party in breach gets the opportunist's payoff and the innocent party gets the sucker's payoff. Future parties will anticipate this and refuse to enter into agreements. The result is a settled pattern of defection and mistrust in which bargaining gains are abandoned, unless the parties can bind themselves through enforceable bargains.

Beneficial reliance

When the parties refuse to rely on each other's promises, the bargaining loss can usefully be explained through the economist's indifference curves. An indifference mapping also highlights the deficiencies in the reliance and benefits explanations of contracting.

When presented with a choice between different goods (represented along axes of a diagram), a consumer will find himself indifferent between various bundles of goods. He might find that five apples and three oranges are just as good as four apples and four oranges. Or ten apples and no oranges. The line that connects all the points of indifference between one combination of goods and other combinations is called an indifference curve.

For our purposes, let us assume that the two goods are consumption today and consumption tomorrow of money. The indifference mapping will indicate the consumer's preferences as between present and future consumption.

In Figure 3.1, the consumer is given $100 which he must spread over two time periods. The straight line between consumption of $100 in the two periods is called the *budget line* and represents every possible combination of present vs. deferred consumption, given the consumer's fixed amount of money. The frugal ant takes a position at one extreme, saving in the present and spending the entire amount in the second period; while the grasshopper lives solely for today and spends the entire amount in the present period.

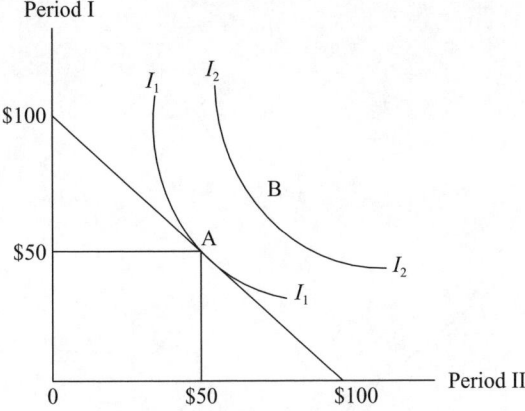

Figure 3.1 The saving decision

At the point of origin the consumer has no goods of either kind. We assume that he always wants more goods and that he will always prefer to be on the highest indifference curve (the one furthest from the point of origin). Given the choice between curves I_1 and I_2 he would, therefore, prefer to be on the latter. As this lies above the budget line, however, it is not a feasible outcome. He simply doesn't have the money. Instead, curve I_1, which is tangent to the budget line at the point of intersection, represents the highest feasible indifference curve available to the consumer with a $100 budget and, as it happens, this assumes equal consumption in the two periods, $50 now and $50 later.[5]

Charles Goetz and Robert Scott have employed an indifference curve model to explain how trust benefits bargainers (see Figure 3.2).[6] Suppose that our subject – call him David – begins with an endowment of $100 and reaches his highest feasible indifference curve at point $A_{50, 50}$, where he consumes $50 now and $50 later. David's Uncle Ebenezer tells David he wants to give him another $100. If Ebenezer makes the gift in the first period, we assume (arbitrarily) that David will move to point $B_{100, 100}$, again dividing consumption equally in the two periods. However, Ebenezer does not have the $100 in period 1, and can only promise to give David the money in period 2. If Ebenezer promises to make the gift and subsequently performs, and if David relies on the promise by consuming his entire $100 in period 1 and the gift of $100 in period 2, then David will be as well off as he would have been had Ebenezer made the gift in period 1.

Now suppose that Ebenezer promises and David relies in period 1, but that Ebenezer fails to perform in period 2. David will now be at point $C_{0, 100}$ and worse off than if he had not relied. Had he refused to trust his uncle, he would be on indifference curve I_{100}; instead, he is now on

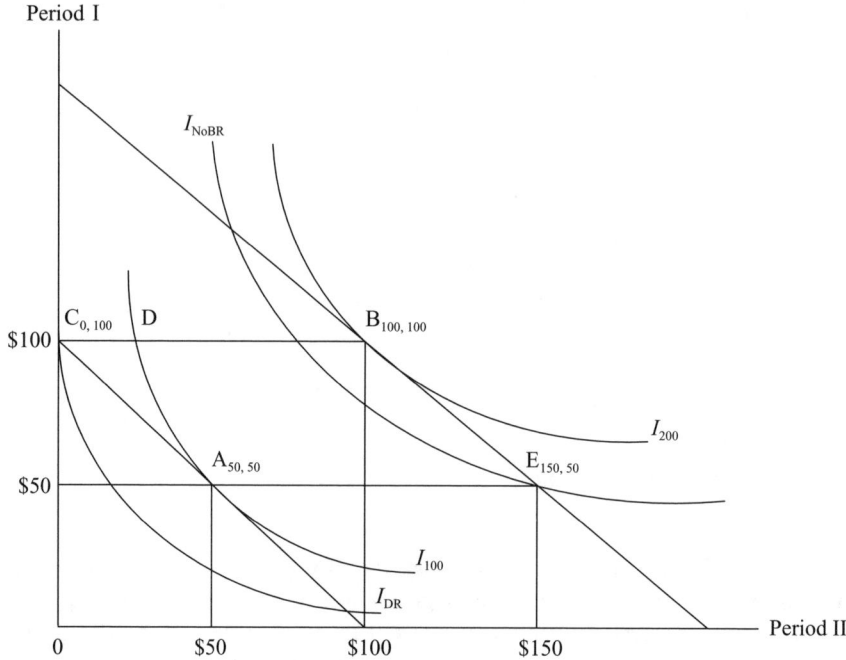

Figure 3.2 Detrimental and beneficial reliance

indifference curve I_{DR}; and the difference represents his detrimental reliance loss. To compensate David for the loss, Ebenezer would have to give David reliance damages of $CD (which as I have drawn it looks to be about $25) to bring him back to indifference curve I_{100} and leave him as well off as if the promise had never been made.

Once bitten, twice shy. The next time Ebenezer makes a promise David does not rely. In period 1 David consumes $50, just as he would have had the promise not been made. If Ebenezer fails to perform, David will consume $50 in period 2 and no harm will have been done from a reliance perspective. But now suppose that Ebenezer does perform in period 2, and that David finds himself at point $E_{150,\,50}$. He is better off than he would have been had Uncle Ebenezer not performed, but not as well off as he would have been had he relied and Ebenezer performed. He would then have been on indifference curve I_{200}; but now is only on indifference curve I_{NoBR}.

The difference between indifference curves I_{200} and I_{NoBR} represents how a promisee may be made better off by relying when promises are performed. He can adjust his behavior in expectation of performance, and Goetz and Scott call this *beneficial reliance*. The Goetz–Scott analysis usefully highlights the deficiencies of the reliance and benefits theories we saw in the last chapter. Reliance theorists incorrectly assume that the only kind of reliance is detrimental (and if they had the courage of their convictions they would ban contracting entirely). What they forget is beneficial reliance, where promisees adjust their behavior in expectation of performance and promisors do, in fact, perform. Similarly, benefits theorists look only to the benefit received by the promisor and ignore the benefit the promisee derives from credible promises. Reliance and benefits theorists both miss the crucial contribution of promises and contract law, as reassurance devices that promote promisee reliance.

Moral philosophers who are unaccustomed to looking at problems from the economist's *ex ante* perspective, and who tend to ignore the incentive effects of legal rules, typically examine the question of promissory obligations from an *ex post* perspective, where the promise has been made and the promisee has relied to his detriment. Since they do not see the *ex ante* side of things they miss the element of beneficial reliance, which is the whole point of the institution. Sadly, the same mistake is made by academic lawyers such as Patrick Atiyah who are unfamiliar with the economic analysis of law.

But why stop at beneficial reliance? The ability of promisees to adjust their behavior seems an instrumental good, desirable only so far as it promotes a higher good. We prize beneficial reliance not because we like reliance, but because it permits the parties to exploit joint projects that make them better off. It fosters the creation of wealth and results in a more prosperous society. This might not come down to a simple utilitarianism, but the overlap is sufficiently close that most scholars in the law-and-economics tradition subscribe to utilitarian moral theories, to the extent that they stray beyond a purely positive view of their discipline.

Credible commitments

The institutions of promising and contract law promote beneficial reliance by imposing a cost on the faithless promisor. A breach of promise is a moral wrong, and the promisor suffers a reputational loss. The moral obligation of promising may thus be employed to make a statement of intention more credible. "You say you will come to dinner – but do you *promise*?" Unless backed by the force of law, however, a promise might not suffice, for talk is cheap and often unreliable. A bare promise, said Thomas Hobbes, is "but words, and breath," with "no force to oblige, contain, constrain, or protect any man."[7] To invite promisee reliance, the promisor might therefore have to show a willingness to incur contractual sanctions for breach.

Without contractual sanctions, markets might collapse in what George Akerlof has described as a "market for lemons."[8] Suppose that there are only two commodities: good used cars and defective used cars ("lemons"), with an equal number of both kinds. The seller can tell which car is which, but not the buyer. Could he distinguish them, the buyer would be willing to pay $10,000 for a good car and $1,000 for a lemon. Not knowing the quality of the car, the buyer would still be willing to pay $5,500 for it if he thought he stood an equal chance of getting one as the other (there being an equal number of both). However, this ignores the game-theoretic nature of the problem: sellers not only know the quality of the car but also have the choice whether to sell or not. A seller who values a good car at $10,000 will not sell it for a market price of $5,500. Instead, he will sell only lemons. Buyers will recognize this, and will rationally refuse to pay more than $1,000 for a car. The market for high-quality cars will disappear and only lemons will be sold.

Akerlof's lemons problem arises whenever a promisee is asked to rely on a promise and reassurance techniques such as contractual warranties are unavailable. This will happen in commercial contracts and in many other bargains as well. Those who think that marriage is a special bond which is threatened by the morals of the market-place sometimes say that "marriage is more than a contract: it is a covenant." But marriage is more than a covenant: it is a contract. Or, rather, it is less than a contract, since in all but two states the parties cannot waive their right to a no-fault divorce.[9] Because of the threat of a break-up, marriage has been weakened as the Akerlof model predicts. Since the passage of no-fault laws, people have been less willing to get married and, once married, to have children.[10] These trends might be reversed were the marriage contract more strongly enforced. Giving the parties the right upon marriage to waive no-fault divorce rights would make the exit option costlier for parties who exercised that option. A husband who sought to abandon his wife could not divorce her without her consent and would find himself paying her to secure it. As fault becomes costlier, there will be less of it, and fewer divorces. Small faults will annoy less. Blemishes that seem oppressive when exit is costless will be far less troublesome when one realizes that the marriage will last. An expansion of free bargaining rights, in which no-fault divorce waivers are made enforceable and marriage vows are made more credible, would therefore protect marriage.

The problem of trust is one of credible commitments, in which promisees must determine which promise can be believed. Bare promises, which are not legally enforceable, might not do the trick, since low-quality promisors could easily mimic high-quality promisors. The promisee will then discount all promises and the bargain will be lost. But this means that good cars will not be sold at their true value in used car markets. High-quality sellers have, therefore, an incentive to reveal the car's true quality, and Michael Spence has shown how they might do so by their willingness to bear the cost of signaling (or information revelation).[11]

When *signaling costs* are the same for both faithful and faithless promisors, the willingness to bear them does not permit promisees to tell them apart. For example, a bare promise costs neither promisor anything, and the result is a *pooling equilibrium* in which the two promisors cannot be distinguished. Because neither promise is credible, nobody would bother to promise. Suppose, however, that signaling costs are differentially borne by faithful and faithless promisors: signaling is costly for both, but much more costly for the faithless promisor. Where these costs exceed his expected gains from the bargain, he has no incentive to signal. But the faithful promisor, with his lower signaling costs, will be willing to bear signaling costs when these are exceeded by the bargaining gains. Game theorists call this a *separating equilibrium*: only the faithful promisor has an incentive to signal, and when he does so his promise is credible. The promisors sort themselves out into two separate groups and the promisee can tell them apart.

The kind of signaling costs Spence had in mind were educational. Schooling is costly, but more costly for slow learners who have to expend more mental toil. Academic credentials might thus permit employers to distinguish on the basis of intelligence and mental grit. Better credentials mean a higher salary, but not enough to make a difference for the slow learner. Spence signaling also explains how contract law can solve the credible commitment problem. The willingness to bear the risk of liability for breach of contract might constitute a signal that credibly identifies the faithful promisor, transforming a pooling into a separating equilibrium. The signal is costly, since breach will impose a financial burden in the form of damages. But these costs will be lower for high- than for low-quality promisors, for whom default is more likely. The sanction of damages may thus provide the crucial test that separates faithful from faithless promisors.

Substitutes for contract law

Remedies for breach in contract are not the only devices that promisors might employ to reassure promisees about performance. In addition, the credible commitment problem might be addressed through (1) piece-work contracting, (2) reciprocal altruism, (3) internalized norms, (4) union strategies and (5) non-contractual bonding. Where the normal writs of the common law do not run, in international law for example, these might be the only available reassurance techniques. Even in common law jurisdictions, the promise might be too vague to be easily enforced (or to trust to a jury). In addition, contracting is sometimes costly, and substitutes might then be cheaper. In spite of this, people do rely on contractual fetters, particularly for significant transactions, and this demonstrates that for a crucially important set of bargains, substitute reassurance strategies cannot take the place of contract law.

Piece-work contracting

In piece-work contracting, an employee is not paid a regular salary; instead, he is paid per unit of output. Piece-work compensation breaks up a long-term contract into small, discrete lumps, and may commend itself when it is impossible to monitor employee performance and a regular salary would invite shirking. The same strategy may be employed in other cases where the promisee is unwilling to bear the risk of making a major reliance investment. For example, the buyer might purchase goods on a per-item basis over time, rather than in gross all at once.

However, there are two difficulties with piece-work strategies. First, promisee reliance might be required even in a piece-work contract. On a per-item basis, buyers might still worry about contract remedies for breach of warranty. Second, the whole point of the relationship between the parties might be to induce the promisee to make major reliance investments. When the goods are expensive to manufacture and idiosyncratic so that no one save the buyer will want them, then a piece-work approach will not promote sufficient promisee reliance. A custom-made piece of expensive, heavy equipment, made to the buyer's specifications and of use to only him, will leave the manufacturer high and dry if the buyer throws up the bargain halfway through. Because of this, the manufacturer will not wish to enter into the relationship without an *ex ante* promise of contract remedies for breach of the entire undertaking.

Reciprocal altruism

Reciprocal altruism is related to piece-work strategies, since in both cases a long-term relationship is broken into discrete elements which are made the subject of separate contracts. The difference is that reciprocal altruism provides an explanation for how trust might develop for the entire undertaking, beyond each individual contract. In reciprocal altruism, a party's cooperative behavior in one move signals a willingness to cooperate in the future and invites a cooperative response in turn.

The Prisoner's Dilemma game we examined above was a one-period game. There was no expectation that the parties would play against each other in repeated games. Otherwise the nature of the game would change, since the parties could signal information about future cooperation by refraining from defecting in a prior move. Once the parties begin to co-operate, they might easily continue to do so. What might result is a pattern of reciprocal altruism through which parties in repeated transactions are able to extract bargaining gains without a formal long-term contract.[12]

The idea of reciprocal altruism was discovered by biologist Robert Trivers and used by evolutionary biologists to explain patterns of cooperation among animals.[13] The extension to game theory came in a famous round of computer-simulated negotiations two decades ago.[14] Game theorists around the world were invited to submit strategies in repeated Prisoners' Dilemma games. In each round, one strategy was matched against another, and at the end total scores were added up. The overall winner was a strategy called "tit-for-tat" (TFT), which resembles the eye-for-an-eye norm of the *lex talionis.* In TFT, a party begins with a cooperative move and thereafter mimics the other player's last move. If the second party always defects (ALL-D), the first party will cooperate on his first move and defect thereafter; if both parties adopt TFT, they will both cooperate on every move. The advantage of TFT is that, while not excessively forgiving, it does not carry a grudge. The defector is immediately forgiven once he begins to cooperate. TFT is also a simple strategy that is easily communicated to the other party. It does not defeat every strategy, however. Played against ALL-D, the TFT player will cooperate and receive the sucker's payoff in round 1, while the ALL-D player will receive the opportunist's payoff. Thereafter, both parties will defect in every subsequent game. Having won round 1, the ALL-D player will beat the TFT player. But while TFT does not beat every opponent, it generally outperforms rival strategies when there is a broad mix of strategies and a large number of rounds.[15] TFT exploits bargaining gains which nastier strategies such as ALL-D sacrifice, and permits the parties to move from a dominant strategy of joint defection in the one-period game to joint cooperation in repeated games. What Axelrod's experiment showed is that, even without contractual fetters, the prudently cooperative TFT strategy encourages the development of trust when a Prisoners' Dilemma game is repeated numerous times.

In practice, parties who have repeated business dealings (called relational contractors) tend to fall into a pattern of reciprocal altruism. Consider the relationship between a large law firm and one of its major business clients that generates millions of dollars a year for the firm. There might be no formal long-term arrangement between them, but only a series of repeated one-shot retainer agreements setting out a specific task to be performed by the firm and the fee to be paid by the client. On any day, the size of the firm's billings is dwarfed by the expected value of future business dealings, since clients seldom transfer their business from one firm to another. What gives the relationship stability is not the individual contracts but rather the personal relationships and trust built up over the years between firm and client.

Long-term relational dealings are often self-enforcing,[16] in the sense that the parties never have an incentive to breach. Where the parties expect to continue dealing with one another in the future, like the law firm and its business client, both might find that the expected value of the long-term business relationship exceeds the gains from breach at every step of the way. The immediate gain from breach is dwarfed by the loss of long-term relational gains, and the parties continue indefinitely in their relationship.

Taking this one step further, the possibility of exploiting promissory gains explains why some friendships are formed in the first instance. This is obviously true of the professional friendships within a firm, but it is also true of the social networks and clubs that serve as voluntary insurance organizations. The relationship of trust lets the parties rely on each other in a way they could not do with strangers. Reciprocal altruism also helps to explain why clans and ethnic loyalties persist. Ethnographers and economists have noted that an ethnic group might come to dominate a particular trade – Jewish diamond merchants in New York, for example – because of reputational advantages within a group.[17] Outsiders will find it hard to compete with members of a group who can seal million dollar deals among themselves with a handshake. What binds the parties is not only personal friendship but also a heightened sense of kinship duty.[18] We distinguish between strangers and brothers, as *Deuteronomy* does in banning usury with the latter but not the former.[19]

Internalized norms

The example of kinship preferences suggests a third way in which a promisor might credibly signal his commitment. When norms of reciprocity are *internalized*, the promisor cannot breach without experiencing psychological discomfort, and this reduces the likelihood of breach by increasing its costs. If the promisor can credibly signal that he has internalized such norms, he can more easily persuade promisees to trust him and to benefit from the gains of joint cooperation.

Internalized norms are the self-policing mechanisms of what anthropologist Ruth Benedict called a guilt culture.[20] When an internalized norm is breached the individual assumes the perspective of an external judge and condemns himself for the fault, even if no one else observes it. When he felt such guilt, Sir Thomas Browne said, "There is another man inside of me that is angry with me." By contrast, in a shame culture such as Benedict's Japan the sanction for breach is a reputational loss when other people notice the fault and revise their opinion of one.[21]

In Homeric Greece, the sense of shame (*aidōs*) was an all-powerful incentive to bravery. When Andromache implores her husband Hector to abandon the battle, he replies that he would feel nothing but shame if he did so. But later Greeks wondered if shame was quite enough, since the unobserved fault escapes sanction. Because of this, Democritus sought to redefine *aidōs* as a feeling of guilt for personal lapses, even if no external shame attached to one's action. Similarly, in *Crime and Punishment* guilt is the crucial moral hurdle for the modern amoralist (Raskolnikov) who lacks the introspection to accept responsibility for his sins.[22]

Reciprocal altruism strategies may thus be seen to rest on a shame culture that awards goodwill points to those who are seen as trustworthy and stigmatizes those who are observed to misbehave. By contrast, in guilt cultures what matters is the signal to oneself through a sense of diminished worth.[23] We see our lives from the outside, like a movie in which we are the hero and have all the best lines. Self-love is one of the most powerful emotions, and we cannot observe ourselves departing from our self-image without severe emotional distress. So strong is the need for self-esteem that we employ sophisticated and powerful excuse mechanisms to block negative self-signals. But these are never entirely effective, and impose their own costs since they blind a person to his faults.

Guilt cultures may, therefore, enjoy a bargaining advantage over shame cultures. When breaches are undetectable or when performance standards are hard to measure, reputational signaling will not deter breaches so well as internalized guilt sanctions. This explains why promisors might want to internalize cooperative norms and make fixed preferences of them. Economist Robert Frank pointed this out with a tongue-in-cheek question: if *homo economicus* had a choice, would he want a conscience?[24] Only if he sincerely wanted to be wealthy, answered Frank. We are less likely to trust those whom we sense are dishonest and more likely to repose confidence in those who evince some sympathy for their fellows. Up to a point, virtue is its own reward.

A sense of personal guilt imposes a cost, to be sure, since it constrains future choices. It makes it painful to betray one's family, and those who have gone through a divorce might have wished that it were easier to do so. But if it were painless to leave one's spouse, marriage rates would be lower, since a man would find it harder to persuade a lady to trust his promises. Binding oneself through fixed preferences restricts future choices, but permits one to exploit bargain opportunities that would otherwise be lost.

Not everyone will find the trade-off desirable. The playboy must avoid entangling alliances to move easily from one woman to another. The result is a separating equilibrium, in which some people invest in stable cooperative preferences and others do not. The latter keep their options open, but sacrifice the long-term relationships that depend on trust. They also impose costs on promise-keepers, since promisees will sometimes fail to trust them because of the difficulty in distinguishing between true and false promises.

How can promisees distinguish between faithful and faithless promisors? What the promisee needs is deception-detection equipment, where he tests promisors for signs of reliability. But how is this done? The answer is written on our faces, the most public part of our body, where our emotions register for all to see. Facial signals reveal our deepest feelings to others, and permit them to make reliable inferences about our future behavior.[25] The rare person whose face never changes expression seems less than human. If he is not severely depressed, he is taken to signal complete indifference to other people.

We may express our sentiments in other ways, of course, but what is special about facial expressions is that they are so hard to mimic. We show our anxiety when lying, for example, and our blushes are therefore a useful commitment device. They increase the likelihood of detection and strengthen the incentive to tell the truth. Others will repose greater confidence in us, and this will permit us to extract increased gains from joint cooperation. Were it otherwise, thought La Bruyère, we might get away with everything. "If a person could blush on command, what crimes, not merely hidden, but public and known, would he not commit?"[26]

We may signal reliability in a variety of ways. Gossip is a trust-enhancing device that forges bonds within a group.[27] Revealing a confidence about oneself gives the listener the power to betray the teller, and by sending a strong signal that he trusts the listener the teller invites return trust. Even a joke might serve as a trust-building device. Sudden genuine laughter is written on our faces by muscles over which we lack full self-control. The counterfeit laugh, produced for purely strategic purposes, is a pale imitation, and easy to distinguish from true laughter.[28]

Union strategies

In union strategies the promisor's incentive to defect is addressed by aligning his interests more closely with those of the promisee, in the manner of medieval princes who sealed a treaty with a marriage. A more modern example would be the buyers and sellers who transform their relationship into a joint venture in which they share project profits. At the limit, the parties might merge. For example, General Motors purchased one of its suppliers, the Fisher car design business ("Body by Fisher"), after the latter hectored GM with demands for opportunistic contract renegotiations at a time when GM was hard pressed to refuse.[29] After the merger, the costs of supplier opportunism disappeared.

Family enterprises are another example of a union strategy, since families enjoy significant bargaining advantages over more impersonal businesses. At one time it was feared that family farms would be replaced by "agribusiness," the free market version of the collective farm. However, farming requires an extraordinary degree of loyalty at crucial times, such as when the harvest must be brought in and everyone must work very long hours. Shirking at this time could mean the loss of millions of dollars if the crops might be lost to a frost. Few employees can be trusted in these circumstances, but with family it is different. Therefore, the family farm remains the most common farming organization – even if the optimum size of the farm has greatly increased because of technological improvements and the number of farms has declined.

Non-contractual bonding

The final substitute for contract remedies is *bonding* or hands-tying.[30] Here, the promisor narrows the range of his future options by making it more difficult or expensive to breach. As Jon Elster has noted,[31] the self-binding promisor is like Ulysses, who wished to hear the song the Sirens sing. The difficulty was that everyone who heard the song was so enchanted that they sailed right up to the Sirens and perished on the reefs. Ulysses solved the problem with the first example of hands-tying. He ordered his crew to lash him to the mast and to stop up their ears with wax. As they rowed past, he heard the music but they didn't. They also didn't hear his pleas to be untied so he could direct them to the rocks. So they rowed safely on.

By binding himself in the first period, Ulysses was able to exploit an opportunity in the second. This is just what promisors would want to do, by removing the possibility of a future breach so as to induce promises to rely. Like Ulysses, the promisor seeks to restrict his future freedom of action in order to take up an opportunity. And, like Ulysses, he might have to bind his hands through non-contractual means where a contract cannot be written. One extreme example was the exchange of hostages through which medieval princes sometimes sealed their treaties, with the grimmest of sanctions levied against promise-breakers.[32] In our day, promisors might adopt similar if less painful reassurance techniques, making default more painful by offering promisees a bond against default. For example, borrowers might physically transfer consumer goods to lenders as a pledge. Alternatively, borrowers might retain possession of business assets but give the lender the right to step in and seize them on default. This is often a powerful signal of the borrower's credit-worthiness, as default would put him into bankruptcy.

Since all these substitutes are available, are the institutions of contract law less important than has been thought? The classic conception of contract law has quite properly been faulted for failing to take account of the ways in which parties might cooperate without formal agreements.[33] But, as bargainers still employ contractual reassurance techniques, bargaining substitutes have manifestly failed to take the place of contract law, and this for three reasons.

First, the substitutes might be costlier than contracting. Piece-work contracting sacrifices the beneficial reliance that a long-term contract might elicit when one party is asked to make a major preliminary investment in the project. And the business mergers of a union strategy might sacrifice the efficiencies associated with deconglomerization and result in a bloated firm. Similarly, extra-contractual bonding strategies might require a party to leave productive assets unused.

Second, substitutes for contract law might simply be unavailable in a wide range of bargaining circumstances. For example, the parties might be too geographically dispersed for relationships of trust to arise without contract law. Alternatively, they might be strangers with no basis for a reputational ranking.

Third, habits of mistrust might be too deep-seated to foster beneficial reliance without the external sanction of contract law enforcement. The kind of pre-contractual society where promisors must fall back on their families was described by Edward C. Banfield in *The Moral Basis of a Backward Society*. Banfield wrote of a society so riddled with envy – an Italian town he called "Montegrano" – that any form of economic progress was unthinkable. The Montegranese thought that every politician was on the take, that every priest was corrupt, that every employer cheated his employees. Only the most basic forms of economic cooperation, within the circle of the family, were possible.[34]

For such societies, contract law and an honest and independent judiciary to enforce contracts, are critical to economic development. Contracts make possible economic cooperation across families, clans and ethnic groups. They permit the stranger, the immigrant, the member of an outcast tribe, to burst the bounds of prejudice and form new ties with others. Free contracting produces a more diverse society, and also a wealthier one.

Summary

The institutions of promising and contract law permit promisors to commit credibly to perform their promises. This promotes promisee reliance and permits both parties to share in the contractual surplus. There are other techniques of promisee reassurance, but none that can take the place of contract law.

4 Fidelity to promising

> We have obligations to mankind at large, which are not in consequence of any special voluntary pact.
>
> Edmund Burke

Unlike rival theories, the economic account of contract law rests on a conception of promising as an institution, and it alone explains why the institution is desirable. By invoking the institution we persuade others to rely on our promises and enter into joint projects with us. But economic explanations are incomplete if they cannot tell us why promisors ought to respect promissory institutions. What is needed is a connecting factor that links promisors to promising and explains why, having invoked it, they cannot walk away from the institution.

While reliance, benefits and will theories cannot explain why promissory institutions should exist, they might nevertheless be thought to suggest a connecting factor that yokes us to it. If the institution is already a feature of our society, might some form of the reliance, benefits or will theories account for personal duties to adhere to its rules? In the end, however, theories that do not concede the institution's value cannot supply the fidelity requirement that oblige us to support it.

Respect, gratitude and consent

For each of the three rival theories of promising, there is a closely related connecting factor that links an individual to the institution. For reliance theories, there is a requirement of *respect* owed to the institutions with which one comes in contact; for benefits theories, there is a debt of *gratitude*; and for will theories there is obligation to comply with the rules of institutions to which one has *consented*.

Respect, gratitude and consent theories do not assume that promissory institutions are valuable and cannot explain why they ought to exist. The indifference of such theories to the economist's beneficial reliance would seem enough to condemn them. In one respect, however, they are more promising than the reliance, benefits and will theories, discussed in Chapter 2, which were unable to explain how promissory institutions arose. Under respect, gratitude and consent theories, the existence of the institution is taken as a given, and the question is, rather, why we are bound to support it. In the end, however, they fail to supply a principle of fidelity that obliges us to perform our promises.

Respect

Respect duties resemble reliance explanations, since the duty of respect asks us to take due care when employing a society's conventions lest others come to harm by relying on us. When driving in another country I should find out on which side of the road people drive, and not only for my sake. Similarly, the tourist from Tonga should inform himself about our promissory institutions. If he should happen to promise he might be found to be bound by the institution and its rules, even if they are not to be found in his country.[1]

The respect account of fidelity requirements is more attractive than reliance explanations of the institution of promising. Unlike reliance theories, the duty of respect does not give rise to problems of circularity since it does not seek to explain why promissory institutions should exist. Under the duty of respect, the visitor takes the institutions as he finds them. He is bound if the promisee acted in conformity with a societal institution, and it is beside the point to argue that the promisee should not have relied.

Nevertheless, duties of respect cannot explain why promisors are bound to perform their unrelied-upon promises. Respect requirements are reliance-based, and the connecting factor does not take hold if the promisee has not relied and no harm has been done. While those who promise and then pull back before the promisee relies might weaken the institution of promising, the duty of respect is agnostic about the institution's benefits. Respect requirements do not ask the promisor to promote the institution but only to ensure that he does not harm others. Thus, the duty of respect cannot satisfy the principle of fidelity to contract law, but only to a truncated version of the institution where the unrelied-on promise is unenforceable.

Gratitude

The next explanation of promissory connecting factors grounds a duty of fidelity on the promisor's receipt of a benefit from the institution and the sense of gratitude he ought to feel as a consequence. It is difficult to speak of an obligation of gratitude, which is a feeling more than an action. People have imperfect control over their feelings, so that an obligation to have a feeling sounds odd.[2] If "ought implies can," how can we blame the person who cannot feel gratitude? Yet we do blame people for their feelings, whether or not they can change them, because they are constitutive of their identities and moral personhood. We blame the sociopath for his lack of affect and the narcissist for his overweening love of praise, just as we blame the ingrate for an impoverished heart.

However, there are other serious objections to gratitude accounts of promissory connecting factors. While gifts call for gratitude, impersonal benefits (like those conferred by the English language) do not. What are needed are givers, quite apart from the institution itself: the gift without the giver is bare, as James Russell Lowell noted. But institutional benefits are scarcely gifts. While we benefit from living in promissory societies, the benefits are derived from the performances of past promisors, through which the institution became a reliable means of promoting trust. But the past promisors did not seek to confer a benefit upon me. They never met me, and I was the last thing on their minds. Their performance was purely self-interested and not an act of charity to anonymous beneficiaries, and this excludes any debt of gratitude.[3]

John Rawls argued that there is a requirement of gratitude to institutions, which he called the *principle of fairness*, under which an institution's rules bind those who have availed themselves of it.[4] Fairness requirements must assume that the institution is morally neutral, and that goods derived from it are not good in a way that has any moral significance. Otherwise, we might dispense with the principle of fairness and ground allegiance requirements on a natural duty to support valuable institutions. Suppose, for example, that international organizations such as NATO and the United Nations are thought desirable institutions, and not morally neutral. Member-states that free ride on them by failing to pay their dues would then have breached a natural duty of support, and the principle of fairness might be ignored.

To say that the institution is morally neutral is to say that it does not matter if it disappears and no one benefits from it in the future. But if so, how can we say that anyone benefits from it in the present? Suppose, further, that we seek to charge someone with a gratitude duty to support the institution of promising. However, he tells us that he derives no benefits from American promises as he much prefers Tonganese promises. We cannot contradict him, so long as no moral value is ascribed to promising.[5]

The difficulty in identifying the benefit (not morally good in itself) that is received by living in a promissory society is analogous to the problem that arises in the law of restitution when unsolicited services are provided. You might think you are conferring a benefit on me if, without my knowledge or approval, you paint my house purple. However, absent something that looks like a solicitation or consent, I should be able to deny that your services were of any benefit to me. As a consequence, officious gifts do not ground a restitutionary claim.

Finally, it is not clear how the principle of fairness could permit us to abandon an institution. Would the principle require the Tonganese to stick with their form of promising and bar them from adopting Western promises? A dynamic account of how new institutions replace old ones would always begin with some first act of disloyalty, and each new institution, unless it rose out of thin air, would be founded on an aboriginal betrayal. This would seem to offend under any reasonable right to freedom of association. Although I derive benefits from the English language I am free to abandon it for Norwegian without any sense of guilt. One has the right to shop around, to be fickle, where the choice matters little. So long as the institution is morally neutral, fidelity requirements do not arise.

Obligations of respect and gratitude (or fairness) are therefore unable to account for the principle of fidelity to promising.

Consent

Consent theories suggest a third explanation for the duty of support. We saw another kind of consent theory in Chapter 2, one that sought to explain how the institution of promising might be created. That theory was quite unsuccessful. The consent theory we consider here assumes the existence of the institution and seeks only to explain how we might be bound to it. In the end, however, it fares no better than the consent theory discussed in Chapter 2.

Once again, the problem of circularity arises. Consent to a particular contract does not result in a moral obligation to support the institution of promising unless one first assumes a moral duty to perform one's promises. The institution might exist, but that does not permit us to derive a moral duty to perform promises unless we begin by assuming that which we set out to prove: that people ought to perform their promises.

Moreover, one cannot be said to have consented to an institution unless there is a meaningful opportunity to reject it. But how can we reject promising? If the argument is that we consent to promising by living in a promissory society, or attorn to contract law by living in a state that enforces promises, Hume's response to tacit consent explanations of political obligation seems unanswerable.

> We may as well assert that a man, by remaining in a vessel, freely consents to the dominion of the master; though he was carried on board while asleep, and must leap into the ocean and perish, the moment he leaves her.[6]

John Simmons argues that we may voluntarily accept goods that we unavoidably receive.[7] French civilians in occupied France could not reject the German invaders, but collaborators did more than sit on their hands: they voluntarily accepted the German rule; and some of them were executed after the war as a consequence. But it is doubtful that any such voluntary acceptance may ground a principle of fidelity to promissory institutions. Before an acceptance is voluntary, the recipient must perform some affirmative act. For collaborators, this was "having intelligence" with the enemy. However, it is difficult to see what the analogue might be in the case of promising. If the acceptance comes from the fact of having promised, this scarcely seems more rejectable. The possibility of eliminating promising from our language seems a little far-fetched.[8]

One last version of the consent theory must be rejected. We cannot derive a principle of consent from hypothetical bargain models that posit a beneficial institution. Hypothetical bargains are often employed as a heuristic device to persuade students to sign on to efficiency norms. If the result is efficient, we tell our students, surely everyone would consent.[9] But actual consent is superfluous if it turns out that we ought to consent. The institution is not just because it is chosen; rather, it is chosen because it is just. Hypothetical bargain models turn out to be nothing more than a covert manner to inculcate allegiance to efficiency norms, and with more candor we would dispense with them and rely on the natural duty to support just institutions.[10]

Natural duties of support

We turn, therefore, from fidelity requirements that refuse to concede value to promissory institutions to the consequentialist theories that do. Promising and contract law promote the beneficial reliance we saw in Chapter 3 and permit the parties to exploit opportunities for gain; and a principle of fidelity arises from the natural duty to support a valuable institution.[11]

To call the duty natural is not to suggest a connection to natural law theories. Instead, it is natural in the sense that it arises without a voluntary act on our part. Our allegiance to the institution of promising resembles Edmund Burke's Tory duty of allegiance to the state.

> If we owe to [civil society] any duty, it is not subject to our wills. Duties are not voluntary. ... [Civil society] attaches to every individual of that society, without any formal act of his own. ... Men without their choice derive benefits from that association; without their choice they are subjected to duties in consequence of these benefits; and without their choice enter into a virtual obligation as binding as any that is actual. ... We have obligations to mankind at large, which are not in consequence of any special voluntary pact. They arise from the relation of man to man, and the relation of man to God, which relations are not matters of choice. On the contrary, the force of all the pacts which we enter into ... depends upon those prior obligations.[12]

There are two kinds of Burkean natural duties. The first are regulative requirements that are owed to other persons (such as parents or God);

the second are fidelity requirements that ask us to support just institutions (such as civil society or promising). In both cases they arise without our consent and trump our rights. There is no right to abandon one's parents, or to waive our duties to a just civil society.

Consent explanations of political obligation turn the principle of fidelity into something very mysterious, since they look for a consent that almost never is given. "The wit of man cannot say more for anarchy," observed Filmer.[13] The error lies in thinking consent a necessary and not merely a sufficient ground of allegiance, such that only consent binds us. But non-consensual duties of support lie all about one, said Burke, to our families, to God, to our neighbors and to the state. Such duties are *positional*, and are owed by everyone who occupies a particular position or station. "The place that determines our duty to our country is a social, civil relation. . . . The place of every man determines his duty."[14]

In rejecting positional requirements, consent theorists argue that we are only bound to perform duties to which we have consented. Otherwise, argues John Simmons, we might be appointed to a position against our will and told to perform its duties.[15] For some positions, such as the President of the United States (with its ceremonious oath of office), consent is clearly a precondition. But Simmons' objection would not be telling unless consent were required for every duty-imposing position, and this is not the case.

Positional fidelity requirements arise without our consent when: (1) it is morally desirable that a state or institution should command our allegiance; and (2) given the failure of respect, gratitude and consent theories, it is impossible to provide a satisfactory account of non-positional support obligations.[16] The second of these propositions is largely conceded by Simmons, who places himself *On the Edge of Anarchy*. If one rejects Simmons' anarchism, what are left are positional duties to support the state, to which one is bound by the not unjust connecting factors supplied by the state's law of citizenship. In morals as in civil law, the right to resist institutional duties must sometimes yield to the superior plea of *raison d'état*.

The philosophical anarchist who rejects all political and legal obligations because consent is lacking begins in the wrong place, with the subject to be bound. The proper place to begin is with the institution. To say that it is morally desirable is to say that it should be preserved. But it could not be preserved without fidelity requirements, as this would give its members free exit rights. If the institution is just, and can be established only through natural duties of support, then natural duties must be deemed to arise, and from them we may derive a principle of fidelity.

As this is not a book of political theory, I need not answer the question whether it is desirable that states should exist. In the case of promissory institutions, the answer is simpler. Promising and contract law promote the beneficial reliance that we saw in the last chapter and permit parties to exploit opportunities for joint gain which would otherwise be lost. Since the institutions would wither were the parties permitted to plead the absence of fidelity requirements, the efficiency gains of promising and contract law supply the natural duty of support that satisfies the principle of fidelity.

Unlike the obligations of promising, fidelity requirements are not normally owed to any person.[17] American citizens owe a duty of allegiance to their country, not to its other citizens. The same is true of British subjects (even if they owe a personal duty to the monarch). Similarly, the duty to support promissory institutions is not a duty to a person. Instead, it is a duty to abide by the rules of the institution when they impose an obligation to a promisee. The idea of a duty owed not to a person but to an institution might seem odd to non-lawyers, but it was just such a duty that sent Lord Haw-Haw to the gallows.

This does not end the enquiry, since the question of who might be bound still arises. If the duty is positional, when is one in the position of membership in the institution? The state might be just, but we still need a principle of citizenship before anyone is bound to offer allegiance. However, there is nothing mysterious in the way we become bound to a state, through just laws of jurisdiction and citizenship. These are specified by the state itself, in its membership rules. So long as these are not unjust, they bind the subjects to whom they apply, and this without a formal act of consent on their part. In short, the problem of political obligation, which has troubled philosophers for centuries, has been quietly solved by private international lawyers and their just rules of personal jurisdiction.

The connecting factors that give rise to natural duties of support need to be clear if they are to command people's allegiance. However, this is not to say that only one kind of connecting factor can be thought just, or that the law of citizenship must be everywhere the same. For example, there are several different tests of legal residency and citizenship. For fiscal legislation, with its need for certainty, there are bright-line standards that depend on the number of days spent in the jurisdiction. For the law of treason, however, the standard might be more expansive, as Lord Haw-Haw discovered. Moreover, tests of residency and citizenship differ from one country to another (which is why tax treaties are needed to resolve problems of double taxation). In devising a just law of citizenship there is a certain amount of rubber; yet so long as the connecting factor is not unjust it still compels our allegiance.

The question of fidelity to promissory institutions may be answered in the same way. If promissory institutions are desirable, the institution should be able to command allegiance. It may, therefore, supply its own rules to identify those who are bound by their promises and contracts. Provided the connecting factor is not unjust, the principle of fidelity is satisfied.

In the case of promissory institutions the connecting factor is the promise itself. As citizenship is to political obligation, so promising is to promissory obligations. The institution specifies that those who promise are bound; and as this is a reasonable connecting factor it satisfies the principle of fidelity. But the promise does not supply the fidelity requirement by itself, as consent theorists would have it, any more than citizenship laws solve the problem of political obligation by themselves. In both cases, fidelity requirements are grounded on a natural duty to support just institutions and not on mere consent.

When we form a new club we may debate its rules and drop out if they do not suit us. It is otherwise when the institution is already in existence. We might propose new rules, but if they are not adopted we are not absolved from fidelity requirements to valuable institutions because better ones can be imagined. Were that the case, the natural duty of support could always be evaded. When the institution is morally indifferent, the duty of support does not arise; and when it is evil there may be a duty of resistance. But when it is valuable, we take the institution as we find it and owe it our support.

A single defection will not greatly weaken the institution. However, this does not excuse the solitary defector, since permitting one person to free ride is tantamount to permitting everyone similarly situated to do so. In that case, the institution would disappear. Whether this would matter depends on whether the institution is desirable. As we saw in Chapter 2, Kant appeared to think free riding bad in itself, but this cannot be right. There is nothing wrong with free riding when the institution is morally indifferent or evil. Where Kant went wrong was in thinking that anti-free riding requirements might supply a moral basis for the institution. They do not, unless the institution deserves to be supported, in which case the natural duty of support would prohibit free riding.

Since promissory institutions are valuable because of the efficiency goals they serve, we may evaluate the connecting factors from an economic perspective. Promisors whose bargains are likely inefficient should be absolved from fidelity requirements; while near-promisors might find themselves brought within the duty of fidelity against their will when this serves efficiency goals.

When promises are expected to be inefficient, promisors are excused from performance under a variety of contractual doctrines. These include the vices of capacity that we will see in Chapter 5 as well as the vices of consent, such as duress, that we will examine in Chapter 8. When a promisor lacks capacity we cannot assume that his bargains will make him better off; and even if he is of full capacity his bargains might leave him worse off if they are tainted by duress or fraud. Bargains might also impose heavy costs on non-consenting third parties, as we shall see in Chapter 7. In all of these cases, the presumption that contracts effect efficiency gains does not apply and the parties are excused from performance.

In cases of near-promising, contractual liability is sometimes imposed where a full promise would have been value-increasing. Under the objective theory of contract we saw in Chapter 1, a promisor is bound where a reasonable promisee would infer a promise had been made, even if the promisor privately withheld his consent through a secret mental reservation. Otherwise, promisors would always have an easy out, and this would be entirely destructive of the beneficial reliance promoted by contract law enforcement. In such cases the law might seize upon the public manifestation of a promise to enforce what would likely have been an efficient contract.

A promisor might, therefore, be bound to perform even if he did not intend to incur an obligation. In addition, he might be bound even if he does not recognize the fidelity requirement to adhere to the rules of the institution.[18] The promissory skeptic who denies the value of the institution, and the reliance theorist who believes that promises are not binding absent promisee reliance, are both liable upon their promises. Neither the promisee nor the judge need enquire into the promisor's philosophical doubts before concluding that an obligation is owed. The alternative would be to offer promisors an easy way out that would weaken the institution.

Summary

Before a person can be said to be bound to an institution, a principle of fidelity must link him to it, making it *his* institution. What is needed is something like the connecting factors of public international lawyers, which link a person or transaction with the laws of a particular state. In the case of promising and contract law, the connecting factor may be supplied by the rules of promising and contract law, so long as these are not unjust, once the value of the institution is conceded. In that case, support duties arise from the natural duty to support just institutions. By contrast, reliance, benefits and will theories that do not concede the institution's value cannot supply a satisfactory connecting factor in duties of respect, gratitude and consent.

Part I of this book has examined the foundations of contract law and has argued that they most plausibly rest upon norms of efficiency. In Part II, I take note of critics who charge that the ethical implications of normative law-and-economics are troubling and that efficiency theories should not determine the content of contract law rules. These objections often strike a sympathetic chord, since many people have an inchoate sense that economic principles should be reined in by a very different set of norms, such as fairness. While these kinds of arguments extend well beyond contract law, I shall not try to address broad concerns about social justice. However, within the narrower ambit of contract theory, I shall argue that such concerns are misplaced. Law-and-economics explains not only the logic but also the limits of free bargaining, and in the chapters that follow I look at how restrictions on bargaining rights might serve efficiency norms.

Part II

The limits of bargaining freedom

5 Soft paternalism

I stumbled when I saw.
  Shakespeare, *King Lear*

Hegel thought that freedom was the foundational good, and that other goods – even morality – were instrumental and valuable only insofar as they promoted autonomy. For most consequentialists, this is exactly backwards: what matters is the end state more than how we get there, what is chosen more than how we choose. This is not to say that consequentialists are indifferent to the quality of the choice. Our choices are means to an end, but as Derek Parfit noted "mattering as a means is a way of mattering."[1] The freely chosen ice cream cone tastes better than the one forced on us, even if it's the same flavor in the end.

Nevertheless, the possibility of bad choices must be troubling to the consequentialist. And to the chooser as well. Could we persuade him that, for certain kinds of decisions, he will systematically make poor choices as compared to those we would make for him, we might persuade him to give us the power to bind him in the tainted class. With the benefit of full knowledge and calm deliberation, he might willingly surrender his free bargaining rights, trading a miserable freedom for a happy slavery.

The least controversial cases for interference with individual choice are minors (children under 18) and the mentally incapable. No adult would want to be bound by all the contracts he entered into when he was a minor, nor would a person who returned to mental health want to be held accountable to the agreements he made when mentally impaired. Neither kind of contract would be likely to satisfy the Pareto standard of efficiency:

> *Pareto efficiency.* A transformation is Pareto-superior if at least one person is made better off and no one is made worse off.

Parties of full capacity will not consent to contracts that leave them worse off; but with minors and the mentally incapable one cannot be so sure and such contracts are presumptively unenforceable. This is not to say that things divide up neatly. We should want some of our minor contracts to be binding and some of our adult contracts to be non-binding. Minors should be able to enter into binding agreements for necessities such as food and shelter. More controversially, restrictions on the bargaining rights of mentally competent adults might be justified on the theories we examine in this and the next two chapters.

Restrictions on a person's choice which are imposed for his own good are paternalistic, and paternalism comes in two kinds: soft and hard.[2] The *soft paternalism* we examine in this chapter second-guesses a person's choices with the goal of giving effect to his true desires. His judgment is clouded by mental biases; or his judgment is clear but he is prevented from reaching the desired end by weakness of the will. Either way, soft paternalism is limited to satisfying the subject's deepest wishes and is powerless against a clear-minded and resolute assertion of individual choice.

There is, however, a harder kind of paternalism under which the state overrules a person's choices even when these represent his true wishes. The problem is not that the subject is unable to identify and pursue his preferences; instead, he has the wrong set of preferences and "does not know what is good for him." In this kind of paternalism the state enunciates a conception of the good life and frowns on choices that are inconsistent with it. Life would be simpler could we label this hard paternalism, but by convention it is called *perfectionism*.[3] Perfectionism makes a strong assumption about the state's knowledge about the good, and is contrasted with an anti-perfectionist *neutralism* which holds that the state should abstain from taking sides about ultimate personal choices.

Minors and incompetents

The soft paternalism that impeaches the contracts of minors is sometimes thought to present a problem for law-and-economics. But it does just the opposite. Minor contracts that are presumptively inefficient would not be enforced from a law-and-economics perspective. Efficiency considerations also explain why an arbitrary event – an eighteenth birthday – serves as the test of capacity.[4]

A rigorous Hegelian would base the test of capacity not on birthdays but on demonstrated reasoning ability. In some respects, this might be a superior system, as there are some minors who deserve to be emancipated and some adults who are anything but mature. But this would impose economic costs that a birthday standard avoids. Proving a person's incapacity in court would be vastly harder than proving how old he was, and mature 19 and 20-year-olds would, therefore, find it difficult to find people to deal with them. In practice, a Hegelian standard would perversely fetter the freedom of true adults and deprive them of the gains of free contracting.

Like a 65 m.p.h. speed limit, the age of majority standard is both over-
inclusive and under-inclusive. It upholds the contracts of immature
19-year-olds and sets aside the contracts of mature 17-year-olds. However,
where the alternative is a costly, case-by-case examination of dangerous
driving or bargaining ability, a bright-line standard is the best we can
do.[5] We settle on what the speed limit should be by determining when
most people begin to drive dangerously; and we select the age to serve
as the test of capacity by determining when most people are able to enter
into value-increasing contracts. The criterion in both cases is driven by
efficiency considerations.

The common law usefully makes an exception to the bright-line standard when the minor bargains for necessities. The child who is cut off
from his parents (for example Macaulay Culkin in *Home Alone*) might
need to pledge his credit to keep body and soul together. If the child's
contracts were unenforceable, the merchant would have a weaker incentive to provide him with food and shelter, and the child might go hungry.
He is, therefore, better off when his contracts for necessities are enforceable and merchants can rely on his promises.

There is no bright-line standard for mental capacity, which is therefore
a tougher nut than minority. The merchant cannot "card" the mental
incompetent, and might identify him only with difficulty or not at all.
Things were easier for the merchant in the nineteenth century, when the
test was the narrow *M'Naghten* criminal law standard: was the party "so
deprived of his mental faculties as to be wholly, absolutely and completely
unable to understand or comprehend the nature of the transaction."[6] Such
defects are apparent to nearly everyone and the merchant is put on notice.
In the twentieth century, however, the definition of incapacity expanded
to reach the case of those who understood the nature of the transaction
but who labored under the compulsion of a mental disorder,[7] and even
beyond this to cases of mental weakness or diminished mental capacity.[8]
These definitions focus upon the consumer's disability and not on the
merchant's notice; and as the possibility of honest mistake is greater,
the merchant will be more reluctant to bargain with borderline cases. If
he does, he can be expected to seek a premium price to compensate him
for the greater risk of unenforceability. The expansion in protection never
comes without a cost to its intended beneficiaries.

Hidden mental illness is like a latent defect that eludes the careful buyer.
The risks that the unsuspecting merchant is asked to bear are nicely
brought out in *Faber* v. *Sweet Style Mfg. Corp.*, where a manic-depressive
real estate developer sought to set aside a land purchase contract on
grounds of incapacity. In August 1961 Faber entered into his manic phase
and stopped seeing his psychiatrist. He "began to drive at high speeds,
to take his wife out to dinner, to be sexually more active and to discuss
his prowess with others."[9] He bought three expensive cars and began to
discuss turning his Long Island bathhouse into a 12-storey cooperative.

Apparently, none of this was known to the seller, but the court still set the sale aside because of the buyer's incapacity.

This result is doubly unfortunate. From the evidence, there was nothing the *Faber* defendant could reasonably have done to cure the problem. But there was something the plaintiff could have done. Manic-depression is treatable with mood-altering drugs, and had the plaintiff sought medication and stayed with it he might never have bought the land. Permitting plaintiffs to plead their incapacity in such cases weakens their incentives to solve the problem themselves.

In other respects, however, the law of incapacity was far broader in the nineteenth century, when African-Americans and women lacked bargaining freedom. As slaves, African-Americans had no right to contract, and even after emancipation their bargaining rights were severely curtailed. For example, southern Black Codes greatly restricted their ability to sell their most valuable asset: their services.

David Bernstein's *Only One Place of Redress* describes one such statute, the emigrant agent laws that restricted the ability of African-Americans in the deep South to take up better-paying jobs in another state.[10] They were valued employees, and employers from other states wanted to hire them. Because moving was costly, the out-of-state employers hired "emigrant agents" to help them relocate. However, deep-South employers resented the loss of cheap labor and the competition from better-paying employers in other states, and imposed prohibitive licensing fees on emigrant agents. Sadly, the Supreme Court upheld these laws.[11] Bernstein's conclusion that a court more concerned to protect freedom of contract would better have served the interests of African-Americans is difficult to resist.

Women's bargaining rights were also severely curtailed in the nineteenth century. Women were excluded from many jobs and required the assent of their fathers or husbands before they could sell or buy property. At marriage a woman lost her capacity to contract. She had no separate legal personality, and marriage transferred everything she possessed to the control of her husband. All this was changed by law reform legislation such as the British Married Women's Property Act of 1870.

The effort to remove the disabilities under which blacks and women suffered was championed by nineteenth-century utilitarians (notably John Stuart Mill) who were the forerunners of the law-and-economics movement. As an economist, Mill recognized the costs that fetters on bargaining freedom impose, and his *On Liberty* remains the *locus classicus* of anti-paternalism. Mill condemned all state interference with individual choice where the sole intended beneficiary is the individual himself. "The sole end for which mankind are warranted, individually or collectively, in interfering with the liberty of action of any of their number is self-protection," said Mill. I may interfere with your choices to protect myself, not to protect you. Harm-to-others is what matters, not harm-to-oneself. "The only purpose for which power can be rightfully exercised over any member of a civilized community, against his will, is harm to others. His own good, either physical or moral, is not a sufficient warrant."[12]

Mill's anti-paternalism had clear political ramifications, from which he did not shrink. He was a passionate abolitionist and one of the earliest liberal feminists. His opponents, such as Thomas Carlyle, ridiculed Mill's concern for blacks and women. It is often thought that Carlyle's put-down of economics as the "dismal science" referred to Malthusian declinism and the (erroneous) idea that free markets would condemn the poor to starvation. In fact, what Carlyle condemned, in the most vulgar manner, was the anti-slavery movement.[13] What was dismal was not economics but Carlyle's anti-market theories.

Within the women's movement, early leaders shared Mill's goals of economic liberty and equality.[14] Elizabeth Cady Stanton and Susan B. Anthony were anti-paternalists who sought to remove legal obstacles to free bargaining. Subsequently, "equity" feminists such as Justice Ruth Bader Ginsburg took aim at economic inequalities that prevented women from participating fully in a liberal society. However, late twentieth-century "gender" feminists abandoned economic liberalism and embraced paternalistic fetters on bargaining freedom. "Radical and socialist feminists," writes gender feminist Alison Jagger, "have shown that the old ideals of freedom, equality and democracy are insufficient."[15]

Though separated by an ideological chasm, there are striking similarities between anti-liberals, left and right, on the subject of bargaining freedom. Nineteenth-century apologists for slavery such as John C. Calhoun and George Fitzhugh were paternalists who sought to defend the institution on the grounds that it benefited the slave as well as the master. Calhoun contrasted Southern slaves with Northern industrial workers, whom (anticipating Marx) he called "wage slaves"; and he concluded that laborers fared better under paternalism than under free contracting.[16] In our day, Critical Race Scholars are no less suspicious of liberal ideals such as free bargaining. The affinities between nineteenth- and twentieth-century paternalists was noted by Arthur Leff, who observed that "the benevolent have a tendency to colonize, whether geographically or legally."[17]

Judgment heuristics

While the history of bargaining fetters is troubling, we are, nevertheless, in the midst of a paternalist revival. But there is a difference. The new paternalist would impeach everyone's judgment, not just that of children or African-Americans or women. He might draw his net more widely, but at least he does not discriminate.[18] Nor is he without empirical support, for he rests his case on current research in cognitive psychology and behavioral law-and-economics that shows how our *judgment heuristics* may mislead. A heuristic device is a tool for learning, such as a teacher's prop; and judgment heuristics are the props or mental shortcuts we employ in all our decision-making. They are the pervasive and indispensable rules of thumb we use when we see everything at a glance, when we infer from scattered bits of evidence, when we rely on hunches and guesstimates.

Were rationality defined in terms of the reasoning ability of an infinitely powerful computer, we would all seem less than rational. Yet, that sets the bar too high, for we should never wish to emulate a computer in our daily lives. Even simple tasks, like looking across the room, would become impossible if we could not abstract from all the information we process. Steven Pinker notes that a potentially infinite number of three-dimensional objects may project the same image on our retinas.[19] That does not happen, however, for we focus on only a small part of all we experience; beyond that, our instincts and patterns of perception and thought take over. Driving down the highway, our minds are occupied with plans and ideas, and our instincts guide the steering wheel. We arrive home on auto-pilot, without fully remembering how we got there. Otherwise, we could not move at all. We would be paralyzed by the mental costs of concentration, information acquisition, information marshaling and evaluation, calculation and decision. To economize on all this, we rely upon judgment heuristics, preferring a rational irrationality to an irrational rationality, a wise ignorance to foolish learning.

Our emotions also economize on calculation costs and, as an "affect heuristic," influence our behavior.[20] The distinction between feelings and calculation is often blurred and many of our judgments are as much one as the other. "We do not just see 'a house'," said Robert Zajonc, "we see a *handsome* house, an *ugly* house, or a *pretentious* house."[21] Similarly, our distaste for liars is both an aversion and a sense of the harm they may impose upon us, with the emotion substituting for a costly cost-benefit analysis. We don't have to calculate the harm they might impose – we simply know we don't like them. Feelings of boredom or disgust also provide us with useful stopping rules that short circuit wasteful mental calculation. The sense of boredom prompts us not to spend too much time at pointless tasks, while a feeling of impending disgust can bring an overlong inquiry to an abrupt halt. Our natural tendency to imitate others also usefully prevents us from continuing on where others have stopped.[22] Finally, a simple preference or aversion may take charge and tell us to stop calculating and get on with it. We might spend an endless amount of time in search of the perfect mate, but falling in love tells us to stop. As does our mate.

The need for a stopping impulse is illustrated by one of neurologist Anthony Damasio's brain-damaged patients. The patient lacked any sense of emotional commitment and spent inordinate amounts of time on trivial tasks. One day Damasio asked him when their next session should take place:

I suggested two alternatives dates, both in the coming month and just a few days apart from each other. The patient pulled out his appointment book and began consulting the calendar. . . . For the better part of a half-hour, the patient enumerated reasons for and against each of the two dates: Previous engagements, proximity to other engagements, possible meteorological conditions, virtually anything that one could reasonably think about concerning a simple date. . . . [H]e was now walking us through a tiresome cost-benefit analysis, and endless outlining and fruitless comparison of options and possible consequences. [W]e finally did tell him, quietly, that he should come on the second of the alternative dates. His response was equally calm and prompt. He simply said: "That's fine."[23]

Damasio concluded that "deciding well also means deciding expeditiously, especially when time is of the essence."[24]

From an evolutionary perspective, our judgment heuristics and emotions economize on the scarcest of resources – the higher consciousness of deliberation and reflection. Big brains are very expensive organs, relative to the rest of our body. At rest, they take 22 times as much energy as an equivalent amount of muscle[25]; and the nervous system, which interacts with the brain, consumes about 20 percent of the body's oxygen system but only 2 percent of its mass.[26] Through judgment heuristics we accomplish the same tasks but at less cost. We work smarter and not harder – just as Dilbert is encouraged to do.[27]

Over time our calculations may turn into instincts. We begin by working out the details of a complex decision, evaluating and weighing all of the possible outcomes, and finally arrive at an overall best solution. When a similar problem arises in the future, the best outcome suggests itself naturally and immediately. Similarly, we feel an instinctive aversion to what resembles a bad choice from the past: "Been there, done that." G.E. Hinton concludes that "people seem capable of taking frequently repeated sequences and eliminating the sequential steps so that an inference that was once rational becomes intuitive."[28]

This is not to attribute inerrancy to the instincts and emotions that economize on calculation. The cognitive psychology literature of the 1970s and 1980s identified several areas where our hunches might systematically lead us astray.[29] Daniel Kahneman and Amos Tversky – the leaders of the cognitive movement – created situations where our heuristics and probabilistic thinking diverge and where we follow our hunches even though they violate the rules of probability theory. When this happens, the heuristics are *biased* and can mislead us. The following is a selection of cognitive biases, where this might happen:

Availability bias. We form judgments about the likelihood of an event on the basis of how quickly instances come to mind.[30] We might, therefore, overestimate the divorce rate if many of our friends are divorced. In another example, film critic Pauline Kael reported that she did not understand how Nixon was elected in 1972, since none of her friends had voted for him. As it happens, Nixon won 49 states in that election, including New York.

Anchoring bias. To simplify decision-making, people may start with a particular reference point (anchor) that shapes their conclusion. In one test, a roulette wheel was spun to generate a number between 0 and 100. Subjects were then asked whether this number was higher or lower than the number of African members of the UN. When the roulette number was 10, the median estimate of African UN members was 25; when the roulette number was 65, the median estimate was 45.[31]

The Gambler's Fallacy. A fair coin is tossed six times and comes up TTTTTT. What is the probability that it will be an H on the next toss? Since it is a fair coin the correct answer is 50 percent. The coin has no memory of previous tosses, and the probability of an H on the sixth toss is the same as it was on the first one. Nevertheless, most people seem to think it must be higher than 50 percent, as though an H were "due." A related judgment bias is called the law of small numbers. In probability theory, the law of large numbers ensures that very large samples (e.g., 1,000 coin tosses) are highly representative of the population from which they are drawn. The law of small numbers refers to the mistaken belief that very small samples are as representative of the population as very large samples.[32]

The Base Rate Fallacy. Assume that one person in 1,000 (the base rate) has a particular disease. You have taken a test for the disease with a 99 percent probability of a correct diagnosis (sensitivity rate), and on visiting your doctor are told that you tested positive. The probability that people who don't have the disease will test positive (false positive rate) is 10 percent. What is the probability that you have the disease? Those who say 99 percent ignore the base rate and commit the Base Rate Fallacy. For those who care to work it out, Bayes' Theorem gives us the correct answer of 0.98 percent:

$$p(H|D) = p(H)p(D|H) \,/\, [p(H)p(D|H) + p(-H)p(D|-H)] \qquad (1)$$
$$= (0.001)(0.99) \,/\, [(0.001)(0.99) + (0.999)(0.1)]$$
$$= 0.0098$$

The probability $p(H|D)$ is the likelihood that you have disease (H) given that you tested positive for it (D), and is a function of the one-in-a-thousand prior probability $p(H)$ that a patient has the disease, the sensitivity rate $p(D|H)$ and the false positive rate $p(D|-H)]$. The correct probability is less than 1 percent, not 99 percent. The mistake was to fix on the probability and not the base rate.

Since the answers provided by probability theory are the right ones, the effect of these experiments is to make people look stupid. But that isn't the view of most behavioral scientists who work in the area. Kahneman and Tversky themselves regarded judgment heuristics as highly efficient rules of thumb.[33] For the average case they work quite well, nor could they easily be improved upon. However, any reservations about the message to be drawn from these experiments have been all but ignored by academic lawyers, who suggest that we rely on our heuristics at our peril and see the evidence of cognitive biases as a permission slip to the paternalist. If our hunches mislead, we should defer to the expert with his statistical tables and manuals of probability theory.

Over the last 20 years, hundreds of law review articles have embraced this kind of *cognitive paternalism*. The approach seldom varies: first, identify a judgment bias from the cognitive literature; and second, propose fetters on bargaining freedom in areas where the bias might obtain. The race is always to find a new area where our judgment seems defective and where we should attend to the law professor to steer us right. Restrictions in bargaining freedom have thus been proposed in consumer lending (where we might underestimate the probability of default and borrow too heavily), family law (where we might underestimate the probability of a divorce) and investment law (where we might underestimate losses and undersave for retirement).

However, the cognitive paternalist sometimes reveals his own biases. In the real world to which he so often refers, our heuristics are far more sophisticated and accurate than he concedes. What he has largely ignored is a more recent counter-revolution in cognitive psychology that emphasizes the overall efficiency of our judgment heuristics, and that suggests five arguments against cognitive paternalism. I label these the *meta-rationality* argument, the *ecological* argument, the argument from *design flaws*, the argument from *indeterminacy* and the argument from the *paternalist's biases*.[34]

The meta-rationality argument

The French mathematician Pierre Laplace posited an omniscient superintelligence which, knowing everything there was to know and possessing limitless intelligence, could predict the future with certainty.[35] However, Laplace's chimera of perfect rationality is a misleading illusion. We live in a world with positive informational costs of gathering data and computational costs of processing it, and to navigate about must rely on our heuristics. Even if these are sometimes in error, it is still efficient to rely on them if the costs of getting it wrong are exceeded by the costs of verifying the hunch and getting it right.

Our heuristics and instincts serve as a substitute for information search and mental computation. Were information and computation costless we could dispense with our heuristics and turn ourselves into Laplace's monster of rationality. But we would want to rely on our guesstimates where the benefits of searching for better information exceed the costs of doing so. And where computation is costly, we would reasonably prefer to go with our hunches if the mental cost of calculation is unlikely to produce a better decision. Sometimes we need precise answers, but for the run-of-the-mill case precision is a luxury we can easily do without, and there our heuristics serve us well. We can gauge how high a ceiling is without breaking out a measuring tape, and estimate how many people live in San Diego without looking it up.

Experimental tests which suggest that our instincts mislead in the individual case do not permit us to pass judgment on our heuristics as a whole. Instead, the appropriate standard is one of meta-rationality, in which we evaluate heuristics holistically for all of the tasks for which they are employed, and compare how they work with the information gathering and mental computation for which they substitute. This is not to say that we must be satisfied with heuristics that work well on average, if a set of more discriminating heuristics would be more accurate when tailored for the idiosyncratic case. Before condemning our heuristics, however, we would have to be sure that the gain in accuracy was not exceeded by the additional information-processing and computational costs.

From the perspective of meta-rationality, our heuristics have more going for them than the cognitive paternalist concedes. They are better seen as the fast and frugal tools identified by Gerd Gigerenzer than as a set of misleading biases. *Fast* heuristics do not require much mental computation, and *frugal* heuristics do not need much information. But while they are low cost, fast and frugal rules can accurately mimic highly complex mathematical calculations. If my dog occasionally fails to catch the frisbee on the fly, it is not because she failed to calculate the flight path to the third or fourth derivative.

Our heuristics also permit us to store and integrate a large amount of information which we can use thereafter. We can disregard extraneous data and bring to mind only the relevant information. We can also make inferences from past experiences without literal recall through simple cognitive tools. The cook who knows just how much spice to add does not remember past successes and failures, but only what feels right between his fingers.

Gigerenzer argues that we are better equipped to handle probabilistic events and statistical evidence than cognitive paternalists let on. For example, the Base Rate Fallacy is less likely to mislead when information is presented in familiar *natural frequencies*.[36] The natural frequency of a disease is the frequency with which it is associated with a symptom, and before there was such a thing as epidemiology that was how physicians diagnosed an illness. Recall the Base Rate example above, and suppose that a physician has seen 5,000 patients, of whom 20 had the disease.

Of these 20, 10 had the symptom. Of the 4,980 unaffected patients, 1,009 had the symptom. The probability that a new patient with the symptom has the disease may then be expressed in the form of a natural frequency:

$$p(H|D) = a/(a + b) = 10/(10 + 1,009) = 0.0098 \qquad (2)$$

where a is the number of infected patients with the symptom, and b is the number of uninfected patients with the symptom. Equation (2) is Bayes' Theorem expressed in the much more accessible form of natural frequencies. With natural frequencies the physician is unlikely to be misled, as he was when he saw the same problem expressed in probabilities. He will quickly see that about 10 in 1,000 people with the symptom had the disease, for a natural frequency around 1 percent. Our heuristics get us to an approximately correct answer quickly and simply, and without the mental effort required to work out Bayes' Theorem.[37]

Judgment biases sometimes work at cross-purposes and might even cancel out, leaving us with hunches that are generally accurate from the perspective of meta-rationality. Consider the following:

> *Optimism bias.* We seem to discount the risks we face. Half of marriages end in divorce, but few couples that marry believe this will happen to them. Because of this, parties might be too ready to enter into agreements, matrimonial or otherwise. A leading cognitive paternalist argues that "unreasonable optimism creates a distinctive problem for conventional objections to paternalism in law."[38]

> *Risk aversion and risk seeking.* In evaluating a gamble involving two favorable outcomes people are risk averse, in the sense that they prefer the sure thing over a risky bet with a higher expected monetary value (probability times magnitude). People would prefer $1,000 with certainty to a coin-toss with a payoff of 0 for heads and $2,100 for tails. But while we are risk averse as to gains, we appear to be risk-seeking as to losses. Risk-seekers would prefer a 50–50 gamble of a loss of $0 or $2,000 to a sure thing loss of $900.[39]

The mix of preferences about gains and losses shown in Figure 5.1 has been labeled prospect theory.[40] Prospect theory posits that our preferences about gains and losses are not linear, as they would be if a straight line were drawn through the origin. Instead, the utility function is the S-shaped curve of Figure 5.1. The curve is steeper for losses than it is for gains, in the sense that a loss of X represents a greater loss of utility than the gain in utility from a win of X, a phenomenon called loss aversion. The curves become flatter as we move from the origin (being concave for gains and convex for losses), which reflects risk aversion as to gains and risk-seeking as to losses.

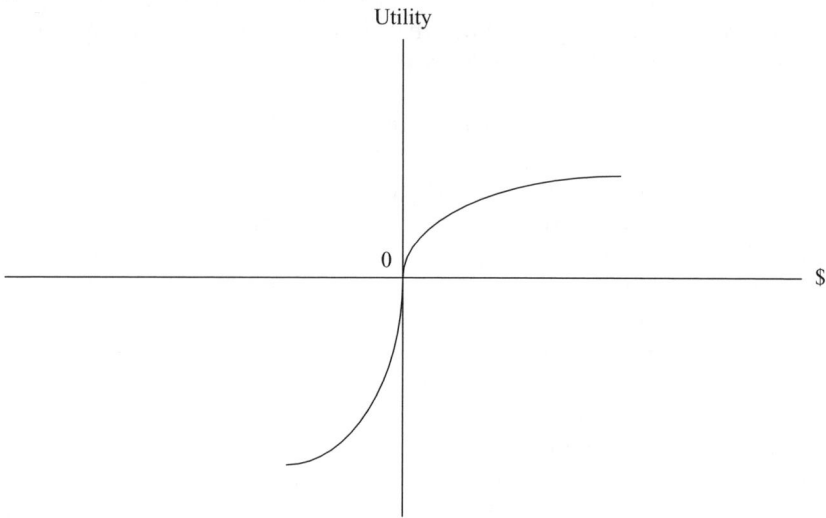

Figure 5.1 Prospect theory: risk and loss aversion

The overly optimistic are too quick to gamble, taking risks whose expected value is negative. For example, they might purchase a $1 lottery ticket with a one in a million chance of $100,000 and an expected value of 10 cents. The risk averse are too slow to gamble, in the sense that they reject gambles whose expected value exceeds the cost of taking up the opportunity. They might refuse to spend $1 on a gamble with an expected value of $2. When the prizes have a negative value, however, the loss averse are too quick to gamble, preferring a gamble with an expected loss of $2 to a sure thing loss of $1. It is difficult to know what to conclude from biases that ride off in all directions, and which all might be invoked in a single business decision with separate upsides possibilities and downsides risks.

Like the One-Hoss Shay, the biases might even be in equipoise so that the entire apparatus hums along nicely. When my impulses balance off each other, my aim is true. Optimism and risk aversion might, together, give us the right incentives to take up valuable opportunities, whose expected benefits exceed their costs. Optimism might also counterbalance emotional barriers to action, such as the natural desire to procrastinate and goof off. Students will find it a lot easier to begin a dreaded term paper if they think they can whip it off. Optimism can also lead to self-fulfilling prophecies, in which the belief that a task may be easily performed makes it easier to perform in fact.[41]

All this is speculative, of course, and might even remind one of Kipling's "Just So" stories that assure us that everything works out nicely, and humorously ascribe a secret purpose to evolutionary flukes ("How the Camel Got its Hump"). But if it is a stretch to describe our overall mix of risk preferences as efficient, it is no less a stretch to see them as woefully inadequate to the task of guiding us through life. In particular, it is wholly unsatisfactory to view each item in our tool-kit of instincts in isolation from every other one. What matters is the ensemble of instincts, not the solitary nudge in a particular direction. The cognitive paternalist derides the *homo economicus*, whom he compares unfavorably to his "real people." But these turn out to be not very real either, when their heuristics are seen in isolation rather than from the perspective of meta-rationality.

The ecological argument

The argument from meta-rationality identifies two weaknesses in the literature of cognitive paternalism. First, the paternalist ignores the information-gathering and computational costs for which our heuristics substitute. Second, the paternalist takes the anomalous case as the standard one and fails to assess the ability of our heuristics to respond to the everyday situations in which we find ourselves. A heuristic that misleads in one case might perform very well in the mass of cases for which it is employed. A related objection to cognitive paternalism is the argument from ecological rationality, which asks how well our heuristics fit the world as we find it. This depends on the match between heuristic and environment, and not on the heuristic standing alone.

Ecological rationality involves the social as well as the physical environment: how useful are our heuristics in our interaction with other people with similar heuristics. If nearly everyone shares the same biases, an idiosyncratic individual might not be advantaged by different heuristics, even if these are objectively just as good. When driving on the road, for example, it helps if we all have the same instincts about keeping to the right.

When ecological rationality is taken into account, our heuristics can more easily be seen as fast and frugal rules that efficiently exploit information for the task at hand. For example, the availability heuristic that brings the most salient information to mind is useful in the general case precisely for that reason. We need it most for the situations with which we are most familiar, and there it is most helpful. The taxi driver knows his favorite shortcuts and the computer programmer his tried-and-true stratagems. For the idiosyncratic problems on which the cognitive paternalist focuses his attention, the heuristic advantages the expert who specializes in those issues and strengthens economies of specialization. The same might be said of the probabilistic puzzles of epidemiology that ask us to work through Bayes' Theorem. In such cases we rely upon the expert and discount lay opinions. Where it matters the heuristic assists; and where it misleads the errors are often of little importance. What do we care what movie critics such as Pauline Kael might have thought about politics?

Similarly, the anchoring heuristic, in which our judgment is shaped by the prompts we are given, is a fast and frugal judgment rule that outperforms any alternative that comes to mind. The prompts which first come to mind are those most familiar to us. When buying a shirt, we remember better the collar size of the last shirt we bought, not the one we bought ten years ago. To evaluate anything we must compare it with something else, and what matters most is ordinarily the comparison that first comes to mind. A rule that asked us to dig up memories of more remote purchases would sacrifice frugality or fastness and impose its own not inconsiderable costs.

Because of the anchoring heuristic, we might be misled by the spin-meister (or the cognitive paternalist) who proposes a particular anchor for strategic reasons. For example, immigration opponents sometimes note that immigration is at a historic high, as measured by the number of immigrants. Whether the number is too high or too low is something about which reasonable men might differ. However, a more accurate way of framing the issue is to recognize that the percent of foreign-born is about half what it was 100 years ago. There are always a number of ways in which issues may be spun, and we may ordinarily rely on the free market of ideas to provide alternative anchors and frames. That might not be perfect – but it usually beats the alternative.

Heuristics might be likened to programs we adopt at birth and can alter only with difficulty thereafter. To evaluate them, we must examine their overall effect on our welfare, since a heuristic that seems to err in a particular case might nevertheless be efficient from a life-cycle perspective. Consider the phenomenon of regret, which is said to be an example of judgment bias:

> *Regret.* You arrive at a play just behind another customer who is told that he has won $1,000 as the theatre's 100,000th customer. Had you not paused on your way to window-shop you would have won the money, and even though there is nothing wrong with window-shopping you might still experience regret. We are upset about losses when these can be traced to some action on our part even when they arise through no fault of our own, and even though the past cannot be changed.[42]

Regret might seem a highly inefficient emotion. When things turn out badly, we regret actions that made sense at the time. Or we magnify our mistakes. Juan Marichal, a superb pitcher, said that he hated giving up walks to batters, because "they always seem to end up scoring." We imagine a counterfactual world, where we acted differently and where things turn out better. However, this is often a valuable exercise. The anxiety we experience through regret is a useful reality check that pierces through our self-esteem and forces us to scrutinize past behavior for signs of error. Without regret, there would be no learning from past errors and an increased likelihood of future errors. Regret is, therefore, a useful adaptive strategy. Like the anchoring and the availability heuristics, it permits us to adjust better to our environment and serves ecological rationality.

The argument from design flaws

Some experimental tests that purport to evidence judgment biases seem to suffer from design flaws, and the results might have a benign explanation rather than one that suggests irrationality. This might happen in one of five ways. First, a subject might reject a seemingly preferable alternative because of a rational concern for status signals. Second, the subject might discount the facts as they are recounted to him by the experimenter. Third, subjects might have the self-correcting ability to correct for probabilistic errors by adjusting the probabilities they assign to individual events. Fourth, subjects might learn from their mistakes in ways not captured by a one-shot experiment. Finally, judgment biases might be corrected in market transactions, where irrationality invites entry by competitors.

Status explanations

Status explanations might account for the seemingly anomalous endowment effect, which has been thought to show that we value goods more after we acquire them. A random group of students was given mugs worth about $5 and then asked for how much they would sell them. Another random group of students was asked how much they would pay to buy the mugs. The selling price exceeded the buying price, and this has been taken to mean that we value goods more once we possess them.[43] However, Richard Posner has suggested a more commonsensical *status* explanation for this result.[44] The mug-seller reveals his preferences about money as well as mugs, and a sale at $5 might be taken to signal that he is hard up. After all, the well-off do not sell their household items. By contrast, the decision to buy a mug is more likely to reveal a pure preference for mugs and not money, since the mug-buyer does not signal his need for cash in buying or refusing to buy a mug. The signal to oneself from mug-selling may also be inconsistent with a superior self-image. It is hard to think oneself above money-grubbing when selling a mug for $5.

Discounting the facts

Subjects might *discount the facts* in the problem set before them, and this might explain the bird-in-the-hand fallacy in which we seem to have an irrational preference for goods received sooner rather than later. In an experiment, subjects were presented with two options with identical probabilities and outcomes but with slightly different temporal dimensions.

In both options the probabilities were broken down into two separate events. In option I the first event had a higher probability of success and the second event had a lower probability; while in option II the probabilities were reversed and the payoff was back-end loaded. When tested, the subjects preferred the first option over the second. Since the expected monetary values were the same, this might seem irrational. However, temporal preferences are not irrational when there is a positive probability of default in the second stage. The experimental psychologist might assure us that this will not happen, but we seem hard-wired to mistrust people who tell us the check is in the mail. We live in a world where the future is uncertain, and where we rationally discount later events and prefer the bird-in-the-hand.[45]

Self-correction

Subjects who err in psychological tests might get it right when the same problems are presented to them in the real world. Psychological experiments which suggest that we handle the rules of probability theory poorly present subjects with simple factual problems, in which the probabilities are taken as given. In the conjunction effect, for example, we are said to overestimate the probability of conjunctive events. Outside of the experimental lab, however, people might react to anticipated judgment biases by adjusting probability estimates, and judgment biases such as the conjunction effect might be *self-correcting* in ways that escape the notice of experimental economists.

The probability that two independent events will occur is the product of the probability of each. If there is a 10 percent chance that it will rain and a 50 percent chance that the Montreal Canadiens will win the play-offs, then there is a (0.5 times 0.1 =) 5 percent chance that both will happen. In tests, however, most people seem to guess higher and this error is labeled the conjunction effect.[46] In one case, subjects were given personality sketches and asked to make inferences about the person described. In one sketch, "Linda" was said to be deeply concerned with issues of discrimination and social justice. Subjects were then asked which was more probable: (A) Linda is a bank teller; or (B) Linda is a bank teller who is active in the feminist movement. More than 80 percent of a sample of undergraduates and half of a sample of psychology graduates picked B. Had they thought about it, they would have recognized that the class of bank tellers must be larger than the class of feminist bank tellers, since some tellers are not feminists.[47]

In experimental tests of the conjunction effect, subjects are typically told what the probabilities are. In the real world, however, events do not come with labels about probabilities, and we have to estimate likelihoods; and a bias in an experimental lab might turn out to be self-correcting in the real world. If we are likely to overestimate the probability of a series of conjunctive events, we might adjust for the error by reducing probability estimates for each separate event. In the above example, we might underestimate the likelihood of one of the events and come up with the correct estimate of the joint probability.[48] We might think that there is a 5 percent chance of both happening because we underestimate the probability it will rain. This suggestion is necessarily speculative and unverifiable. But if it is speculative, so too is the assertion that we do not adjust probability estimates in this way and that we should place much weight on experimental tests of the conjunction effect.

Learning from mistakes

Psychological experiments seldom try to capture the possibility of *learning*, where people learn from their mistakes and adjust their hunches. Hitting a home run is said to be the most difficult skill in sports. Yet, over time a baseball player may learn how to increase his slugging average. He might adjust his stance or his swing, and correct for such instincts as the compulsion to drop to the ground when a curve ball is thrown towards his head. Similarly, people might learn how to adjust for the availability or anchoring heuristics, when they see that they are misled.[49]

This is not to suggest that we can unlearn all our biases and come up with a perfectly accurate set of heuristics. Our tendency to overestimate our abilities might resist learning because it helps in overcoming a natural inertia.[50] Like the little engine that could, I am well served when "I think I can," even if sometimes I can't. However, the possibility of learning weakens the case for cognitive paternalism.

Correction of judgment biases in market transactions

Finally, a business that sought to exploit faulty heuristics would invite entry by competitors, and this might drive the biased firm out of business. This might not eliminate judgment errors, since there is reason to believe that they persist in the most efficient markets, such as the stock market. There is a lengthy literature on stock market inefficiencies, such as price bubbles and profit opportunities from lagged insider trading data.[51] That said, there is evidence that the violations of rationality norms in experimental settings tend to disappear in *market transactions*.[52]

The argument from indeterminacy

It is often difficult to draw normative conclusions about legal rules from behavioral experiments, since it may be unclear whether a judgment heuristic should be seen as a constraint to be respected or a prejudice to be overcome. For example, the preference for goods in our possession, which behavioral theorists call the endowment effect, might argue for either reinforced or relaxed property rights. If we assume that the owner's deepest desire is to retain his assets, he might seem entitled to a premium on expropriation, since giving him the market value might seem to under-compensate him.[53] But when he is compensated the owner can go out and buy other goods with which he might bond just as closely, if all that drives his preferences is an abstract endowment effect; and this suggests that any endowment effect might be ignored. "Move a person from a city house to a country house and, lo and behold, he is quite likely to prefer the country house more than he did when he resided in the city."[54] When opposite conclusions may be drawn for the same theory, it can hardly be thought to offer a satisfactory basis for legal intervention.

The problem of indeterminism makes it difficult to derive policy prescriptions from our attitudes to risk. The phenomenon of optimism suggests that we might enter into unwise contracts in which we bear a low-level risk of a crippling loss, and this has been thought to justify restrictions on our bargaining freedom.[55] For example, state paternalism in the form of mandatory pension plans has been thought an appropriate response to optimism errors.[56] Unless we are forced to save we will throw our money away on foolish schemes. However, the opposite inference would be drawn if these problems were approached from the perspective of the risk aversion heuristic, under which we are fearful of risky upsides and reluctant to invest or gamble. Where the optimism bias makes us too ready to gamble, risk aversion makes us too reluctant to gamble. Once again, it is difficult to base policy prescriptions on biases that seem to point in both directions.

The failure to consider the indeterminacy of the experimental evidence sometimes makes cognitive paternalism look like special pleading. For example, Thomas Jackson has argued that mandatory personal bankruptcy laws respond to our tendency to overestimate the probability of conjunctive events and underestimate the probability of disjunctive events.[57] For Jackson, upsides are always conjunctive (my gold mine will succeed if interest rates are low *and* the price of gold is high) and downsides are always disjunctive (my gold mine will fail if exploration costs are high *or* the chance of finding gold is low). Under these unrealistic assumptions, mandatory bankruptcy rights might correct the debtor's tendency to over-estimate upside gains and underestimate the likelihood of default. However, there is little reason to suppose that the world will systematically line up this way. In choosing between a worldly and an ecclesiastical career, *Le rouge et le noir*'s Julien Sorel had different alternatives in mind, so that his upsides were disjunctive (Le rouge *ou* le noir). Similarly, a person's downside risks will often be conjunctive, and depend on the combination of separate events. Antonio, the Merchant of Venice, could withstand a single shipwreck but not several independent ones. In short, the debtor would seem as likely to overestimate as to underestimate default, to make too few and not too many risky investments.

The argument from the paternalist's biases

Behavioral theories might even be consistent with anti-paternalism, since judgment biases seem at least as likely to affect the paternalist as his subject. The paternalist asks legislators, judges and juries to evaluate individual choices, without pausing to reflect that the same judgment biases might color their decisions. For example, the hindsight bias is less likely to affect individuals than those who sit in judgment on them:

> *Hindsight bias.* Hindsight is not 20–20, and looking backwards we are apt to ascribe a false wisdom to our decisions. We knew precisely when to pull the pitcher in yesterday's ball game. Tolstoy described another example of this bias in *War and Peace.* General Kutuzov thought he had lured Napoleon into the heart of Russia for the purpose of destroying his army. The reality, according to Tolstoy, was that Kutuzov was a blunderer who never planned to give up Moscow to the French. The French army was defeated by the Russian winter, and not by any general.

There might be a benign explanation for the hindsight bias. In forming our judgments we adjust our inferences by recalling past decisions and re-estimating future results, with the perspective shifting between the retrospective and the prospective. The hindsight bias might thus be seen as a by-product of an adaptive process in which we update our knowledge after feedback.[58] We sharpen our judgment by learning from past mistakes and forming amended rules for future behavior. However, we remember the amended rule more easily if we think we have always adhered to it. Because of the psychic cost of disintegration, of the sense that more than one person has inhabited our life and that I am not I, we need to feel that our life story belongs to a single person. Failing to do so weakens any lesson we can take from our experience. The back-and-forth process of shaping our judgment is therefore assisted if we can see our lives as a consistent story in which we have always adhered to the amended rule, with a plausible explanation for any deviation. Remembering that we were once mistaken might confuse us, but thinking that "I knew it all along" burns the message into our memory.

However, the hindsight bias is more likely to mislead when we sit in judgment over others and it is all retrospective. A jury might think an accident to have been far more likely than it really was, and impose liability in negligence upon defendants who took reasonable precautions to guard against events with very small probabilities. At the moment of contracting, when the future lies ahead and a million different outcomes are possible, the consumer might wisely discount the possibility of a one-in-a-million defect. But looking backward, after the future has revealed itself, a judge with the robust self-confidence of a Lord Denning is apt to think that things had to turn out just as they did and find a manufacturer negligent for a design flaw. Nor was Lord Denning the exception. Judge Steven Williams is one of the relatively few judges to see through the hindsight bias to notice that, when plaintiffs complain they should have been warned of some future accident, "failure-to-warn cases have the curious property that, when the episode is examined in hindsight, it appears as though addition of warnings keyed to a particular accident would be virtually cost free."[59]

The hindsight bias plausibly explains the judicial fascination with contractual exemption clauses that absolve a seller from liability. *Ex ante*, the likelihood of the event that would trigger the clause might have been exceedingly small; but *ex post* it always seemed inevitable to Lord Denning, who was quick to impeach the exemption clause and find the seller liable. Ironically, it was the paternalist whose judgment was off.

Not surprisingly, therefore, much of most sophisticated work in behavioral law-and-economics deals with jury error,[60] and is thus more anti-paternalist than paternalist in its direction. If the consumer has better judgment, it makes little sense for the jury to play the role of paternalist. Behavioral theories also buttress the conservative case for narrow liability rules in corporation and tort law. Given the possibility of hindsight bias, the business judgment standard, which absolves managers from liability for good faith breaches of the standard of due care, is eminently reasonable. Otherwise, courts would second-guess business decisions that made sense at the time, and this would weaken management's incentives to take up valuable but risky opportunities that have a high expected return but a broad spread of possible outcomes.[61] For the same reason, courts should not be over-ready to impose liability for negligence upon manufacturers in tort law.[62]

In addition, the highly salient costs that attract newspaper coverage appear to attract excessive regulation, as the availability heuristic would predict. One example is the Superfund liability imposed on polluters and successor land owners for environmental clean-ups where the clean-up costs vastly exceed any possible health or aesthetic benefits from a cleaner environment.[63] From an economic perspective it makes little sense to get the last particle of a pollutant out of the ground. Nevertheless, the salience of the story attracts public interest groups who find it easy to bring their tale to the media and pressure the EPA for action.

In sum, the academic lawyer's facile paternalism, based on psychological experiments from 20 or 30 years ago, now seems dated. A more recent counter-revolution in experimental psychology has done much to rehabilitate the idea that our heuristics are coded with valuable signals on how to behave. Indeed, there might be little reason to think that we could improve on them. The anti-paternalist might even advance an Efficient Heuristic Hypothesis under which any change in our heuristics would be for the worse. Small improvements suggested by cognitive paternalists for the idiosyncratic case would be swamped by the costs of worsened heuristics in our everyday decisions or by the costs of information gathering and calculation for which the heuristics substitute.

This suggestion is necessarily speculative. Since mental calculation is costly, there is an irreducible and radical uncertainty about the payoffs from our choices and the efficiency of our heuristics. Determining the best course of action can never be like George Stigler's optimal stopping rule, where someone who wants to buy a used car will stop looking for a deal when the cost of one more search exceeds the benefit of a further search.[64] This works only if the searcher knows the distribution of prices in advance. Where the distribution of prices is unknown, the searcher can only guess at the benefit of an additional search. If he wants something more precise, he would have to bear search costs in order to determine whether it is cost-effective to bear search costs, and an infinite regress would set in.

We face the same problem in evaluating the efficiency of our choices when rationality is costly. At first glance, the problem looks like the routine exercise of factoring in one more cost: in stage I we assume that mental calculation is costless, and that the subject maximizes gains subject to non-mental cost constraints (such as money); and in stage II we add in the mental calculation costs we suppressed in stage I. But when we add in the new stage II costs we have to recalculate the first-stage optimization problem (money and mental labor together). So we need a stage III to revisit the optimization problem, and a fourth stage to add in these third-stage costs, and so on. We are like a builder who fashions a scaffold to see his building whole; and then makes a further scaffold to see the building and first scaffold together, and so on and on. Like the builder we must make an end and accept the necessary uncertainty in evaluating our choices.

Herbert Simon expressed this uncertainty in his theory of *bounded rationality*.[65] Given information and mental calculation costs, we cannot weigh all the possible outcomes of our actions and then apply the rules of probability theory to come up with the best overall plan. Instead, said Simon, we make decisions by *satisficing*: setting an aspiration level to aim for that leaves us happy enough, and reaching for it. After house-shopping for a time, we find something we like and settle on it, even if the absolutely perfect house might have been the next one on our list. We can't tell whether we might have done better with a bit more search, but we can end up with a good enough result.

Since our rationality is bounded we can never have a definitive evaluation of the efficiency of our choices, or test the Efficient Heuristic Hypothesis. To do so, we would have to evaluate our heuristics from the perspective of costless rationality. That is, we would have to step outside our heuristics and work out all our choices with a calculator. But it is precisely because the costs of calculation are so great that we learned to rely on our instincts in the first place.

If the Efficient Heuristic Hypothesis is speculative, however, so too is the cognitive paternalist's suggestion that our heuristics are inefficient.

Simon's bounded rationality is not irrationality. A belief in goblins is irrational; but reliance on judgment heuristics is wholly rational and should never be confused with the kinds of mental illness that lead to a finding of contract law incapacity. Our heuristics economize on costly calculation, and are much more accurate than cognitive paternalists seem willing to concede. Turning every daily decision into a matter of mathematical calculation would give us more accurate information, but the game would not be worth the candle.

Before second-guessing our heuristics, therefore, we should pose Jack Nicholson's question in *As Good as it Gets*. Do you suppose, he asked the waiting room of psychiatric patients, that it doesn't get any better than this? Even if a heuristic might mislead around the edges, it might still outperform all rival heuristics for the overall environment in which it is employed. One would be rash to trade our present set of heuristics for some other set, given the chance to do so.

This is not to say that cognitive paternalism must everywhere be rejected, and that laws mandating seat belts and safety helmets are unnecessary. Neither side in the "rationality wars" has won a decisive victory.[66] If our heuristics are not a coggery of defects, neither are they LaPlace's perfect calculating machine. We do not eliminate biases by learning our way out of them, and increasing the monetary payout does not seem to make us better calculators. One study concluded that "there is no replicated study in which a theory of rational choice was rejected at low stakes ... and accepted at high stakes."[67] Nor can we eliminate the problem by delegating our decisions to an expert. (If we could, we should have found the perfect paternalist.) Experts are, themselves, subject to judgment biases, even in their own field of expertise.[68]

However, the counter-revolution in behavioral law-and-economics does argue for a far more discriminating approach to bargaining fetters which recognizes that our heuristics are more accurate than the cognitive paternalism literature has suggested, and that the paternalist might, himself, lack unclouded judgment.[69] Our heuristics are more sophisticated and accurate than the quick-and-dirty algorithms derided by the cognitive paternalists. To the extent that our hunches sometimes mislead, it is also unclear how a legal response might be framed. Are we too risk averse or too risk loving? And if we bond in some way with our property, as the endowment effect would have it, does that argue for stronger or weaker legal recognition of property rights? Finally, the argument from judgment biases has greatest bite when employed to impeach the paternalist's judgment, and thus might weaken the case for paternalism.

Weakness of the will

A more traditional form of paternalism focuses on the need for strength of purpose or will to choose rightly. Let us suppose that a person's mind is unclouded by judgment biases. He knows precisely what he must do to achieve his highest ends. He can measure every possible end-state, so that he knows his best ends along with the best means to get there. Would such a person always choose rightly? Not if he lacks the strength of will to put his best life plan into effect. Where no external impediment blocks his way and where he sees the good clearly, his lack of inner resolve might still prevent him from reaching his goal, and his weakness might supply a second explanation for paternalistic restraints on free choice.

The weak-willed person is the problem drinker, the binge-eater, the drug user. He is the impulse buyer and the credit card junkie. He is the gambler, who knows just how much his habit harms his family but who cannot help himself when he sees the green baize spread in front of him. He is the child whose preferences are all in the present, and the expectant heir through whose pockets money burns a hole. He is the prodigal son for whom the spendthrift trust was invented. He is the myopic criminal, for whom the prospect of tomorrow's punishment weighs lightly against the benefits of today's crime. He is Racine's god-possessed Phèdre and "Venus incarnate, attached to her prey" (Vénus tout entière a sa proie attachée). He is St Peter asleep at his post. He is Aristotle's *akrates*, the man who lacks self-control. He is you and I.[70]

Forms of akrasia

There are five models for weakness of will or akrasia. First, the akrates is the person in the grip of an overwhelming, irresistible passion. Second, he might be seen as a divided self where a strong- and weak-willed person war in the bosom of a single breast. Third, a person might regret a choice made in the past as weak-willed after a change in his preferences. Fourth, he might deceive himself about his strength of will and tumble into bad habits. Finally, he might place an absurdly high discount rate on future happiness and over-consume in the present.

Overwhelming passion

First, the akrates might be *overpowered by his passions*, like Racine's Phèdre with her lust for her step-son Hippolyte, and for this reason might seem less than sinful. "Her crime is more a punishment of the gods than an act of will," explained Racine.[71] Since she cannot be blamed for her passion, Phèdre is a "righteous sinner" who strives to be good but whose moral fate is beyond her control. As such, she testifies to the teachings on the indeterminacy of God's grace which Racine learned at a Jansenist school. For Jansenists, God's grace is a free gift which He can bestow on anyone, and the righteous sinner might thus be condemned in spite of his moral worth.[72]

If the weak-willed are passionate, it follows that the non-passionate are not strong-willed. The innately moderate person who lacks the disposition to misbehave might live a virtuous life, but as he has not been tested he does not display strength of will. Perhaps no such people exist, since we all have an inclination to sin. But some of us lack the desire to indulge in a particular vice and there is nothing strong-willed about abstaining from sins that do not tempt one. There is an element of cynical truth in La Rochefoucauld's observation that "if we resist our passions, it is more because of their weakness than our strength."[73]

Strength of will is measured by resistance to temptation, and as the temptation increases so does the self-control needed to resist it. But this is not to say that strength of will must be accompanied by the will theorist's teeth-clenching act of will that we saw in Chapter 2. In arguing that some people are weak-willed, it is unnecessary to posit a special faculty called the will or a mental act of exercising our will. We show greater self-control when we dismiss a real temptation without an agony of self-doubt and hesitation.

The divided self

A second way of thinking about akrasia is to abandon the assumption of a unitary personal identity and posit a *divided self*. A unified self has a consistent set of preferences but a divided self might have conflicting ones. The strong-willed part of one's psyche might hate gambling in general while the weak-willed part loves blackjack in particular, especially when in Las Vegas and after a few martinis. The idea that we might be inhabited by different people is not a novel one, and Freudian psychologists will identify the different parts of our personalities as the strong-willed super-ego and the weak-willed ego.

The divided self is conflicted. One part of him wants to gamble; the other part regrets the desire to gamble. If it could, the calmer self would replace the preference for gambling with, say, the desire to read French novels. These preferences about preferences (or "meta-preferences") are common to all of us, and an essential prelude to the task of reforming our character. In such cases, it might not be clear who the "true" self is, and whether the desire to quit gambling is more than a pose. Yet, the familiar sense of deliberating about which set of preferences should be satisfied reminds us of the conflict in our desires.[74]

A self might also be divided in time. Things we did many years before sometimes seem to have been done by another person, a person who somehow saddled us with his debts and guilts. And trying to imagine what that person thought and felt requires just the same kind of empathy as the imaginative act of putting oneself inside the mind of a stranger. Maurice Barrès tells of a meeting with Tolstoy that makes the point:

> "Hello, Count Tolstoy," he greeted him.
> And was told: "You're mistaken. I'm not who you think I am. What do you want with Tolstoy?"

"I come to greet the author of *Anna Karenina* and *War and Peace*."
"That person is dead."
"Then I come to greet the author of *Redemption*, of . . ."
"That person is me."[75]

Today's self is like the manager of a firm who is charged with the respon-sibility of determining the payoffs to present and later selves. A prudent manager will seek to maximize the sum of the payoffs and smooth out consumption between different periods. However, a misbehaving manager is more closely allied to today's self and will stint later in favor of present selves. Though free of judgment biases, today's self might thus be unable to implement a utility-maximizing life plan because of a conflict of inter-ests. He might transfer excessive wealth from future to present periods, over-consuming in the present and under-consuming in the future. When the future comes he will regret his choice, but by then it is too late.

Reversal of preferences

The analogy to a manager with a conflict of interest assumes that a person can foresee what his preferences will be in the future. He knows he will subsequently regret over-consumption in the present and simply cannot help himself. But the change of heart might be wholly unanticipated and result from a transforming *reversal of preferences*, and this might consti-tute a third kind of akrasia. The kinds of plans we make before a religious conversion, before we fall in love, before a child is born, are very different from the plans we make afterwards, and a later self might regret choices made by a former self and even ascribe them to weakness of will.

The *Baby M* litigation can be seen as an example of this kind of akrasia. Mary Beth Whitehead agreed to be artificially inseminated for a fee of $10,000 in a surrogacy contract which specified that she would give up the child at birth to a childless, professional couple and do whatever was necessary to terminate her maternal rights. She wanted the money, and she also wanted to give the other couple "the gift of life." She did not think she would regret her decision. But when the child was born Mrs Whitehead was a very different person and realized she could not part with it. She surrendered the child but soon became suicidal. She received permission to see the child and fled with it 1,000 miles away, where she lived in hiding in a series of motels until the police found her three months later.[76]

At the moment when she signed the surrogacy contract, Mary Beth Whitehead would not have described her decision as weak-willed. Possibly it was made after calm deliberation, unlike her frantic decision to run off with her child. But after she realized how attached she was to the baby she would likely have described her former self as weak-willed. She sold a child for money, and what could be more weak-willed than that?

There are two ways of characterizing Mrs Whitehead's decision to enter into the surrogacy arrangement. First, it might simply be seen as an objectively bad choice. The problem was not that her decision failed to reflect her preferences; the problem was that she had bad preferences. Impeaching her decision for this reason implies not soft paternalism but hard paternalism or perfectionism, and we will examine it under this rubric in the next chapter. Second, the surrogacy decision might be second-guessed because it conflicted with her preferences at a later time. Today's self had not undergone the transforming experiences of childbirth and separation, and was in conflict with tomorrow's self. If we accept the second set of preferences as better reflecting the true Mrs Whitehead, then a restriction on surrogacy contracts is a form of soft paternalism.

Self-deception

The fourth kind of akrasia arises through a person's *self-deception* about his character or preferences.[77] Recently, newspapers reported that 98 percent of Americans thought they were going to Heaven – and that only 70 percent thought that Mother Teresa would make it. One doesn't have to be a cynic to suspect that the 2 percent of doubters were better people than the presumptuous 98 percent. We seem to inflate our own worth relative to everyone else, and the self-deception might lead to akratic behavior. The self-deceiver might thus be a weak-willed person who tumbles into vice because he imagines that he has more control over his emotions than is really the case.

Self-deception is not the same thing as akrasia, however, since some self-deceivers are strong-willed. Those who lie to themselves, like those who lie to others, might deviate on either side of the mean of accuracy. They might claim virtues they lack, like Aristotle's boastful *alazon*; or they might sell themselves short, like his ironic, self-deprecating *eiron*. The *alazon* will imagine himself more strong-willed than he really is, while the *eiron* might be a moral martinet who maintains an over-rigid code because he underestimates his power of self-control.

Nor is every akrates a self-deceiver. The self-aware might perform a harmful act knowing it to be harmful, but believing that, just this once, it will not weigh very heavily in the balance. We might know how many calories there are in a forbidden dessert, but think that by itself it will not much affect a diet. The self-aware sinner might also be a thoroughgoing reprobate who knows precisely what he is doing. About to go under the surgeon's knife, Oscar Wilde (no coward in real life) prayed, "Lord, spare me physical anguish. As for moral anguish, I can handle that myself." By contrast, true self-deceivers are often figures of fun, such as M. Jourdain in Molière's *Bourgeois gentilhomme*.

So, far from being akratic, self-deception is sometimes a useful adaptive strategy. It is often painful to know what others think of one or (what may be worse) how little they think of one, and psychologists report that the people with the most accurate understanding of how they are viewed are the clinically depressed. Self-deception might also turn out to be a useful signaling strategy for those who seek to present a positive image of themselves to others. To signal our worth we might accentuate the positive and hide the negative; and these signals become more credible when we believe them ourselves.[78] Those with a settled, if inflated, estimate of their worth do not give themselves away with a blush or downcast eye.

Some philosophers define self-deception as a simultaneous belief in inconsistent things.[79] That is, self-deceivers believe in p and not-p. So defined, self-deception is harder to understand than akratic preferences for p (the weak-willed choice) and not-p (the strong-willed choice). After all, a strong-willed adherence to a consistent life-plan imposes an emotional cost which the akrates might be unable to bear. The self-deceiver is a tougher nut, on this definition. How might he come to believe in two inconsistent things at the same time? There are two answers. First, we need not define self-deception to mean a belief in inconsistent things.[80] Instead, the self-deceived might simply place an inflated value on their own worth. Second, a belief in inconsistent things is no harder to understand than akrasia, when facing the truth about oneself imposes emotional costs. Denial is not a river in Egypt, and Pascal's observation that "ordinary people have the ability not to think about things they do not want to think about" is generally accepted by psychologists.[81]

Hyperbolic discounting

The last way of portraying akrasia is as a problem of *hyperbolic discounting*.[82] Ten dollars received a year from now is worth less than $10 received today, given the time-value of money and the possibility of investing today's $10 for a greater sum in a year's time. Future outcomes must therefore be discounted to arrive at their present value. However, some people discount the future more heavily than others because they prefer present to future consumption, and they are called hyperbolic discounters.

With an annual discount rate of r (say, the T-bill rate of interest), the present value PV of a future outcome FV received in one year is $PV = FV/(1 + r)$. For a sum received t years in the future, the formula becomes $PV = FV/(1 + r)^t$. This assumes that the discount rate r is a constant which does not change over time, and that people are strong-willed and have "time-consistent preferences." That is, they value future lives as highly as present ones and the utility or gain associated with consuming $10 today is the same as consuming an amount with the present value of $10 five, ten or fifteen years from now. On testing this, however, experimental economists report that the discount rate people actually apply seems hyperbolic rather than constant, declining sharply in early periods until it levels off in future ones, and their time-inconsistent preferences imply akrasia.

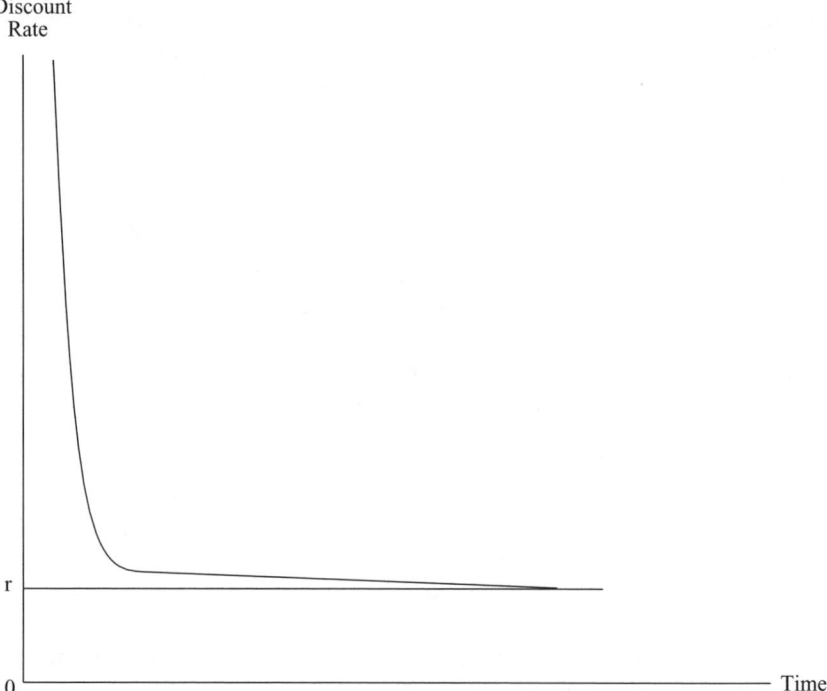

Figure 5.2 Hyperbolic and constant discounting

Under hyperbolic discounting, preferences about the discount rate change over time. For example, a hyperbolic discounter might prefer $100 today to $105 tomorrow, even though he prefers $105 in a year and a day to $100 in a year.[83] The discount rate between today and tomorrow is a short-term high discount rate; while the discount rate between two far off periods is a long-term low discount rate. Like the child before the candy store, the hyperbolic discounter wants it *now*.

Whether hyperbolic discounting really exists has been disputed. In experimental tests, subjects are more likely to discount hyperbolically when small sums of money are at stake,[84] which is consistent with the bounded rationality effects we saw in the last section. For large amounts of money the subjects have an incentive to calculate present values; for small amounts of money, the difference might not be worth the mental effort. Were this all that was going on, hyperbolic discounting would be classified as a judgment bias and not as a form of akrasia.

Tests of hyperbolic discounting might also suffer from a design flaw. A non-hyperbolic discounter might reasonably approach such problems with a concern for the risk of promisor default and apply a heavy discount to promises of future payouts. As we saw, a bird-in-the-hand bias is rational if there is a positive probability that the bird in the bush will fail to materialize. When the promisor might default, when the check in the mail might prove bogus, the choice of $100 today versus $105 tomorrow is not equivalent to the choice of $100 in a year versus $105 in a year and a day. Where the promise is not entirely credible, $100 in cash today might be worth more than a promise of $105 tomorrow. However, this difference does not arise for promises to perform in a year, since the problem of credibility is the same. A promise of $105 in a year and a day is therefore worth more than a promise of $100 in a year. Even if the subject is told that future payments are sure things, this might not overcome a healthy, ingrained suspicion about cheap talk.

Status concerns might give rise to another design flaw, since the choice of $105 tomorrow over $100 today might reveal an ignoble concern for chump change. The accountant might come back tomorrow for the five dollars, but not the aristocrat. Status signals are weakened when consumption is delayed for a year and the decision looks more purely financial. A preference for the $100 in a year might also signal the lack of intelligence to see that $105 in a year and a day is a better investment.[85]

Nevertheless, the real-world decisions of individuals do seem consistent with hyperbolic discounting. A large number of people receive tax refunds each year from the IRS. As they have overpaid their taxes, they might have increased their wealth by reducing their withholding payments and saving the difference for taxes. Presumably they do not seek to make a gift of the float to the fisc. But this might be a hyperbolic consumer's rational self-binding strategy, since it reduces the temptation to waste money in present periods and ensures there will not be a cash crunch when the tax bill is due. Further evidence of hyperbolic discounting is provided by tax shelters, which permit prudent savers to save to lower their tax burden. Non-hyperbolic taxpayers will take full advantage of tax shelters; and since many taxpayers fail to do so, the message from the Tax Code seems to be that some of us are akratic and some of us not.

Does akrasia exist?

The Mary Beth Whiteheads who experience a reversal of preferences are not hyperbolic discounters. Their desires have changed, but not their discount rate. That apart, there is a considerable overlap in the other four kinds of akrasia. The weak-willed who surrender to their passions without a care for subsequent consequences reveal hyperbolic preferences, as do those who prefer today's self over that of tomorrow, as well as those who deceive themselves about the costs that today's behavior will impose on future lives. They all seem to discount future pleasures relative to present ones.

There are advantages to making hyperbolic preferences the touchstone of akrasia. It avoids philosophical problems about personal identity and sidesteps the question of whether there really are weak-willed people. Aristotle doubted whether weakness of the will exists, since he found it difficult to imagine how someone with knowledge of the good would lack the strength of purpose to reach for it.[86] We might repent acts committed in the past, but the intuitive sense of having succumbed to temptation need not signify akrasia since we often regret past actions that were truly desired at the time.

This is not to say that, to be akratic, the act must be actively regretted in the present, even as we are doing it. The compulsive gambler does not regret his weakness when he gambles, but he is still weak-willed. Were it otherwise, were weakness of will confined to acts regretted when performed, Aristotle would have been right to question the existence of akrasia. We do not do that which we do not want to do. But that is not what weakness of will means. We can reach for the extra slice of pie without thinking, or make the foolish impulse purchase because we have persuaded ourselves that, just this once, it doesn't count. We might forget the rules we have set for ourselves because the pie in front of us has more salience, or because the drink is offered to us in a pleasant social setting.[87] We can do that which we would have known was bad for us had we not shut down our critical faculties, and in doing so we are weak-willed.

Akrasia can be distinguished from the judgment biases we saw in the previous section. Weakness of the will is not a mental lapse, even if the akratic appear to have an inconsistent set of preferences. Mary Beth Whitehead had inconsistent preferences about surrogacy, and the hyperbolic consumer has time-inconsistent preferences about saving. If the rational consumer has consistent preferences, inconsistency implies irrational preferences and might seem to suggest a judgment bias. However, rationality does not mean that one must have the same set of preferences all through one's life. Mary Beth Whitehead did not have consistent preferences over time but she was no less rational for her change of heart. Nor is the hyperbolic consumer necessarily irrational. Instead, he might be weak-willed and unwilling to bear the emotional costs of sacrificing present gratification to make his actions conform to a consistent set of preferences. The mistake is to think that the effort to achieve consistency is purely a mental, computational exercise and not an exercise of will that imposes an emotional burden. Finally, a person might simply favor consumption today to consumption tomorrow, today's person over tomorrow's person. Such time preferences are neither rational nor irrational – they are simply preferences. Some people like vanilla and some people are hyperbolic discounters.

Figure 3.1 illustrated how a bias for consumption solely in the present might be described as rational. The diagram described a consumer's time preferences, with his optimal choice represented by the intersection of the budget line with his highest indifference curve. Any other choice would be higher than the budget line and infeasible (in the sense that it would ask the consumer to spend more than he has) or inefficient (in the sense that the consumer could move to a higher indifference curve while still remaining on the budget line). When rational choices are defined as feasible and efficient, any choice not at the intersection of budget line and the highest indifference curve is irrational. But standards of rationality do not tell us where the two lines must intersect. The indifference curve might be drawn so that the intersection takes place at any point on the budget line, including the corner solutions of consumption only in the present and consumption only in the future.

Jon Elster argues that a bias in favor of present consumption must be irrational because it will be regretted in the future.[88] But the experience of regret proves nothing, since the prudent saver may regret postponed joys. Regret is a by-product of the conflict between today's and tomorrow's person, and does not tell us who should win the contest. Deferred consumption will be regretted by today's person and present consumption will be regretted by tomorrow's person. However we choose we will experience regret. Nor should we always want to defer to tomorrow's person. Rather than postpone the trip to Europe to a time when other joys have faded, we might reasonably prefer to experience it in our youth when it might be savored more intensely and remembered for a longer period. Jeremy Bentham thought that rational agents would have a bias for the present and we cannot say that he was wrong.

Rational addiction

It is often difficult to identify akrasia, since the choice of one's best life plan is a vastly complicated matter. Those who seem weak-willed might simply be making their best personal choices. The beau ideal of a saintly figure who does nothing to excess, who does not smoke or overindulge, who gets just the right amount of exercise, and whose life is in every way as nicely moderated as that of a law professor at one of our better schools, supplies one definition of perfection. As George Orwell noted, however, "the essence of being human is that one does not seek perfection. . . . No doubt alcohol, tobacco and so forth are things that a saint must avoid, but sainthood is also a thing that human beings must avoid."[89]

Nietzsche called the person who worries obsessively about health and personal safety the Last Man. Modern man, said Nietzsche, had forgotten his heroic past and was evolving towards a state of ignominious degradation. The evolutionary decline will end with the Last Man, who is contented with his mediocrity, who risks nothing, "who makes everything small." Such people are well balanced, and if there are few epiphanies in their lives they at least have mastered Benjamin Franklin's rules for success. "They have their little pleasures for the day and their little pleasures for the night: but they respect health."[90] Nietzsche contrasted the Last Man with the risk-taking and life-affirming Superman whom he presented as his ideal.

Those who pretend to possess a set of strong-willed rules for the good life, who never let themselves go, have missed life's very point. What life calls on us to do is to open ourselves to the numberless occasions for joy it affords us, and this requires the kind of spontaneity that a set of rules would kill. People who live their whole lives according to rules are marionettes, whose actions are circumscribed and mechanical. Like machines, their actions follow a determined program, and they are comically inadequate to the dexterity society requires of us. This is why we laugh at the machine-man. "Society requires something more," said Henry Bergson. "It is not satisfied with living, but wants us to live *well*."[91]

The sensible paternalist is apt to regard Orwell's sinner and Nietzsche's superman as suitable cases for psychiatric treatment. Yet, the decision to drink or smoke might be consistent with one's best life plan, even if the drinker or smoker develops a dependence on his vice. Gary Becker has noted that addiction may be rational, in the sense that one might choose to become addicted with eyes wide open, provided that the addict's life is happier than the abstainer's.

> *Addictive good*: Becker defines an addictive good as one whose utility is a function of previous consumption: the more one has consumed in the past, the better one likes it in the present.[92] With increased consumption, the good becomes harder to give up. So defined, addictive goods include not only cigarettes and liquor but also classical music and romantic love. In falling in love one takes one's chances, but the possibility of heartbreak will not deter most of us. Like the rational smoker, the rational lover recognizes the possibility of a Beckerian addiction but believes the benefits exceed the costs.

Figure 5.3 represents three forms of addiction, for classical music, coffee and heroin, with time measured on the horizontal axis and utility on the vertical axis. Line OA represents the utility level of the person who abstains from all three goods. The utility level of the classical music addict is shown in line OB. Since listening to classical music is pleasurable and CDs are cheap, his addiction decision is efficient: it leaves him better off than he would have been as an abstainer. His addiction is also time-consistent: there never is a time when he regrets his addiction. The addiction to coffee, represented by line OC, is efficient and time-inconsistent. Because it is efficient, the coffee-drinker is better off overall than the abstainer; but because it is time-inconsistent there comes a time when he would rather give up coffee. Where his utility curve drops below the horizontal line which represents the abstainers' utility level, he would prefer not to drink coffee; but being an addict he cannot give it up. Withdrawal has simply become too painful. Line OD represents heroin addiction, which is both time-inconsistent and inefficient. The heroin addict experiences a preference reversal in which he regrets his addiction decision; and he is worse off overall than the abstainer.[93]

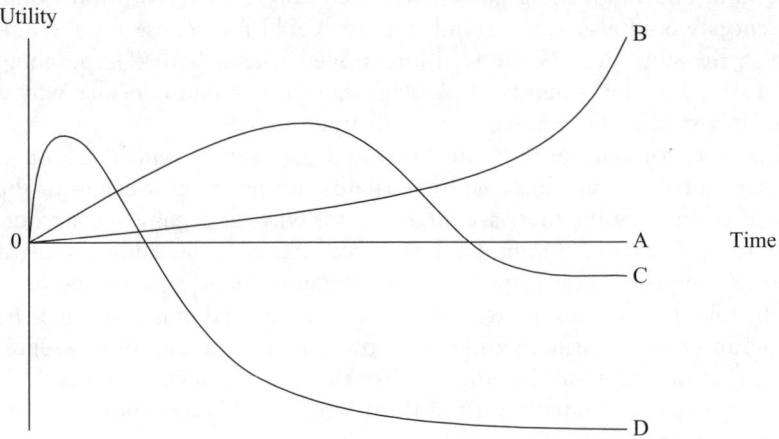

Figure 5.3 Addiction

Becker does not assume a constant discount rate and equal preferences for present versus future consumption. To make his model work in the case of heroin, therefore, we might imagine the rational addict to be a hyperbolic discounter who places a high weight on present gratification and a low weight on later misery.[94] This runs strongly against the intuitive norm of a constant discount rate and consumption-smoothing (where the goal is equal pleasure in every time period), and seems imprudent. Were a friend to tell us that he really has no concern for tomorrow, we would surely try to persuade him to become more like La Fontaine's ant who stored his food for the winter, less like his grasshopper who preferred to play. We would describe a later life of hardship and penury. But if he persisted, we would have little to say against a settled bias in favor of present consumption.

The Beckerian addict is not irrational, since in each of the three cases he is doing precisely what he wants to do at the moment when he becomes addicted. Moreover, the classical music and coffee addicts are not weak-willed; even the strong-willed would become addicted were the payoffs those of Figure 5.3. The heroin addict might tell us he is not weak-willed either. It is not that he lacks the strength of will to satisfy his preferences; instead, he has the wrong set of preferences. But if he is not weak-willed, no one is. The heroin addict might be rational, but a perverse preference for present over future consumption shows weakness of will.

Does akrasia argue for paternalism?

Let us suppose we could not persuade a friend to abstain from addictive goods. Would we force him, had we the power to do so? Few of us would be so bold; and if so, the argument for state interference with individual preferences would also seem to fail, for we would not repose more confidence in the state than in the well-intentioned friend. Before impeaching individual choice on grounds of akrasia, then, we should consider why a person might hesitate to impose his will upon a friend.

Arguments for interfering with individual preferences which assume a perfectly motivated and informed paternalist are naive, as we saw in the last section. In addition, there are three reasons why the argument for paternalism from akrasia might fail. First, the decision to become addicted might represent a person's best response to the circumstances in which he finds himself. Like the decision to acquire a taste for classical music, it might be efficient and time-consistent; and even if the person comes in time to regret the decision, it might still be efficient, like the coffee drinker's choice.

Second, when presented with the third kind of addictive choice, which is both inefficient and time-inconsistent, the individual might employ his own self-binding strategies to remove temptation from his path. Weakness of the will is sometimes thought to provide a rationale for legal barriers which impeach the choices of akratic subjects. However, this ignores the self-control or self-binding devices which a person might himself employ to solve the problem, without relying on mandatory legal rules.

Thomas Jackson has advanced a self-binding explanation for the debtor's mandatory discharge rights under the Bankruptcy Code.[95] Since the debtor cannot waive his right to seek a bankruptcy discharge in the future, these are paternalistic fetters on individual choice. Jackson argues that, absent mandatory bankruptcy barriers, the hyperbolic consumer would mortgage his future to fund present gratification. To prevent this, the individual would want to bind himself against such decisions. By restricting the scope of the assets he may pledge, the mandatory bankruptcy discharge does exactly this. Because he cannot agree to surrender all of his assets to his creditor on default, the debtor's ability to borrow is constrained.

However, self-binding explanations of mandatory rules assume a failure of self-control strategies that the individual might personally adopt. Those who can bind themselves against unwise future choices have no need for legal fetters. Ulysses did not need legal rules to protect him from the lure of the Sirens' song, having earplugs and cord on board his ship. Mandatory legal barriers are thus unnecessary where present selves can bind future selves on their own. And borrowing might constitute just such a strategy.

Borrowing is a form of dissaving, in which debtors draw down on future earnings to fund present consumption. For most of us, saving connotes frugal virtue and dissaving (or spending) suggests prodigality and imprudence. But these are often crude caricatures. Leverage permits the debtor to smooth out consumption so as to avoid feasts and famines, by saving and dissaving at different times in his life cycle. The prudent consumer will save in the fat years and dissave in the lean ones. For example, he will save while he is earning and spend his nest egg during retirement.

Saving might thus be excessive when the miser hoards present wealth beyond the reasonable prospect of future consumption, either for him and his cherished descendents or for the charities he supports. Similarly, dissaving is prudent when the gains from present consumption exceed the costs associated with deferred future consumption. The miser might be a withered, cold-hearted wretch, like *L'Avarre*'s Harpagon; but he might also be the no-longer-youthful curate who postpones his wedding till he obtains a living in Arthur Hughes' painting *The Long Engagement*. Or the professionals who defer having children, like the adoptive parents in the *Baby M* case. Sometimes it is more prudent to burn one's candle at both ends, and save in the middle years.

The borrowing decision might also be a rational self-binding strategy. Suppose that a person lacks assets to take up a valuable investment opportunity, and to finance it must choose between issuing an equity claim (in the form of a partnership interest) or a debt claim (by borrowing). He might prefer to issue debt because the possibility of default (which does not exist in pure equity financing) binds him to pursue and exploit the opportunity. The obligation to repay moneys in the future also disciplines the borrower against future profligacy, just as high leverage binds a firm against the accumulation of "free cash flow" in Michael Jensen's model of corporate borrowing.[96] Jensen argues that the requirement that corporate debt be repaid, usefully prevents a firm from hoarding revenues from investors and investing profits in wasteful opportunities. High leverage might thus be seen as a prudent self-binding strategy, in which the debtor's promise of efficient management is made more credible. In the same way, the obligation to repay personal debt prevents the accumulation of personal free cash flow that the borrower would otherwise squander.

Home purchases are one example of this strategy. While borrowing is usually thought to transfer money from future to present periods, the direction of the wealth transfer is reversed in home mortgages. While the debtor lives in the house he consumes a portion of its value. But he is also saving for future consumption, since houses are durable and appreciable goods and therefore represent an investment. Indeed, houses are an individual's largest asset and his most important private source of retirement savings.[97] On retirement, he will ordinarily cash in the house by trading down to a smaller house, using the proceeds of the sale as a nest egg.

The tax subsidy for debt financing of home purchases (through mortgage interest deductibility) might thus be seen as an incentive to increase retirement savings,[98] like the favored tax treatment for retirement savings accounts. What paternalists such as Jackson have failed to note is that borrowing might be a self-control technique and not a weak-willed consumption activity. It might transfer wealth from present to future persons, rather than from future to present ones.

Some forms of behavior that might otherwise seem quirky or wrongheaded can also be seen as self-control strategies adopted to address akrasia problems. The mental accounting rules identified by Richard Thaler might be one such example. Thaler tells of staying over in Switzerland after giving a talk there. While the hotel price was very high, he told himself that he was only spending the honorarium check. "Had I received the same fee a week earlier for a talk in New York though, the vacation would have been much less enjoyable."[99] Thaler had one mental account for the honorarium and another account for all other moneys, even though in the end they both fell in the same pool. Similarly, Graham Greene set himself a daily 500-word goal when writing a novel. When he reached the last word he stopped, even if he was in the middle of a sentence and even if it was only 9:00 a.m. Like Thaler, he had divided his life into separate mental accounts. From an *ex ante* perspective, however, Greene's mental accounts served as a self-disciplining device, since they forced him to keep to his schedule, even if it took him well into the afternoon to reach his goal. The prospect of quitting early on occasion made the self-control device easier to sign on to and stick with. So, too, the prospect of spending an honorarium check on a holiday might tempt academics to deliver papers abroad when they would otherwise prefer to stay at home. Seen in isolation Greene's 500-word goal and Thaler's Swiss holiday might look indulgent but, overall, the implicit rule might be a prudent self-control strategy.

George Ainslie has suggested that we might adopt compulsive patterns of behavior to prevent ourselves from yielding to temptations.[100] And where the temptation is greater, there is a need for even stronger self-denying rules. The moderate drinker might limit himself to one glass of wine at dinner, but the alcoholic may find it necessary to abstain completely. In the same way, the natural spendthrift might become a miser and the natural sluggard a health fanatic.

These examples show how self-control may shade into over-control, how a person might sacrifice present real pleasures because he fears they might lead to future over-indulgence. The possibility of over-control highlights the difficulty of identifying akrasia. When the abstainer takes a glass of wine at dinner, is he displaying weakness of the will or is he wisely relaxing an excessive self-control program? It may be hard to say, and it might be equally difficult to stigmatize the first cigarette or the first use of narcotics as weak-willed. The first lapse is for philosophy, said Voltaire, and only the second for vice.

The literature about akrasia commonly identifies strength of will as a rigid adherence to a set of rules. The self-controlled *enkrates* adopts a set of stringent requirements, which he thereafter follows without the slightest deviation. It is difficult to imagine a more joyless existence. The rule-follower is Bergson's machine-man, who imagines that life can be reduced to a simple program. He takes a few principles and absurdly extends them beyond their reasonable scope. He is the miser, the teetotaler, the health

Nazi. What he has forgotten is that "willpower is an awkward expedient, not the ultimate rationality."[101]

Faced with a choice between the moral martinet's over-control and the moral sluggard's under-control, a person might reasonably decide upon a mixed strategy that avoids both extremes. He might follow a self-control strategy but allow for occasional backsliding, and provided the exceptions do not eat up the self-control rules this might permit him to achieve a higher level of well-being than fanatical abstinence or dissolute intemperance. Such a strategy resembles the Aristotelian virtue of moderation, which is a middle way between extremes of behavior and which, for Aristotle, is very nearly the definition of virtue itself. Aristotle's great-souled man is truthful, and speaks neither too highly nor too lowly of himself; he is neither miserly nor prodigal, but generous; he is sensible in his diet and neither abstains from fine food and wine nor overindulges. He takes a reasonable amount of exercise, and is neither a health fanatic nor a sluggard. His life seems incontestably happier than that of those who live at the extremes of self-control and akrasia.

There is a third reason why the argument for paternalism from akrasia might fail. People might prefer to make their own choices, even where the paternalist is more likely to get it right, because of the independent value associated with the exercise of self-control. John Stuart Mill analogized the will to a muscle, which atrophies when it is not used. By deliberating over one choice, even or especially when this is painful, a person might subsequently find it easier to make the correct choice over an entirely different matter. Further, there is a joy associated with free choice itself. Robert Nozick asked us to imagine whether we would be satisfied to be tied to a machine that made all our choices and provided us with a level of bliss that exceeded anything we could expect to experience on our own.[102] Would we wish to connect ourselves to the machine, he asked? The question answers itself, both for the hedonist and for the person of faith who sees this life as the field upon which we are to work out our salvation in the next.

In sum, the paternalist's argument from akrasia might fail for three reasons. First, the officious paternalist might mistake an efficient addiction, which leaves the subject better off, for an inefficient one. Second, the paternalist might increase the problem of which he complains if he ignores the possibility of private self-binding strategies. Mandatory rules are unnecessary where self-binding strategies effectively remove temptations. Finally, even if private self-control strategies sometimes fail, we might still prefer to leave the individual to wrestle with the problem of resisting temptation.

Screening

The third kind of soft paternalism restricts bargaining rights in order to reduce information costs. As we saw in Chapter 3, each party faces an informational problem about whether the other party will faithfully perform his obligations. Unless the parties can trust each other, the bargain opportunity might be lost. Contract law enforcement addresses the problem of trust by imposing a cost on promise-breakers in the form of damages. But this does not eliminate the problem, if some parties might enter into an extremely one-sided contract without paying much attention to what they are doing. A ban on such contracts might therefore economize on the information production or *screening* costs that parties must bear to understand their contracts.[103] After these contracts are cleaved off, it is more likely that the mass of enforceable contracts that remains reflects the bargainers' true preferences.

Richard Hare suggested a rule of soft paternalism based on screening costs to impeach contracts of slavery.[104] The relation of master and slave is everywhere illegal because the slave has not consented to it, but what Hare had in mind was a contract of slavery to which a hypothetical slave gave his consent. Let us suppose that only one man in a billion would ever do so, and that he is before us. Would we enforce his agreement? Before doing so, we would have to take extra steps to ensure that this really was that one-in-a-billion case where the consent was real. And because the consequences of getting it wrong are so drastic, we would require very strong evidence about the reality of consent. The costs we would have to bear in satisfying this evidentiary burden would be enormous, as would the costs of judicial error where we mistakenly enforce a contract of slavery. Against this, the benefit from enforcing the one-in-a-billion contract could only be trivial. On efficiency grounds, this argues for a complete ban on contracts of slavery.

Screening theories explain why other very harsh contracts are banned as a matter of public policy. For example, a contract to subject oneself to physical abuse will not be enforced, since it is very unlikely than anyone would freely agree to this. We examine other cases where harsh terms are not enforced at common law in Chapter 8, under the rubric of substantive fairness. Such cases apart, however, there must be few contracts so egregiously unfair that a court would ban them on these grounds. Were it to do so, it might find itself banning beneficial, idiosyncratic agreements. A promise which most people would find very burdensome might turn out to be a piece of cake for me.

Summary

State interference with individual preferences is labeled paternalism when its goal is to make the person better off. This chapter examined a soft paternalism that restricts bargaining rights for the purpose of giving effect to the subject's deepest preferences. Soft paternalism comes in three varieties. The argument from judgment biases suggests that our instincts might lead us astray and that the wise paternalist should correct for these biases by restricting our choices where we are likely to get it wrong. The argument from akrasia asserts that we are sometimes too weak-willed to pursue the good even when we recognize it. Finally, the argument from screening identifies a narrow range of cases where mandatory legal rules might economize on the costs of information production.

The first two varieties of paternalism enjoy a great deal of popularity in academic circles but are weaker than has been thought. Our heuristics are far more powerful than they have been made out to be, and might more easily impeach the paternalist's judgment than that of the bargainer. The argument from akrasia fares little better. It is very difficult to distinguish akrasia from an idiosyncratic but willful choice which leaves the subject better off. Screening provides a plausible rationale for mandatory rules, but only in a very narrow range of cases.

6 Private perfectionism

> Perfecting consists in the production of the most powerful individuals, who will use the great mass of people as their tools.
>
> Nietzsche, *The Will to Power*

There is a radical difference between the soft paternalism that we saw in the last chapter and the perfectionist's hard paternalism. Soft paternalism restricts our bargaining freedom, but only in the name of satisfying a deeper set of our preferences, which might be moral or immoral, noble or base. By contrast, the perfectionist is a moralist who is prepared to ignore our deepest wishes when these are deemed unworthy. Instead, he identifies the good ends that we should pursue and directs us to seek them whether we want them or not. The failure to distinguish between the two species of paternalism has confused analysis and permitted the perfectionist to rely on appeals to deep preferences which only the soft paternalist may assert.

Perfectionism might take two forms. The *private perfectionism* we examine in this chapter is a form of paternalism which seeks to restrict a subject's choices for his own benefit. The harm is self-regarding and concerns only him. By contrast, the threatened harm in *social perfectionism,* which is discussed in Chapter 7, is other-regarding and enforces morals for the benefit of third parties. Even as a person might corrupt himself through his actions, he might corrupt others by his example. Social perfectionist laws that fetter a person's choice to prevent him from imposing moral harm on innocent third parties cannot be described as paternalistic, since they do not seek to reform the individual for his own sake. Nevertheless, they are a means of enforcing morals and are a form of perfectionism.

The terms paternalism and perfectionism are often used interchangeably but mean different things. The paternalist second-guesses a person's choices with the goal of making him better off; the perfectionist interferes with a person's choice to promote a theory of the good. The two categories overlap in private perfectionism (or hard paternalism), where the interference seeks to make a person better off by impugning immoral choices. For example, a ban on heroin might address the problems of both akratic and ignoble choices. However, perfectionism and paternalism do not overlap when the soft paternalist's cognitive biases get in the way of morally indifferent choices. They also do not overlap in social perfectionism, which has a theory of the good but seeks to promote the welfare of people the individual influences and not the individual himself. One can be a paternalist without being a perfectionist, and a perfectionist without being a paternalist.

Private and social perfectionism are often confused. For example, the private perfectionist might appeal to the third-party consequences which are the province of social perfectionists. But while it is important to distinguish between the two forms of perfectionism, in practice they frequently overlap. When "extreme boxing" is banned because it would corrupt spectators, the concern is for third-party effects; where it is banned because it would corrupt (as well as injure) the boxers themselves, the prohibition is paternalistic. Both kinds of prohibitions are prompted by the idea that the state has a role in promoting personal virtue, and both are forms of perfectionism. Whether private or social, the perfectionist identifies a vision of the good which he would enforce through legal rules.[1]

Another example of the overlap between the two kinds of perfectionism is provided by concerns about *commodification* (turning things into private property that are best left unowned). Friendship should not be commodified, and a contract for friendship services would be a vain thing. It would also corrupt both parties to the bargain, and if such contracts became common and replaced authentic friendship they would corrupt society as well.

Perfectionism and neutralism

Anti-perfectionists who reject the legal moralism of state-enforced norms are labeled neutralists, and for our purposes might be private or social neutralists depending on which form of perfectionism they oppose.[2] In both cases, neutralists might be subjectivists (or moral relativists) who think that moral and aesthetic claims are devoid of meaning except as statements of personal preferences.[3] However, there are few real subjectivists around. More often, subjectivism is a pose adopted to silence an opponent in a debate. "You're so judgmental," we say to the moralist, as though we, ourselves, aren't judging him. Most often, what bothers is not the fact of judging but the content of the judgment. In the debate over abortion, affirmative action and the other hot button issues of the culture wars, the charge that an opponent is judgmental usually masks the belief that he is objectively wrong.

The subjectivist's denial of all moral values is also self-defeating. If values were wholly subjective and no one had standing to condemn another, we could not object to the perfectionist who sought to impose his moral views upon us. To take part in the debate about perfectionism, either for or against, one must first abandon relativism. As Joel Feinberg has noted:

> The liberal . . . had better beware of ethical relativism . . . for his own theory is committed to a kind of absolutism about his favorite values. If his arguments conveniently presuppose ethical relativism in some places yet presuppose its denial elsewhere, he is in danger of being hoist with his own petard.[4]

The neutralist might nevertheless reject subjectivism and still think that the state should stay out of the business of defining what gives value to life. He would legalize vice without celebrating it. He might prefer truth to falsehood, knowledge to ignorance, courage to cowardice and kindness to spite. He might think beauty more valuable than ugliness, and deny that these terms are meaningless. But he might still not want the state to promote any one of these alternatives. Like John Stuart Mill in *Utilitarianism*, he might have a discriminating moral and aesthetic sense; but like Mill in *On Liberty* he might want the state to abstain from taking a position on any of these issues.

The neutralist must prize tolerance. However, what tolerance might mean has changed over time. The modern definition refers to the respect we are asked to accord to every other system of belief or behavior. In this sense, we display intolerance when we condemn anyone else's practices, and this comes down to subjectivism. But there is another, older sense of tolerance which is explicitly judgmental. Here, we tolerate what we reject, not what we accept. We tolerate fools, but do not embrace them; we tolerate pain, but do not enjoy it. We tolerate other religions even though we think them mistaken, and we tolerate other political beliefs even though we think them wrong-headed. Crucially, we are unwilling to proscribe that which we tolerate.

Toleration is an ambiguous virtue. It is not a virtue for a policeman to tolerate crime. But intolerance may be a vice, even in the older sense, where the activity ought to be tolerated; and the toleration for other religions or political opponents is ordinarily admirable. The neutralist might therefore condemn the wrongful or mistaken behavior he tolerates. He might accept that some actions are base while permitting their practice because he believes that proscribing vice would be impracticable.[5] The neutralist might be tolerant without being a subjectivist.

The neutralist might be a subjectivist, but not the perfectionist. If the state is to promote a vision of how we should live, it must be meaningful to speak of the good. The perfectionist is therefore apt to regard neutralism as morally immature if it rests on a foundation of subjectivism. If it does not, if the neutralist does have a conception of the good and denies that the state should enforce it, the perfectionist might suspect that the neutralist lacks confidence in his beliefs. Why not promote the good, asks the perfectionist, if its existence is conceded? The perfectionist might thus regard *On Liberty*'s neutralism as inconsistent with *Utilitarianism*'s deep moralism.

It is tempting but misleading to identify perfectionism with utilitarianism and neutralism with non-utilitarian theories about abstract human rights.[6] The neutralist might be a non-utilitarian libertarian who seeks to preserve a realm of private liberty grounded upon respect for individual rights; but he might also be an anti-statist utilitarian like Mill and Frederick Hayek, whose opposition to perfectionism was based on prudential concerns about the possibility of excessive state interference. And while the perfectionist might be a meddling, Benthamite utilitarian, he might also be a non-utilitarian rights theorist with a thin conception of individual rights and a thick conception of equality rights. The ACLU liberal who believes that the state should actively promote racial tolerance at the expense of personal liberty might be such a person.[7]

Until relatively recently, perfectionism was the dominant view. Aristotle thought that the very purpose of the state was to make men moral. "Excellence must be the care of a state which is truly so called," he said. Otherwise, it is simply a collection of people and not a state:

> [A] state ... is an association of families and aggregations of families in well-being for the sake of a perfect and self-sufficing life.... [P]olitical society exists for the sake of noble actions, and not of living together.[8]

Aristotle would, therefore, deny that the modern neutralist state is really a state. While moderns will find this peremptory, the classical tradition was thoroughly perfectionist, from Aquinas in the thirteenth century to the Founders in the eighteenth century.

With the rise of nineteenth- and twentieth-century liberalism, however, neutralism became generally accepted. In a time of rapid social change, it had the virtue of flexibility and could adapt more easily to new moral codes. "It is no accident," notes George Sher, "that neutralism has become popular when long-cherished values are being eroded by powerful social forces, and when many of those same values are under attack by resourceful critics."[9] Neutralism was also more consistent with modern egalitarian sentiments that privilege individual conceptions of the good. In Charles Taylor's ethic of respect, people are entitled to have their personal views of the good taken seriously by others even if they might disagree with them. Otherwise, a person is "disrespected." At the limit this implies neutralism, since if every idea about the good deserves respect, if every opinion is equally valuable, there is no room for perfectionism. Yet, if a radical egalitarianism implies neutralism, it does not follow that anti-egalitarians must be perfectionists. Matthew Arnold had a sharp critical sense and a hierarchical view of society, but he shuddered to think of the pompous political hacks who would be appointed to an English version of the Academie Française. For societies that lack a well-accepted cultural hierarchy, cultural neutralism is an eminently sensible position.

Private neutralism might commend itself for other prudential reasons. An individual will ordinarily have a better conception of the conditions in which he will flourish than the state. As Mill noted, "with respect to his own feelings and circumstances the most ordinary man or woman has means of knowledge immeasurably surpassing those that can be possessed by anyone else."[10] If deciding how to live were a technical question, like the choice of bathroom drains, we might delegate it to an expert. But living well is the most complex of arts and a set of mechanistic rules could never do justice to the suppleness needed to extract happiness from life. Because of this, said Mill, "[t]he strongest of all the arguments against the interference of the public with purely personal conduct is that, when it does interfere, the odds are that it does interfere wrongly and in the wrong place."[11]

If there were one simple program we each should follow, if the same set of ends should govern everyone's behavior, we could perhaps defer to the expert or the perfectionist. However, what an individual must do in order to flourish must depend largely on his own particular attributes. The single "good for man" is elusive, and we should not expect everyone to seek the good in precisely the same way. Fortitude and charity are virtues, but just what they might ask of us depends importantly on who we are. There is a fortitude for a soldier and a fortitude for a widow, and they are not the same thing. Virtues may be agent-relative and depend for their content on the individual's qualities without at the same time being subjective.[12]

Nor is there a single rubric by which lifestyle choices might be evaluated. Instead, there is what Charles Taylor calls a "diversity of goods."[13] We are asked to aspire not merely to moral excellence but also to aesthetic taste and an appreciation for the opportunities for joy that life affords. It might even be impossible to rank different lives or goods because they are *incommensurable*.[14] Things are incommensurable when they are not of the same value and yet are neither better nor worse than each other. We might think that Pascal, Bernini and Louis XIV's general, Marshall Turenne all led admirable lives, and still be unable to say which life is best. That is, the lives of the writer, sculptor and war hero might be incommensurable. Even with all possible information about their lives, we might still be unable to choose between them.

In this sense, incommensurability means a value-pluralism, where different conceptions of the good, which cannot be compared in value, coexist. This does not imply subjectivism, since we might agree that Bernini's life was better than that of a schlock artist, Turenne's better than an inglorious general. Still, it means that there is uncertainty at the top, and for a certain kind of liberal this argues persuasively against private perfectionism. In particular, Isaiah Berlin's liberalism rested on value pluralism and the acceptance of irreducible conflicts in visions of the good life.[15]

A state that seeks to micromanage private virtue might also be distracted from the more serious business of protecting life and limb, or even the less serious but still important business of fixing potholes. Criminalizing vice also drives it underground, where organized criminals prey upon ordinary citizens, and where desperate gangs shoot it out on the streets. The War on Drugs has not been an unqualified success, to put it mildly. Legislating virtue also empowers police and prosecutors to harass citizens and opens the door to political abuse. It caters to the prurient, the snoop, the busybody, the blackmailer. It can easily become priggish and invite the kind of drubbing it received in a satire from *THE ONION*:

> Alarmed by the unhealthy choices they make every day, more and more Americans are calling on the government to enact legislation that will protect them from their own behavior. ... Bernard Nathansen, an attorney for the Personal Rights Deferred Center in Oakes, VA, is one of many individuals working to promote "governmental accountability." His organization arranges class-action lawsuits on behalf of Americans who have been hurt by the government's negligence, including individuals who suffer health problems related to overexposure to sunlight. "We can all agree that many choices are too important to be left up to a highly flawed individual," Nathansen said. . . . To this end, Personal Rights Deferred has compiled an action list of more than 700 behaviors it wants regulated by state or federal authorities. The list includes such risky behaviors as swimming in cold weather and staying up all night playing video games.[16]

There might even be something a little vulgar about paying too close attention to the small misdeeds of others. A gentlemanly disregard for gossip and scandal-mongering cannot fail to elicit our admiration. Nor can we read the magnificent encomium to personal liberty in Pericles' Funeral Oration without feeling that we have arrived at one of the peaks of civilized life, that we have left the lowlands of envy, resentment and meanness behind:

> The freedom which we enjoy in our government extends also to our ordinary life. There, far from exercising a jealous surveillance over each other, we do not feel called upon to be angry with our neighbor for doing what he likes, or even to indulge in those injurious looks which cannot fail to be offensive, although they inflict no real harm.[17]

The private perfectionist's attempt to make people moral might also be thought to be self-defeating. We cannot blame people for acts which they were compelled to do, or praise them either. Coerced choices are not moral choices, and people cannot be legislated into Heaven. This was Locke's argument for religious toleration in his *Letter Concerning Toleration*: since conversion requires private assent it cannot be mandated. Similarly, the paternalist who seizes control of my will and turns me into a zombie can make me do anything he wants – except perform a moral act. Machines are neither moral nor immoral, and people who are not responsible for their actions are also beyond good and evil.

Nevertheless, there has been a revival of perfectionist ideas, from various directions. Perfectionists have emerged from a newly strengthened natural law tradition, and still others have expressed dissatisfaction with internal weaknesses in the neutralist position. Able and articulate conservatives such as Robert George have advanced a sophisticated perfectionism, and what was regarded as a closed issue 30 years ago is now very much an open one.

As the new perfectionists have noted, legal moralism is not self-defeating. Laws that promote what Robert George calls a benign moral ecology do not compel virtue in anything other than a metaphorical sense and might contribute to a more moral society composed of more moral subjects.[18] Imposing a tax on vice does not force us to give it up, but merely influences us to do so by changing the calculation of costs and benefits. In contract law, the doctrine of illegality makes immoral contracts unenforceable but does not deprive anyone of his free choice. Even criminal laws do not compel virtue, but only increase the costs of deviance.

In addition, the argument from incommensurability can be carried too far. A thick incommensurability would imply subjectivism if it meant that no two lives could ever be compared. While an extensive perfectionism that would overrule minute personal choices would be objectionable, Mill's argument is less than telling against the thin perfectionism of common law illegality, which does not seek to dictate an extensive code of personal conduct but merely refuses to enforce immoral contracts.

Endogenous preferences

The private perfectionist seeks to convert his subject to the virtuous life. It is not enough to change his behavior without changing his preferences. The hardened criminal might be deterred from crime by the threat of punishment, but this cannot satisfy the perfectionist. Otherwise, every law that seeks to modify behavior would constitute perfectionism. The goal is to make people more perfect, not simply more law-abiding, and this entails a society of individuals who act morally, choosing the good because it is intrinsically desirable and not because cost-benefit analysis tells us that this is the more prudent thing to do.

What the private perfectionist seeks to do, therefore, is change our preferences. He assumes that they are *endogenous*, in the sense that they are shaped by the laws he proposes.[19] For example, the Civil Rights Act of 1964, which penalized certain forms of discrimination, might have changed people's attitudes to race relations in areas beyond the scope of the statute. Of course, one is never sure about the direction of causation, and a prior change in preferences about race might have produced the statute, rather than the other way around. However, it is not implausible to suggest that causation works in both directions and that legal changes can shape our preferences.

The idea that perfectionist legal rules change our preferences by expressing societal displeasure about an offence is referred to as law's *expressive* function.[20] For example, we ban trading votes for money, in part, because we wish to express the view that voting is a civic duty. Voting does not affect the outcome of an election unless one casts a tie-breaking vote, and since ties are almost unheard of in public elections (even in Florida) the question is why anyone votes. The puzzle dissipates when one recognizes how our laws and institutions affirm our support for democratic institutions and the moral duty to vote.

The belief that the law should concern itself with expressive effects transcends ordinary political labels. Liberals support laws that seek to shape our preferences about racial and gender issues, and many conservatives have their own perfectionist agenda. After the Supreme Court set aside a law that criminalized flag-burning, some conservatives proposed a constitutional amendment to restrict free speech rights when it comes to desecrating the flag. Conservative opposition to same-sex marriage is also premised on a fear of expressive effects, in this case the possibility that it would change our preferences about marriage for the worse. For that matter, lifestyle liberals who support same-sex marriage do so because they want to change attitudes to homosexuality. People who disagree strongly about social issues might nevertheless agree that legal rules should seek to mold our preferences.

The neutralist might reject legal moralism but he cannot ban expressive effects. Whether he likes it or not, laws necessarily express approval or disapproval. At most, the neutralist might ask the legislator to ignore all such effects. Yet even this seems dogmatic. In evaluating a statute we should be entitled to take all consequences into account, including expressive ones. Moreover, the neutralist who wishes to limit the role of the state might find it easier to argue for smaller government when he is able to rely on expressive consequences. The social stigma that is implicit in the expressive function economizes on legal penalties, and makes it easier to get by with a thinner set of legal prohibitions. For example, a hortatory human rights code that condemns discrimination without penalizing it might effectively deter misbehavior through the stigma, and permit a state to promote its vision of a just society without heavy-handed criminal sanctions.

Endogenous preferences are a necessary but not a sufficient condition for private perfectionism. They are a necessary condition, since private perfectionism would be a non-starter if our preferences could not be shaped by legal rules. But they are not a sufficient condition, and do not by themselves justify interfering with people's preferences. There is a logical leap from the claim that our preferences are shaped by legal institutions to the assertion that the state has free rein to interfere with our choices. Otherwise, everything would be up for grabs. The state could intervene whenever it saw fit, nor could anyone complain of the interference. Like a moth to a flame, a facile paternalism is drawn to the idea of endogenous preferences; but something more is needed before interference with personal choice is warranted.

Internalities

By committing one sin we weaken our moral sense and increase the likelihood that we will commit other sins. Thomas De Quincey humorously described this kind of moral corruption in his 1827 essay *On Murder as One of the Fine Arts*. In De Quincey's satire, a group of aesthetes, who see crime from a purely artistic perspective, ask whether murder might possibly be *wrong*. Surprisingly, the answer is yes. "If once a man indulges himself in murder, very soon he comes to think little of robbing; and from robbing he comes next to drinking and sabbath-breaking, and from that to incivility and procrastination."

The satire amuses, but De Quincey's point was serious, for he thought that the disregard for morality would corrupt the artist. The theme of corruption is a frequent one in literature, as seen in the soul-decaying lust of an Anthony besotted by Cleopatra or a Rinaldo enchanted by Armida. Besides lust, other sins might corrupt, like the simple unpremeditated lie in George Eliot's *Romola* and the momentary cowardice in *Lord Jim* that decide men's fates. In a chilling portrayal of moral decay, J.M. Coetzee's *Disgrace*, an academic's pride leads to the destruction of his career and the disintegration of his personality.

The gateway sins which lead to other sins are the theologian's capital or deadly sins, so called because they lead to the sinner's moral death. For each of the capital sins there is a corresponding capital virtue which is its antidote. For envy there is brotherly love; for pride, humility; for avarice, liberality; and so on. And like the capital sins, the capital virtues have spillover consequences for our character, the difference being that they strengthen it.

The capital vices and virtues that lead us to commit other vices and practice other virtues have been labeled "internalities."[21] Unlike externalities, whose effects are felt by third parties, internalities affect the subject himself, by changing his tastes and preferences. When the internalities are positive he is changed for the better, as where his character is strengthened through good habits. And when the internalities are negative he has been morally corrupted.

Like the drug habit that can be maintained only through crime, a sinful passion might feed on other sins. First Anthony falls, and then he pays for his lust with dishonor in battle. Some vices, such as pride, attack the moral sense more directly. Coetzee's David Lurie has the modern academic's contempt for the common sense morality that polices misbehavior, and foolishly destroys himself as a consequence.[22] Similarly, the spiritual indifference (the theologian's *acedia*) leads to an ignoble, second-rate life. This is the vice of Aristotle's small-souled man,[23] who robs himself of what he deserves. Because he attempts little, his humility is a greater failing than vanity. The vain man tries to perform honorable deeds and, not knowing his limits, fails. He might look foolish, but at least he has made the effort.

Faced with the prospect of internalities, a person might take particular care not to make the first misstep. Because she loves the duc de Nemours and cannot trust herself with him, Mme de Lafayette's Princesse de Clèves retires to the country where they will not meet. The self-binding strategy is costly, since she also leaves her friends behind, but the risk of succumbing to an adulterous passion would be costlier still. The fear of yielding to temptation also powers the literature of high imperialism, where the colonist who "went native" soon lost his self-respect and habits of self-control. The extreme example is *The Heart of Darkness* and Kurtz, whom Conrad contrasts unfavorably with an accountant who had devised a way of having his collars starched in the jungle. "[I]n the great demoralization of the land he had kept up his appearance. That's backbone."[24]

The argument from internalities assumes that our emotions are bound together, not separated in watertight compartments. One emotion might rub up against another, either to dull or sharpen it. If so, this raises the stakes, for both vices and virtues. The capital sins are more dangerous, the capital virtues more beneficent, and the case for paternalism more compelling. The argument from internalities would justify a stiffer dose of perfectionism than we should want in a world without capital sins.

Liberal perfectionism and conservative neutralism

In the debate over perfectionism, opponents often seem to talk past each other. With a fine eye for victims, neutralists sometimes present pornographers as martyrs for the First Amendment; while they portray the perfectionists who seek to curb obscenity as priggish Savonarolas who would restrict political free speech, if we gave them half a chance. But many modern perfectionists such as Joseph Raz have more modest goals and would employ more modest means to achieve them.[25] Raz's brand of perfectionism would advance aesthetic and moral ideals through state-funded museums and public television, without criminalizing immoral acts that do not physically harm third parties. People such as Raz, who balance their perfectionism with a strong defense of personal autonomy, are termed *liberal perfectionists*.

Neutralism and perfectionism are sometimes misleading terms, for while they imply different views about legal intervention, the form of the intervention matters greatly. The kind of perfectionism Matthew Arnold mostly had in mind, where the state promotes culture through the public education of schoolchildren, is not very intrusive. There is also an important difference between criminalizing vice and conditioning the receipt of a benefit such as welfare on participation in a program with paternalistic ends such as workfare.

As this is a book about contract theory we will restrict our scope to the liberal perfectionism that is implicit in the doctrine of illegality in contract law. Certain kinds of contracts, considered more closely in the next chapter, are deemed immoral at common law and not enforced. For example, sexually immoral contracts and contracts to break the law have been held illegal and unenforceable. These are examples of liberal perfectionism, since the interference with personal choice is not intrusive.

Where the question is one of enforcing a contract, the prudential argument for neutralism is weaker. The doctrine of contract law illegality cannot be abused by overreaching politicians, prosecutors and policemen. And if all he can do is hold illegal contracts void, the perfectionist has a much reduced ability to trump private preferences. The determined immoralist can still pursue his vices privately, and he can even employ the non-contractual self-binding techniques we saw in Chapter 3. For example, he might develop a pattern of reciprocal cooperation, which effectively substitutes for contractual enforceability.[26] Or he might pay cash for his vices.

In defending the doctrine of contract law illegality, the liberal perfectionist also sidesteps a challenge the neutralist might pose. Since perfectionism presupposes a theory of the good, the neutralist might ask for a full accounting of human goods. Some perfectionists seem willing to meet this challenge. For example, natural lawyer John Finnis writes that knowledge, play, aesthetic experience, sociability, practical reason and religion constitute life's basic goods.[27] Not everyone will agree with this list, and the fact of disagreement might seem a flaw in perfectionism. Quite apart from disagreements about basic goods, there is less than a consensus about what constitutes a virtue. Christian humility offends against the Aristotelian norm of truth-telling; Aristotle's liberality is not at all the same thing as Christian charity; and the chaste commit the Aristotelian vice of anaisthesia because they fail to enjoy sex. But the liberal perfectionist cannot be faulted for an imperfectly theorized doctrine of illegality since he is not required to come up with a complete account of the good. Instead, he might simply defend a case-by-case perfectionism, in the manner of a common lawyer. He might disclaim a grand theory of aesthetics or religion, but still insist on banning particular immoral contracts.

Private perfectionism is also less troubling where individuals have exit rights. In a federal state, migration offers a means of escaping a burdensome perfectionist for a neutralist state, and the cheaper the exit option the weaker the case for neutralism in the exit state. Where migration is costless and where there is a choice between perfectionist and neutralist states, a state's perfectionist requirements will seem less objectionable since people could easily undo them by moving elsewhere. Of course, moving is not costless. But where nearly half of Americans live in a different state than the one they were born in,[28] the question for many of us is not whether but whither we will move.

Migration permits us to sort ourselves out by preferences. A conservative Virginian might think that there are foolish laws in California; but he might ask himself why he should care if their effect is confined to that state. However, were perfectionism imposed at the national level, and Virginians and Californians required to conform to the same regime, a good many people in both states would be dissatisfied. Such complaints are fewer when the laws are passed at the state level and people "vote with their feet" for the regime they prefer.[29] In a federalist regime, we can also expect states to tailor perfectionist laws more closely to the local population. As the Supreme Court has noted, "a decentralized government ... will be more sensitive to the diverse needs of a heterogenous society."[30]

Imposing perfectionism at the local level might even be thought to expand (positive) liberty by expanding the range of choices. Zoning requirements might do precisely this when members of a highly mobile society can choose to live in any one of a number of small towns in the same area. In Northern Virginia, for example, people may choose to live in modern communities with lax zoning laws such as McLean, or in the older city of Alexandria with its tough zoning laws. Many of the homes in the older part of Alexandria are more than 200 years old, and its zoning board sends people who "want to make a statement" with concrete and glass houses to the cul-de-sacs of McLean. The result is that people who want to live in a city with Federal style homes are better able to do so where some cities enact zoning laws. In the same way, a local option to enact perfectionist laws about urban blights, such as aggressive panhandlers and ugly graffiti, expands the choices for social conservatives and liberals and permits them to sort themselves out according to their taste for vulgarity.[31]

While the debate over neutralism and perfectionism is often shrill, behind the rhetoric the real differences might not be substantial. Though accused of immoralism, the neutralist might have as deep an appreciation of the importance of private virtue as the perfectionist, but differ on whether virtue flourishes more strongly when it is legislated. A *conservative neutralist* might believe that, left to their own devices, people would organize themselves under norm-generating institutions such as religions, and that this would more effectively police misbehavior than any number of laws. For example, he might support voluntary faith-based associations and vouchers for parochial schools.

Conservative neutralists see private perfectionists as closet statists who seek to expand the role of the government and weaken subsidiary institutions. In the debate about the Boy Scouts' policy of excluding homosexual scoutmasters, it was the perfectionist who sought to impose antidiscrimination requirements on a private organization and the conservative neutralist who wished to limit state interference with individual choice.[32] So too, a perfectionist who would restrict the exercise of religion by banning religious education would expand the role of the state at the expense of the individual. The perfect is often the enemy of the good.

The differences between conservative neutralism and liberal perfectionism might be slight. Liberal perfectionists like Raz have a strong appreciation for human autonomy, and might even seem more disposed to promote free choice than some neutralists. The doctrine of illegality flourished in the nineteenth century, which many would regard as the high-water mark of bargaining freedom. The idea that a man should always be held to contracts he signed and that bargainers should be permitted to arrange their affairs with the least government intrusion coexisted easily with the idea that immoral contracts should be set aside. While contracts for sexual favors were banned, ordinary contracts were rigidly enforced. Subsequently, in the twentieth century, the doctrine of illegality was relaxed in matters of sexual immorality, but in other areas bargaining rights were restricted through principles of unconscionability and economic regulation. Contracts that strike a judge as unfair are more likely to be set aside today than they were a hundred years earlier. The modern egalitarian neutralist is more likely to approve of these changes than the nineteenth-century perfectionist, and it is by no means clear that the former is the stronger supporter of liberty.

Nineteenth-century judges did not see a conflict between the ideal of bargaining freedom and the perfectionism that was implicit in common law illegality. On the surface the conflict is there. The doctrine of illegality promotes a more moral society by removing the option of contractual enforcement. However, the fetters on choice are relatively weak and do not greatly hinder the determined immoralist. Nineteenth-century judges let the individual work out his own salvation, but did not offer him the assistance of the courts when his choices were immoral.

Gregory Alexander distinguishes between alternative conceptions of property in the early Republic: property as a market commodity that might be bought and sold, and property as the foundation of a social order that prizes individual responsibility.[33] In the same way, we may distinguish two ways in which nineteenth-century courts regarded bargaining freedom: as a market process that promotes wealth creation, and as a device that encourages virtue by making the individual responsible for his choices. In both cases, the second conception is the older one, and looks back to an era when no one doubted that the state had a stake in the private virtue of its citizens and that it might seek through its law of contract to shape their characters.

This is not to say that the doctrine of illegality is entirely toothless. A court that refuses to enforce a covenant in a real estate or trust deed which restricts conveyances or grants to members of a particular race or religion might significantly alter residential patterns and the direction in which moneys flow. Moreover, the doctrine of illegality illustrates how the expressive function of the law might effectively shape behavior without strongly interfering with private autonomy rights. It is reasonable to think that, once restrictive covenants were held up for public opprobrium, private expressions of racial and religious prejudice became more costly, and this without the officious barriers to free choice of which neutralists rightly complain.

7   Social perfectionism

The mischief which a person does to himself may seriously affect . . . those
nearly connected with him and, in a minor degree, society at large.
John Stuart Mill, *On Liberty*

John Stuart Mill,
By a mighty effort of will,
Overcame his natural bonhomie
And wrote "Principles of Political Economy."
Edmund Clerihew Bentley

Civilians commonly begin their treatises on contract law with the doctrine
of illegality, under which contracts that offend against public order or
good morals are set aside. By contrast, common lawyers place illegality
in the middle of their textbooks. The civilian approach has much to
commend it, since the doctrine of illegality marks off the border between
public and private ordering. Within the bounds of private ordering the
parties are free to contract over whatever they wish. As in promising,
their obligations are content-independent, with the duty to perform resting
upon the promise and not the nature of the thing promised. But when
the contract is illegal we are in the realm of public ordering and private
bargaining rights are withdrawn. Content-independent promising between
the parties is trumped by content-dependent duties to third parties or to
society at large.

Moral externalities

When we move from private to public ordering, we leave the immediate
parties to the contract and consider its effects upon third parties.
Paternalists, soft and hard, would override the subject's choices out of
concern for the subject himself. But the subject's actions may have the
third-party spillover effects that economists call externalities. What I do
affects others, for good or for ill, and this may supply a reason to restrict
bargaining freedom. The economist's assumption that a person will not

agree to a contract that leaves him worse off might have little traction when the costs are borne by an unwilling third party.

Contracts often have third-party consequences. Positive externalities confer third-party gains, and negative externalities impose third-party costs. However, externalities disappear (are "internalized") when the third parties become parties to the contract; and they might have an incentive to do so to ensure that efficient levels of benefits and costs are conferred. For example, the downstream recipients of sludge might offer a side payment to the upstream polluter to reduce the pollution (assuming he has a right to pollute).

Absent barriers to bargaining, the Coase Theorem posits that all opportunities for gain will be exploited through private contracting.[1] Third parties would bargain for inclusion in contracts that affected them adversely and eliminate any inefficiencies that arise through externalities. However, the barriers to bargaining, which Ronald Coase thought the very point of his Theorem, will often prevent this. These barriers are called transaction costs and include the cost of producing the information about the externality and the contract, identifying the affected parties and negotiating the contract, as well as dealing with holdouts. Where only one third party is affected by the contract and he knows the contractors, transaction costs are low and we would expect him to bargain away any externalities problem. But where the externalities affect thousands of people, as often happens in cases of water and air pollution, the transaction costs will ordinarily make it impossible to bring all third parties into the bargain.

The barriers to bargaining might argue for a governmental response. Because "public goods" that confer positive externalities (such as museums) might be undersupplied, the state might subsidize them. Alternatively, the state might take over production of the public good itself, as it does for national defense. And because "public bads" that impose negative externalities (such as the polluter's sludge) might be oversupplied, the state might penalize them through criminal or civil sanctions. Alternatively, a court might invoke the doctrine of illegality and refuse to enforce a contract because it imposes third-party harms. There is no reason to think that a contract between A and B to impose physical harm on C will be value-increasing if C is not a party to the contract.

We are accustomed to think of externalities as physical things, such as B-1 bombers and sludge. But externalities might also be moral in nature. I am manifestly better off when I live in a society composed of honest, trustworthy people. Such people possess high human capital, and economists call the spillover benefits produced by other people's talents and virtues *social capital*. We are wealthier when we live in a trusting society, and the deviousness and bad faith that weaken trust in Banfield's Montegrano harm everyone in the society. From this, many people would agree with communitarian philosopher Charles Taylor that the state should seek to inculcate a set of social virtues. It is important for an individual that certain activities and institutions flourish in society. It is even of importance to him what the moral tone of the whole society is ... because freedom and individual diversity can only flourish in a society where there is a general recognition of their worth.[2]

I have defined social perfectionism as state interference with personal choice that is prompted by a concern for moral externalities. Compared to private perfectionism, social perfectionism offers a more appealing justification for impugning personal choice, and this explains why it is useful to keep the two kinds of perfectionism separate. We are more willing to let a person dig his own grave, less willing to let him drag others into it. Our contempt for the truly corrupt leaves us indifferent to their fate; we are more sympathetic to the more innocent person who is corrupted by them. And while the private perfectionist seeks to reform only one person, the social perfectionist seeks to protect the many who might be harmed by the moral spillovers. Finally, private perfectionism is more demeaning than social perfectionism. The private perfectionist is a paternalist who impeaches the subject's choices "for his own good"; while the social perfectionist respects his sovereignty and restricts his autonomy only where it affects other people. That is why moralistic legal restrictions on free bargaining are usually framed in terms of negative externalities.

Externalities are ubiquitous, however, and not every spillover effect rises to a level of concern. External goods include the benefits people in wealthy societies derive from the economic activity of others. External benefits also include the passerby's pleasure when he sees a well-dressed woman or a classically designed building. There are a vast number of such benefits and it is absurd to suppose that every recipient has an obligation of financial support.[3] Similarly, not every third-party bad imposes a duty upon its creator. We do not impose aesthetic taxes on ill-dressed louts or concrete-slab buildings.

Nor do spillover effects always result in inefficiencies. Where my actions confer positive externalities, it does not follow that I will undersupply the public goods unless others chip in. For example, my garden might be a public good to the extent that passers-by derive pleasure from it. But this is not to say that I have inadequate incentives to take care of it and that a coalition of passers-by would wish to pay me to trim the boxwood. I might simply enjoy gardening, without the need for a social gardening contract. A little knowledge about public goods can bewitch one into thinking that the mass of gardens will be weed-filled eyesores, but the reality is very different. Whether from vanity or public-spiritedness, we ordinarily have adequate private incentives to keep up our gardens or dress nicely, or do any of the thousand things from which others take pleasure, without a subsidy from them. What matters is whether, at the margin, public goods are undersupplied and public bads oversupplied, and not whether there are third-party effects.[4]

This explains why the doctrine of illegality is narrowly drawn and does not impeach every contract that imposes costs on third parties. The classic case of an external bad that courts ignore is envy. One person's gain is another's loss, if the second person envies the first. Envy is therefore a negative externality of another's gain. But since almost every gain might excite envy, few contracts would be enforceable were courts to take account of envy externalities and every opportunity for self-advancement would be suspect. This explains why envy is thought a moral fault. In the Catholic tradition envy is one of the seven capital sins; and in the Jewish tradition covetousness is the only sin of intention, where the mere desire is wrongful even if it is not acted on.

As the desire to deny goods to one's neighbor, envy is the opposite of the principles of sympathy and benevolence which Adam Smith and Bishop Butler thought the foundational moral sentiments.[5] It is also the sin against capitalism that infected Banfield's Montegrano. Where other people's gains are seen to come at one's own cost, the only sensible strategy is to refuse to bargain with the enemy. All gains from joint cooperation would thus be lost, and what would remain would be Max Weber's "universal reign of absolute unscrupulousness" that is wholly destructive of economic growth.[6]

Common law illegality

A contract that imposes negative externalities cannot be said to satisfy Paretian standards of efficiency, since at least one person is worse off. Were that the test of illegality, few if any contracts would be enforced. However, the doctrine of illegality has wisely been kept within strict bounds, and the legal standard more closely resembles the Kaldor-Hicks criterion of efficiency: a contract is *Kaldor-Hicks efficient* if gains to winners exceed losses to Paretian losers.[7] This standard is sometimes called "potential Pareto-efficiency." It does not require winners to compensate losers for their losses, but does imply that if they did so no one would be worse off since total gains exceed total losses by definition. As a test of illegality, the Kaldor-Hicks standard is thus less rigorous and more realistic than Pareto-superiority. Kaldor-Hicks ignores envy externalities and upholds my contracts in spite of the fact that my success might upset another.

Under Kaldor-Hicks, trivial third-party losses are presumed to be trumped by bargaining gains. Of course, not every negative externality is trivial, and contracts to commit a crime are ordinarily found to be illegal.[8] Even if the criminal statute does not expressly ban the act, a court might still find that contracts to perform it are unenforceable under the doctrine of contract law illegality. Nor need the offence constitute a crime, so long as the statute or regulation was enacted or proclaimed for the protection of the public, like the requirement that stock brokers take out a license in the early case of *Cope* v. *Rowlands*.[9] Yet even this might unduly expand the doctrine of illegality, since it is easy to breach an administrative requirement in a regulatory state, and more recently a transport company was unable to set aside a contract of carriage by arguing that it had secretly failed to obtain the requisite driver's license.[10] As Lord Wright observed, public policy might be "better served by refusing to nullify a bargain save on serious and sufficient grounds."[11]

Where the bargained-for act is not prohibited by statute or regulation, the contract might still be illegal at common law on grounds of public policy. For example, a popular entertainer's contract with a ghostwriter was held to be void in *Roddy-Eden* v. *Berle*.[12] The plaintiff had agreed to write a novel entitled "Sit Still My Soul" in which television's Milton Berle would be credited as the author. The title invites ridicule, but Berle was happy with it. Later, however, he refused to permit publication under his name and the ghostwriter sued. In dismissing her claim, the court said that "agreements which tend to or have for their purpose to defraud the public generally, even though they may not amount to a criminal conspiracy, are illegal and void." As between the ghostwriter and Berle there wasn't much to choose. But the agreement had the broader effect of harming the general public by weakening their reliance on the name under the title, and it was set aside.

The public interest resists precise definition and the list of illegal contracts is open-ended. "[G]aps remain and will always remain," said Lord Simonds in *Shaw* v. *D.P.P*, "since no one can foresee every way in which the wickedness of man may disrupt the order of society."[13] The sale of a public office is illegal,[14] as is a contract with an alien enemy during wartime.[15] So too was the surrogacy agreement in the *Baby M* litigation. The court held that such agreements ignore the best interests of the child, and also saw broader reasons why they are repugnant:

> Putting aside the issue of how compelling [the surrogate mother]'s need for money may have been, and how significant her understanding of the consequences, we suggest that her consent is irrelevant. There are, in a civilized society, some things that money cannot buy.[16]

A state that upholds surrogacy contracts imposes negative moral externalities if it weakens family bonds, and this would leave us all the poorer.

But for the concern about negative externalities, the case against surrogacy or adoption contracts would be much weaker and, in a controversial article, Richard Posner has argued that such contracts should be enforced. The prohibition suppresses the market-clearing functions of efficient markets and creates a waiting list for adoptions and a glut of unadopted children in foster homes. Moreover, concerns about the validity of the consent of surrogate mothers might be addressed through cooling-off rights which might even extend for a period following the birth. Nor is there much reason to fear that purchasers would buy a baby in order to abuse it, said Posner. "Few people buy a car or a television set in order to smash it."[17] What Posner's argument misses, however, are the negative spillovers of a coarser society when baby-selling is legalized.

The concern for negative externalities also informs the barriers against contracts that promote sexual immorality. In *Pearce* v. *Brooks*, the lessors of a specially designed carriage were unable to recover rent owed from a prostitute when they knew that she intended to use it to attract clients.[18] In addition, courts formerly struck down contracts to compensate mistresses because this had the tendency to weaken the institution of marriage.[19] Such cases would likely be decided differently today,[20] and the idea that the state should promote traditional sexual morality is thought a relic of a Victorian past. However, current attitudes on matters of race have plausibly been altered by modern civil rights law, with cases like *Brown* v. *Board of Education* and the 1964 Civil Rights bill, and rightly so in the opinion of most people. The focus of concern has shifted from sexual behavior to racial prejudice, but there has never been a time when morals were not enforced at law.

The harm-to-others principle

On the face of it, the concern for third-party moral harms is consistent with John Stuart Mill's harm-to-others principle, which we saw in Chapter 5. However, Mill's injunction is really two principles in one. First, it is a theory of anti-paternalism so far as parties to the contract are concerned, since it conclusively presumes that bargainers are the best judges of their own welfare. The contract might be set aside if tainted by a vice of consent, such as misrepresentation, mistake or duress, or if tainted by a vice of capacity, such as childhood or mental disability. That apart, Mill would enforce the contract. Second, the harm-to-others principle is a theory about what counts as a harm, since Mill rejected the idea that the state might rely upon moral externalities to impeach a contract. He would have banned contracts that impose physical harm on a third party and upheld contracts that impose non-physical social and moral third-party harms.

Mill was a consistent neutralist. In his anti-paternalism he was a private neutralist; and in his refusal to recognize moral externalities he was a social neutralist. The failure to observe the difference between the two kinds of neutralism often leads to confusion. For example, libertarians and social conservatives would likely agree about waivers of no-fault divorce rights and disagree about same-sex marriages. As a private neutralist, the libertarian would enforce a waiver of divorce rights; and as a social neutralist he would recognize homosexual marriages. He would permit the parties to enter into a binding "covenant marriage" in which the right to a no-fault divorce is waived, because restrictions on the right to elect the form of marriage are paternalistic; and he would permit homosexual marriages because their moral costs, as perceived by conservatives, are not a physical harm. Like the libertarian, the social conservative would enforce divorce waivers; but he would do so because of the social harms associated with divorce. And unlike the libertarian, he would ban same-sex marriage out of a concern for moral spillover effects.

Disputes over moral externalities are factual ones. To say that immoral contracts would coarsen us is to make a prediction about the kind of society we should have were they enforced. Similarly, we might ask whether other, more besetting, pathologies would flourish in a state that tolerates hard drugs. Or whether violent crime rates would rise in a state with high illegitimacy rates. These questions, like most disagreements about moral issues, aspire to the condition of economics, could the data problem be solved. The quantification problem might be vexed, but that does not change the nature of the problem or turn an empirical enquiry into a philosophical one.

"Not everything that counts can be counted," said Einstein, and reasonable men may differ on the subject of moral externalities. However, the philistine's bare denial of the existence of negative moral externalities is a clumsy attempt to win a debate without argument. The costs of moral externalities might be high or low; there is no reason to think that they must be zero. For this, we should have to assume that no one through his behavior could ever influence another. A parent who sincerely believes this would be indifferent about whom his child chooses as a friend, and we should all be quite unaffected by our companions, whether we find them in a faculty tea room or a prison yard. This is obviously not the case, and like Walter Berns we might sympathize with the parent who seeks to insulate his child from the corrosive effects of vulgarity.

> Consider the case of the parent who wants to convince his children of the impropriety of the use of the four-letter verb meaning to copulate. At the present time the task confronting him is only slightly less formidable than that faced by the parent who would teach his children that the world is flat. Just as the latter will have to face a body of scientific evidence to the contrary, the former will have to overcome the power of common usage and the idea of propriety it implies. ... The parent will fail in his effort to educate because he will be on his own, trying to teach a lesson his society no longer wants taught – by the law, by the language, or by the schools.[21]

Mill rejected the easy way out of assuming away moral externalities. "I freely admit," he said, "that the mischief which a person does to himself may seriously affect, both through their sympathies and their interests, those nearly connected with him and, in a minor degree, society at large."[22] The more sophisticated version of social neutralism, which Mill adopted, admits that private contracts may impose moral costs, but nonetheless ignores this because of a concern for excessive interference with personal preferences. Almost anything, Mill feared, might count as a third-party moral cost. To keep the doctrine of illegality within reasonable bounds, therefore, Mill's prudential neutralism would require a physical harm before setting aside a contract. We should then have to put up with real moral externalities, which do impose spillover effects. But this, said Mill, is an "inconvenience ... which society can afford to bear, for the sake of the greater good of human freedom."

Mill's *On Liberty* is chiefly remembered for its trenchant anti-paternalism, for its attack on laws that overrule a subject's preferences with the goal of making him better off. But Mill reserved his harshest criticism for laws that address moral externalities and which seek to benefit not the subject but those he affects. This "monstrous" principle is without limits. "There is no violation of liberty which it would not justify; it acknowledges no right to any freedom whatever, except perhaps to that of holding opinions in secret."[23] Indeed, the scope of social perfectionism is broader than that of private perfectionism, since faults that the private perfectionist might overlook might justify bargaining fetters when third-party spillover effects are taken into account. Private perfectionism is directed to one person, social perfectionism to the many. The private perfectionist might, therefore, be more prepared to tolerate obscenity than the social perfectionist.

In place of legal sanctions, Mill preferred social sanctions, which he described with Victorian hauteur as "the *natural* penalties which cannot be prevented from falling on those who incur the distaste or contempt of those who know them."[24] Yet, even here Mill decried what he saw as the deadening hand of social norms. Perhaps there was an element of personal resentment. When he was 25, Mill met Harriet Taylor, a married woman with two small children, and for 20 years they continued a liaison that shocked their friends. The relationship was apparently chaste, and on the death of Mr Taylor in 1851 the couple married. Nevertheless, the public scandal left Mill embittered against restrictive social norms. Because of "the despotism of custom" and a "dreaded censorship," eccentricity was treated as a crime and a sterile religion of duty shut out avenues of joy. Real progress, which depends on the individuality of men of genius, cannot thrive where we are governed by a regime that requires "ape-like" imitation.[25]

While Mill accepted the reality of moral spillovers, his final position was very close to those who deny them. All sanctions, whether legal or social, that sought to police negative moral externalities were condemned as excessive restrictions on personal liberty. The plea for toleration, the aversion to anything that might encumber personal tastes, the contempt for social conventions, remain a *locus classicus* of neutralism almost 150 years after publication. But the bluff self-confidence of the Victorian rationalist wears less well today. The lofty defense of individualism and of "experiments in living" became, a century later, a special pleading for the psychopath in Norman Mailer's notorious essay "The White Negro."

Mailer urged the reader to reject the "square's" common sense morality and adopt what he described as the superior primitiveness of the underclass, with its perversion, promiscuity and drug addiction, where all preferences are equally valid.

In Mill's day divorce required a special Act of Parliament, and Charles Stuart Parnell was driven from politics when he was named as the co-respondent in a divorce petition. In our day, one in three children is born to an unmarried mother, and in the inner city the ratio approaches 70 percent. Of the two-thirds of children born to married parents, nearly half the marriages will end in divorce before the child reaches 18.[26] What might have seemed a benign plea for toleration when social norms were strict began to seem a squalid defense of deviance when they were wholly relaxed.

The disintegration thesis

The case for and against laws that respond to moral externalities was argued in a well-known debate between Lord Devlin and H.L.A. Hart 40 years ago. In 1957 the Wolfenden Report in England had recommended that homosexual acts between consenting adults should no longer be a criminal offence. The Report was criticized by Lord Devlin in *The Enforcement of Morals* and supported by Professor Hart in *Law, Liberty, and Morality*, and the two little books remain leading statements of their respective positions.[27]

Devlin was a social perfectionist, for he rested his legal moralism upon a concern for moral externalities. Mill had conceded that we might be injured by the example of an immoral fellow subject. If so, said Devlin, the state has a prima facie right to penalize such behavior. "A nation of debauchees would not in 1940 have responded satisfactorily to Winston Churchill's call to blood and toil and sweat and tears."[28] Moreover, said Devlin, moral externalities might do serious harm to society at large. We are so bound together in the moral enterprise of good governance that a state might disintegrate if it failed to enforce its moral code.

> Society means a community of ideas; without shared ideas on politics, morals, and ethics no society can exist. ... If men and women try to create a society in which there is no fundamental agreement about good and evil they will fail; if, having based it on common agreement the agreement goes, the society will disintegrate. For society is not something that is kept together physically; it is held by the invisible bonds of common thought. ... The bondage is part of the price of society; and mankind, which needs society, must pay its price.[29]

Devlin's disintegration thesis is a normative theory, as it assumes that society's preservation is a moral good. Doubtless, some societies deserve to disintegrate, but this was not true of England. Nor did Devlin think that the common sense morality he sought to enforce was unjust. There are wrongful prejudices that should not be legislated, even if necessary in some way to preserve a society, but Devlin did not think this was the case before him.

In response, Hart described the disintegration thesis with withering contempt: Devlin was "confused and confusing" and "not very perspicuous;" "no reputable historian" would agree with him; and his "absurd" views were not entitled to any more respect "than the Emperor Justinian's statement that homosexuality was the cause of earthquakes."[30] Forty years on, after the homosexual rights revolution, Devlin's social conservatism will seem even more retrograde. Norms change all the time; and the change is often for the better. In any case, said Hart, a change in social norms does not destroy a society.

However, the disintegration thesis cannot be so easily dismissed. In particular, Devlin's claim that a society is constituted in part by its moral code is unexceptional. English society in 1959 had particular views about sexual deviance, and these views along with an ensemble of beliefs and practices about culture, government and history made up what was meant by England. In the celebrated phrase of Benedict Anderson, nationalities are imagined communities, defined by something more than mere geographical residence.[31] Ernest Renan had a very similar idea of what it means to be French: one is not born French, he thought; instead one becomes French by acquiring a particular culture, with its special canon of literature, song and historical truths and fictions.[32] So, too, a shared moral code and a common habit of looking at certain things with "intolerance, indignation, and disgust"[33] go to define a society.

A softer form of the disintegration thesis might, thus, commend itself. A change in social norms that does not pulverize its pebbles and salt its fields might nevertheless profoundly alter a society. Similarly, a person might be radically changed, for good or ill, through a conversion experience. "Presume not that I am the thing I was," Henry V told Falstaff. And *non sum qualis eram* is our plea to every Cynara. Today's America is a different country from the one it was in 1960. In part, it is a better country, in part worse. But it is not the same country. Something that was a part of us, something that defined who we were, has disintegrated.

Radical changes in society might be troubling in four different ways. First, an *ecological* version of the disintegration thesis would mourn the passing of a society because a distinctive way of living dies with it. In the same way, the disappearance of languages makes the world a less diverse place. The difference is that, while new languages do not arise to take the place of disappearing old ones, a new society emerges out of the ashes of the old. The loss in diversity might then seem greater when languages disappear. Possibly, in their embrace of modernism, the new societies that have emerged across the globe more closely resemble each other than their predecessors, so that the general tendency is to uniformity and a loss of diversity. But even if not, the disappearance of a society will seem problematical to many. It is an odd sort of ecology which regrets the disappearance of an animal species but not a human society.

The nostalgia for the world we left behind us is on view in every tourist colonial farm and pioneer village. Nevertheless, it is difficult to see how such expressions of sentiment might ascend to the level of a policy argument. People left the older societies willingly. They moved from farms and villages to cities; or, staying home, they purchased the transforming cars and appliances that freed them from the drudgery of life in a colonial village. To coin a phrase, the Williamsburgs of the world are a nice place to visit, but you wouldn't want to live there. We left the past with a sigh, but the psychic cost of staying was greater than the cost of leaving.

This assumes that the move to modernity, with its increased life expectancy and greater social mobility, was an improvement. Social conservatives might contest this, but even if they are right no one had a duty to remain in Oliver Goldsmith's *Deserted Village*. The change from that world to this might have occurred through a series of incremental steps, none of which were wrongful. Not every bad grounds a legitimate grievance against someone. There may be evils without evil-doers. Some bads are "free-floating" and give us no one to blame.[34] Changes in technology that sweep away former patterns of life are of this kind, if the change is indeed evil. And without a wrong-doer, without a duty to desist which might be imposed upon any person, the ecological version of the disintegration thesis lacks any traction.

Second, Robert George has proposed a *communitarian* reinterpretation of the disintegration thesis.[35] The change in social norms might produce a more alienated society, he suggests. The sense of attachment to and sympathy with others, which is called solidarity and which is one of the most basic of human goods, might be weakened when common values are no longer shared. Even if a society does not disintegrate, it might divide into hostile camps, with a no-man's land separating former friends. Something like this happened in France during the Dreyfus affair, and at other times in that country's turbulent history.

As a general matter, however, this is speculative. It is not easy to compare the strength of communitarian bonds across different societies or the same society over time. Is America a more communitarian society today because racial and religious prejudices have weakened over the last 40 years? Or does tolerance impose its own costs on communitarian values? A society in which the only shared value is tolerance might be harmonious, but it would not be particularly communitarian. The society of the tolerant might include all world federalists and unitarians, and this is not a society. It is a mistake to think that, in evaluating communitarian sentiment, only the most encompassing groups count. What this overlooks is that we cannot take the side of one community without taking sides against another. We cheer for our high school team against that of its rival. Every community worthy of its name excludes non-members. There is a community of Cheeseheads who support the Green Bay Packers, but no community of NFL fans or of sports fans everywhere.

Nevertheless, it is not clear that the sense of American community was weakened as it became more inclusive. Ten years ago it seemed that way to many conservatives. Now, after 9-11, the sense of unity and community is much more apparent. The threatened disintegration has not taken place, and as the title of a recent book proclaimed we are still "one nation after all."[36] Moreover, the virtues of individual courage and resilience seem as alive in post-9-11 America as ever they were during the frontier period. The set of virtues are different, but the sense of national identity and the virtues needed to maintain the state still seem strong.

When comparing the America of today with that of the past, the most striking difference is arguably integration, not disintegration. Racial and ethnic groups that formerly were marginalized made gains that were almost unthinkable in 1960, and opportunities for women vastly expanded. The changes were powered by legal reforms that worked out the implications of constitutional protections, but were also accompanied by a profound shift in popular attitudes. What produced the change is an unanswered question. The relaxation of social prejudice eased the way for legal reform, but it is also plausible to suppose that the legal change weakened social prejudices, as the Devlin thesis would have predicted. Devlin's mistake was to assume that the change in social norms must be for the worst.

The third form the disintegration thesis might take is the argument from *moral repugnance* suggested by James Fitzjames Stephen. Like Mill, Stephen was a member of a prominent liberal, intellectual family. His brother was Leslie Stephen and his niece was Virginia Woolf. But Stephen's utilitarianism took a very different form from that of Mill. So far from deprecating social norms, Stephen celebrated them as a necessary foundation for any society, and in *Liberty, Equality, Fraternity*, written a decade after Mill's *On Liberty*, he argued that "the custom of looking upon certain courses of conduct with aversion [is] the essence of morality."[37] When inured to evil we lose our sense of moral outrage and learn to tolerate the intolerable.

While rationalists might object to the idea of moral emotions, another tradition sees feelings such as disgust as central to our moral life. As Aristotle noted, being moral is not simply a matter of right action; it also involves having the right sentiments. We can and do blame those whose feelings are inadequate, who cannot feel friendship, love, patriotism, anger or joy when these are called for.[38] In part, this is because we bear a responsibility for shaping our feelings. Alternatively, we might blame people for their feelings, whether or not they can change them, because they are constitutive of their identities and moral personhood. La Bruyère noted that "to say of an angry, unjust, quarrelsome, depressed, punctilious or capricious person, 'that's his humor,' is not as is generally believed to excuse him; but to aver without giving it much thought that his great faults are irredeemable."[39]

On the argument from repugnance, our emotions sometimes provide a more reliable moral guide than our reason, and this was Edmund Burke's great theme in his *Reflections on the French Revolution*. The English, said Burke, "are generally men of untaught feelings," so that "instead of casting away all our old prejudices, we cherish them to a considerable degree, and, to take more shame to ourselves, we cherish them because they are prejudices." The appeal to prejudice was a rejection of political rationalism, and most particularly of Richard Price's sermon in support of the French Revolution. Burke contrasted Price's didactic sermon with the theater, which must move our emotions to succeed, and which he thought must afford more reliable moral instruction. "No theatric audience in Athens would bear what has been borne" by Dr Price's friends.[40]

The argument from repugnance was recently revived in the debate over cloning. There may be excellent prudential reasons why the prospect of cloning a person is dangerous, but Leon Kass, the chair of the Presidential Council of Bioethics has advanced a very different kind of argument, based on natural feelings of disgust.

> We are repelled by the prospect of cloning human beings not because of the strangeness or novelty of the undertaking, but because we intuit and feel, immediately and without argument, the violation of things that we rightfully hold dear. Repugnance, here as elsewhere, revolts against the excesses of human willfulness, warning us not to transgress against what is unspeakably profound.[41]

The very distinction between reason and passion is often suspect, as we saw in Chapter 5. Cartesian dualists identify emotions with sensations, like heat or cold, or with the brute physiological events in our brain to which they are correlated. Emotions are more than that, however, and philosophers have begun to conceive of them as an intelligent way of responding to choices dominated by desires.[42] Behind Adam Smith's sentiment of benevolence, for example, is the thought that we should act in a kindly fashion to others, and this is no less a thought for the fact that it has the salience of an emotion. If our emotions are sometimes foolish, they might at other times be wise, and sometimes are even more insightful than the calm deliberations we call reason.

This is not to suggest that our emotions cannot mislead. The breakdown of racial prejudice in America was a positive good. Other emotions, such as envy, might result in social norms that are best suppressed. It does not follow, however, that our emotions are presumptively untrustworthy, and that moral questions are always to be decided according to the dictates of pure reason unaided by emotion.

Nor is it clear that our sense of moral condemnation has shriveled, as the argument from repugnance would have it. What offends is different today, of course. Moral codes are never stationary. Had you asked someone in the sixteenth century what virtues he most admired he might have mentioned honor and courage. He would certainly not have spoken of kindness, which became the central virtue of the nineteenth century. Nor is change always in the direction of laxity. The advent of the Victorian era, when Regency dandies and rakes gave way to earnest philanthropists and pious Tractarians, must be thought to have strengthened the moral code. In our day a very different set of virtues, such as tolerance, is prized, and a very different set of vices condemned. The following is a list of modern vices, to which very few people would have objected 40 years ago:

- Driving an oversize vehicle
- Wearing a fur coat
- Smoking
- Hunting
- Not exercising
- Unsafe sex
- Zionism
- Ageism

Compare this list to the seven deadly sins and it's hard not to feel a sense of decline. Social conservatives such as Devlin will object to the preciousness of modern vices, some of which seem to have originated in Brentwood salons. Modern sins are also more likely to be self-referential and deal with the ways in which we might improve ourselves (such as by exercising) without regard to other people. In addition, the concern is for physical rather than spiritual harms, and the idea of moral corruption, so vivid to the Victorians, will now seem almost quaint to many moderns. Finally, political allegiances matter more today than private character. Provided a candidate has the correct views on a hot button issue like abortion, his personal misbehavior is very nearly irrelevant to many people. Our collective sense of outrage remains as strong as ever; it is simply not triggered by transgressions against traditional morality. For those who continue to subscribe to older codes of conduct, therefore, our moral sense will seem withered and the argument from moral repugnance compelling.

The very words used to describe moral corruption seem to have been lost, like a forgotten language. Talk of evil makes moderns uncomfortable and is very much a social faux-pas. Even the interior sense of evil seems to have been dissolved by the cheap grace of a relaxed moral code. Macbeth is the extreme case of a person who is inured to evil, but the more typical case is closer to home, in the man who cannot remember the last time he had a crisis of conscience.

Finally, an argument from *corruption* supplies the fourth version of the disintegration thesis. The argument from repugnance also describes a form of corruption, but here the term refers to the slippery slope in which the practice of one vice leads to deeper sins. This might happen in two ways. The first kind of corruption is the internalities we saw in Chapter 6, where A's commission of capital sin X leads him to commit sin Y. The second kind of corruption arises through moral externalities, where A's moral faults might rub off on B and in this way go on to corrupt an entire society.

The moral spillover costs of matrimonial bad faith seem particularly high. We used to think, with *Jules and Jim,* that we might "start from zero and rediscover the rules."[43] But when we did so we imposed a good deal of pain all around, particularly to the children of broken homes. There is a good deal of evidence that divorce harms children, and stepparents do not appear to make things any better for them.[44] In one of the most respected longitudinal studies, Mavis Hetherington examined preschoolers after divorce, comparing them with a control group of children in intact families. At two months and a year after the divorce, children in divorced families were found to function worse on a number of psychological tests than those in intact families. While the children of divorce had improved substantially two years after the divorce, boys in divorced families continued to be less compliant than boys in intact families six years later.[45] In addition, the children of unwed mothers are more likely to fall afoul of the law and become unwed parents themselves.[46]

When Vice President Dan Quayle in 1992 criticized the *Murphy Brown* television show for portraying unwed motherhood in a positive light, he became a national laughingstock. Over time, however, the laughter died down. For 40 years we had thought that Hart had demolished Devlin and that there were no such things as moral spillovers. But now the evidence is in, and it is less clear that Devlin lost the debate. Stable marriages are better than broken ones, and illegitimate children fare poorly compared to those raised in family structures.[47] Divorce is something more than the morally neutral personal choice we thought it was. From today's perspective, it is Hart who looks naive and Devlin who appears the realist.

Other forms of deviant behavior have been embraced in the name of an ethic of egalitarian, non-judgmental respect. In *The Death and Life of Great American Cities*, Jane Jacobs described how crime is reduced when people feel safe in their community and make their presence felt on its streets. Strangers are noticed and suspect behavior quickly attracts watchful eyes. However, when the first graffiti appeared on subway cars it was thought a little churlish to make a fuss, and progressives such as Norman Mailer celebrated the birth of a new art form. The apotheosis of this kind of cultural relativism was perhaps *Kreimer* v. *Town of Morristown*.[48] Kreimer was a homeless man who refused to bathe and who acquired the nickname of "Smelly Bum." He took to spending his days at the Morristown, NJ library, where he stared down patrons and spoke loudly and belligerently to librarians and patrons.[49] The library responded with a set of admission guidelines which, not surprisingly, excluded Kreimer. Kreimer sued and the library policies were struck down at trial as unconstitutionally vague and restrictive. "The greatness of our country," wrote the judge, "lies in tolerating speech with which we do not agree; that same toleration must extend to people, particularly where the cause of revulsion may be of our own making."[50]

What this denied was the importance of moral externalities. Subway cars that are covered with graffiti and libraries that welcome people like Kreimer are repulsive and frighten away their patrons. When that happens, the self-policing which the patrons themselves provide is lost as well, and we have bought crime with ugliness.

The case for neutralism

This section examines three objections to social perfectionism. First, the objection from public discourse sees the perfectionist's conception of the good as incompatible with egalitarian duties of respect for different beliefs. Second, the objection from impossibility suggests that morality can never as a practical matter be legislated. Third, the objection from political misincentives suggests that any attempt to legislate morals must necessarily lead to oppression. Of these, the last objection is the strongest, and was the one primarily relied on by Mill in *On Liberty*.

The objection from *public discourse* would be unpersuasive if it simply came down to subjectivism. A subjectivist ethic of egalitarian respect, which shields the pimp and vagrant from criticism, is destructive of moral discourse and every ethic, including that of respect. If the pimp is beyond criticism, so is the perfectionist. If it has any purchase, the objection from public discourse must be more limited; and this is the kind of neutralism advanced by Ronald Dworkin.[51] Dworkin rules out of order any perfectionism founded upon a religious conception of life, as this in his view would amount to establishing a religion. Religious views about the good are to be excluded from political discourse; and what is left are the kinds of public reasons which can be accepted by people of any religion.

There are several difficulties with Dworkin's argument. A neutralism that excludes from public debate those whose political opinions are founded on religious belief is anything but neutral and might even seem discriminatory and anti-democratic. Second, there is no reason to set a priori limits on political debate from the perspective of Dworkin's public reasons. For example, it would be perfectly rational for a non-believer to vote for a party aligned to a particular religion if he concludes that their views are likely to promote the best overall results. Finally, the social perfectionist does appeal to public reasons when his conception of the good can be justified on neutral, non-religious principles. If immoral contracts or easy divorces impose public harm, as the social perfectionist asserts, the question of moral externalities rests not on a religious conception of human nature but, rather, on a humble calculation of costs and benefits. A harm is a harm and there is in principle no reason to distinguish between species of ills so long as their deleterious effects are conceded.

The empirical nature of the dispute between social neutralists and perfectionists is on prominent display in the controversy surrounding same-sex marriages. Neutralists argue that same-sex marriages would not impose social costs, or that any such costs are exceeded by the social benefits of more stable same-sex relationships. For their part, conservatives argue that legalizing homosexual marriages would devalue marriage for heterosexuals, and that this would result in a costly decline in marriage rates and in the number of children born into married families. If we could stipulate what the consequences of legalizing same-sex marriages would be and detail the costs, one side or the other would find itself bereft of arguments. The social perfectionist would have little to fall back on if same-sex marriages did not affect heterosexual marriages after all. He might seek support from natural law theories about human nature, but it would be an odd natural law that had no social consequences of any kind, nor would we have occasion to pay much attention to a set of rules that changed nothing. A natural law devoid of earthy effects might be a natural law for planet Pluto, but not for the planet we live on. Nor would we wish to pay much attention to a social neutralist who promotes a truly harmful institution.

The social perfectionist assumes that the state through its laws can influence behavior. On the objection from *impossibility*, however, laws are unable to do so because the impulse to transgress is so strong. It is difficult to resist Hume's conclusion that "all plans of government, which suppose great reformation in the manners of mankind, are plainly imaginary."[52] The horrifying example of twentieth-century schemes for enforcing morals through such creatures as New Soviet Man suggests that the true conservative will shrink from political theories that take human nature to be entirely malleable, as Samuel Johnson did:

How small of all that human hearts endure
That part which laws or kings can cause or cure.

Theories of evolutionary biology that ascribe a genetic basis for our emotions might appear to support the objection from impossibility. Were our behavior wholly determined by our genes the legal regime would be quite irrelevant. However, no serious evolutionary theorist would make such a claim. The sharp divide between the unwed birth rates of Western societies and those of Japan and Korea, and between the divorce rates of Ireland and America, as well as within America over time, evidence the continued salience of cultural and legal explanations of behavior.

This is not to deny the force of genetic constraints on our behavior. The incest taboo, which Freud thought a product of our culture, is likely genetic, since it is a feature of all cultures, human and animal. There are, in addition, a good many other sexual practices and gender roles that have a genetic basis and that resist wholesale legal intervention. But this is not to say that our sexual practices cannot be influenced by legal rules. Instead, it is precisely these cases where social norms are usefully supplemented by legal constraints, as in criminal sanctions for rape.

Freud was right about the need for social repression, even if he was wrong about the strength of biological explanations of behavior. While he was thought a radical in his day he is a conservative in ours, since he had no illusions about primitive innocence and argued that civilization required the repression of individual desires. Civilization does not promote self-expression so much as repress it, he thought, by restraining the ego's sexual and aggressive impulses.

> Civilization has to use its utmost efforts in order to set limits to man's aggressive instincts and to hold the manifestation of them in check. ... Hence, therefore, the use of methods intended to incite people into identifications and aim-inhibited relationships of love, hence the restriction upon sexual life. ...[53]

These methods would, presumably, include the refusal to enforce sexually immoral contracts under the doctrine of illegality. Like Devlin, Freud thought such barriers indispensable to civilization. Even if they do little more than restrain the basest kind of misconduct, they at least do that. The alternative, according to Freud, is the "disintegration" of society. There is no evidence that Devlin had read Freud, but Freud's term is the same one that Devlin employed and which Hart ridiculed. Devlin made an easier target than Freud, but their conclusions are identical and, as we have noted, the empirical evidence about the effects of divorce and single motherhood are more consistent with the conservatism of Freud and Devlin than with Hart's liberalism.

The last objection to social perfectionism is an argument from *political misincentives*. As we saw in Chapter 5, there is no reason to think that the paternalist's incentives are perfectly aligned with those of his subjects. Public Choice models, which see politicians as maximizing their chances of re-election and bureaucrats as maximizing the size of their budgets, have strong predictive power, and neither of these goals might have much to do with the interests of their subjects. Ignoring such problems is an example of what economist Harold Demsetz called the "Nirvana fallacy," where fallible markets are compared to infallible government, and where individuals err but the perfectionist never gets it wrong.[54]

Within its limits, the objection from political misincentives is eminently sensible. However, care must be taken to distinguish reasonable concerns about political misbehavior from the argument from Hitler, which demonizes the perfectionist. As an example of the latter, Hart compared Devlin's belief that morals should be enforced through the criminal law with "the idea to be found in German statutes of the Nazi period that anything is punishable if it is deserving of punishment according 'to the fundamental conceptions of a penal law and sound popular feeling'."[55]

While this is mere name-calling, the incentive problem remains and requires an answer. In an empirical vacuum, one falls back on first principles. For social neutralists such as Mill, the fundamental principle is one of liberty and free contracting, and this amounts to an irrebuttable presumption that bargains do not impose external costs. Since almost anything might count as a social cost, and since such costs are so difficult to measure, taking them into account might result in the adoption of illiberal laws. The neutralist would, therefore, assign a value of zero to the social consequences of private acts, not because they are costless, but because the costs of illiberal laws would exceed their benefits were we to legislate morality so finely.

To the social perfectionist, the neutralist's assumption of zero social costs looks suspiciously like a preference for round numbers (there being none rounder than zero). For, if the neutralist is willing to concede some social costs, why assume zero costs rather than a more plausible higher number? But if a higher number, then what should that be? The problem is that no higher number readily suggests itself, and for this reason zero might commend itself as a simple and commonly ascertainable focal point. If we must have a number, but cannot agree on its value, then the virtue of zero is that it is clear and easily operationalized: at zero social costs, all contracts are enforced unless they impose physical harm on third parties. By contrast, if we assume that social costs are some higher but undefined number, then how will we ever have an agreement about what that number is, or what contracts will be enforced?

This is an abstract and philosophical argument. Can the social perfectionist rebut it? I believe he can, with an empirical and not a philosophical answer. The neutralist's claim is that any attempt to legislate social norms will lead to a moral tyranny. And this claim is asserted so often and so confidently that the neutralist is apt to forget that it is really an empirical claim. If meaningful, it amounts to a prediction that relaxing the assumption of zero social costs will result in a moral tyranny. Had Hart been right, for example, the creation of a novel common law offence of conspiring to corrupt public morals in *Shaw* v. *D.P.P.* would have led to a moral fascism. But nothing of the kind happened, and Hart's fears were plainly excessive. A panderer was convicted and England remained a free, democratic state.[56]

Some civil libertarians make a like mistake in suggesting that a minute relaxation of American constitutional guarantees would send us down a slippery slope to political repression. Unless Americans are very different

from Englishmen, such claims betray an ignorance of comparative constitutional law. American-style constitutional rights are not a feature of the
British constitution, and yet the British government does not take every
power to the limit. With very different constitutional structures, but with
similar cultural traditions, Western common law countries have ended up
in a very similar place. Moreover, if broad constitutional differences have
not much affected basic liberties, how much less dangerous is the thin
perfectionism of the doctrine of illegality.

Where critics such as Hart went wrong was in taking Devlin's concern
for the preservation of society as an excuse for an overreaching, thick
perfectionism. Devlin had argued for minimal legal intervention, and in
referring to the possibility of society's disintegration meant to signal how
little, not how much, he would interfere with individual choice. According
to Devlin, legal intervention should not be intrusive, but should respect
the individual's privacy. Its goal is a commonsensical *via media* between
illiberal legal moralism and a social neutralism that wholly discounts moral
externalities. The doctrine of illegality should be reserved for the hardest
cases; beyond that, "[t]here must be toleration of the maximum individual
freedom that is consistent with the integrity of society."[57] And this, thought
Devlin, the common law did.

The debate about moral externalities is sometimes expressed as a
question about the validity of slippery slope arguments.[58] Such arguments
typically assert that a change that might otherwise be benign will prove
dangerous because it will lead to the adoption of unintended harmful
consequences. What is not well recognized is how both sides in public
policy debates might rely on slippery slopes. Social neutralists ridicule
the social perfectionist's slippery slope argument that a policy change
(such as recognizing same-sex marriages) will lead to undisputed harms
(such as weakening the bonds of traditional marriages). But social neutralists also employ a slippery slope argument in suggesting that legal moralism
always leads to holy fascism; and as between the two slippery slope
arguments it is by no means clear that the neutralist has the advantage
in the argument.

Social perfectionism is an empirical more than a philosophical problem,
and cannot be resolved by an appeal to first principles, whether found in
libertarian ideals or in a conception of human nature. What is needed
instead is a comparison of the benefits and costs of interfering with individual choices. Nor is either side able to administer a knockdown blow
to its opponent. In particular, reasonable men may differ on the moderate
perfectionism implicit in the doctrine of illegality in common law. In deliberating over whether to enforce a contract, we are not asked to choose
between moral tyranny and the destruction of society. The stakes are
lower than that, all around.

8 Substantive fairness

If one does not lose, the other does not gain.
St Augustine

In Chapters 5 and 6 we examined the argument for paternalism when a bargainer's cognitive abilities, will or preferences are thought to be flawed. Chapter 7 considered the related problem of third-party externalities. The case for enforceability is weakened when contracts are tainted with any of these defects, since the agreement might not effect Paretian or Kaldor-Hicks improvements. In this chapter we turn our attention to the perennial problem of fairness in contracting. Might a contract that leaves a party better off nevertheless be impeached because his share of the bargaining surplus is too small?

A contract is *substantively unfair* when its terms or price are excessively one-sided. Substantive unfairness may be distinguished from the procedural unfairness of misrepresentations that induce a party to enter into a contract. If procedural fairness concerns the bargaining inputs that precede the formation of the contract, substantive unfairness refers to the output of the resulting contract. The classic example is the medieval theologian's unjust price, where one party is seen to charge too much for goods or services. The two kinds of unfairness are quite distinct. When a contract is impeached for procedural unfairness, it is not a defense that the price was right. And a contract might be substantively unfair even if both parties entered into it with eyes wide open and its procedural fairness cannot be questioned.

Most economists regard substantive fairness as a pseudo-problem of merely historical interest. Pre-economic theologians thought that they could fix the just price of commodities, but that was because they believed that value was objective and not subjective. Were values objective, however, bargaining would not create value. I would give you an apple worth a dollar for a lemon worth a dollar, and nothing would have changed. Why anyone would enter into a contract would then be a puzzle. The mystery disappears when value is seen as subjective, not objective. As we saw in

Chapter 3, goods are valued differently by the parties, which is why both may be made better off by contracting. If I trade you an apple for an orange, we must presume that I prefer oranges to apples and you prefer apples to oranges. Thus the trade makes us both better off.

If value is subjective, the problem of substantive fairness would seem to dissipate. Determining whether a contract is substantively fair would entail measuring each party's gain, and that would mean peering into the bargainers' psychic states. As this is ordinarily beyond the competence of a court, the search for a substantively fair contract will seem elusive. We are both better off on our oranges-for-apples trade, but how could we tell whether my gain exceeds yours? The conclusion most economists have drawn is that there is little justification for impeaching a contract for substantive unfairness when this would sacrifice the efficiency gains of the bargain.

In spite of this, common law courts do not enforce extremely one-sided contracts, and in this chapter I argue that their refusal to do so might actually serve efficiency goals. I identify three ways in which substantive fairness policing is value-increasing. Before doing so, I examine game theoretic solutions to the bargaining problem which suggest how bargaining gains might be divided, to see whether they might help explain the substantive fairness norms which courts enforce.

Game theoretic bargaining solutions

There is a paradox at the heart of economics. As understood today, economics is a mathematical science which studies that which can be measured. When we leave the realm of the quantifiable for the qualitative, we move from economics to history, literature and philosophy. But one of the core ideas in economics is that a procedurally fair exchange satisfies Paretian standards of efficiency, with at least one party better off and no one worse off. This, in turn, might seem to assume that human happiness or utility is measurable on an objective scale in the same manner of Jeremy Bentham's felicific calculus. Bentham thought that happiness could be quantified in units of "utils," and his fundamental ethical injunction was to act in such a way as to maximize the total utility of all individuals. Bentham's utilitarianism has taken a fair number of knocks, but few things have seemed more ridiculous than his idea that one can assign so many utils to a poetry recital and so many to a football match.

Classical economists such as Ricardo, Marx and John Stuart Mill were not troubled by the problem of quantification because they subscribed to supply-side theories in which long-run prices were determined solely by relative costs of production (usually, relative labor costs). This would dispense with the subjective desires of consumers and the problem of measuring utils. The neoclassical economists of the late nineteenth century shifted their attention from supply to consumer demand, but also sidestepped the problem of measuring total utility on an objective scale. While their leaders, men such as William Jevons, Alfred Marshall and F.Y. Edgeworth, agreed with Bentham that utility could in principle be measured, they showed how demand theory could dispense with the need to do so by focusing upon marginal and not total utility.

In a Benthamite world, total utility is the number of utils for each quantity of goods consumed. Marginal utility is the first derivative of total utility, or the difference in total utility as one moves from one unit of consumption to another. If two scoops of vanilla gives one a total of 20 utils, and three scoops 25, the marginal utility of the third scoop is 5 utils. One might therefore think that, in shifting the focus to marginal utility, the problem of measuring utility remains. However, Jevons showed otherwise, by proposing that the ratio of exchange between the parties is the reciprocal of their marginal utilities.[1] That is, the ratio of the marginal utility of oranges to apples for the two of us tells us how many of one fruit we will trade for the other. If I *really* prefer oranges to apples, and you are largely indifferent between them, then I'll give you a lot of apples in exchange for a few oranges. Jevons' model assumes the existence of total utility (even as in calculus the derivative assumes an integral). However, the neoclassicists found they could get along without actually attempting to measure utility.

The neoclassical theory of exchange was enormously strengthened by the indifference curve analysis pioneered by F.Y. Edgeworth. Through the simple preference mapping we saw in Figure 3.2, Edgeworth explained how value-increasing exchange could be modeled with an *ordinal* ranking (first, second, third . . .) that does not assign a measurable *cardinal* value (one, two, three . . .) to personal utility. A move to a higher indifference curve represents a gain in utility, but the diagram does not permit us to quantify the difference. With Jevons' model, Edgeworth's indifference curves resulted in an ordinalist revolution that dispensed with measurable, cardinal utility.

Edgeworth also showed how an infinity of bargaining outcomes are possible in his "Edgeworth Box Function" of Figure 8.1. Jevons had postulated that exchange would take place when the parties' indifference curves are tangent (or touching). But what Jevons had failed to realize was that this might happen at more than one point.

Figure 8.1 resembles the mapping of indifference curves in Figure 3.2, with the difference that Figure 8.1 portrays the preferences of two consumers. For party A the point of origin is at the lower left hand corner of the box, representing a zero endowment of the two commodities x_1 and x_2. Party A's most desired state is the upper right corner, where he has all of the two commodities and party B has none of them. For party B the point of origin is the upper right hand corner, and the most desired state is the lower left hand corner. For simplicity we assume that there are only two commodities and that anything not owned by party

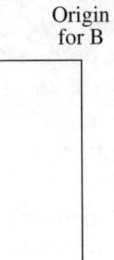

Origin
for B

I_{B1} P_1

P_3

P_2

P_4

I_{A1}

Origin
for A

Figure 8.1 Edgeworth Box Function

A is owned by party B. The Edgeworth Box may thus be seen as two indifference curve diagrams, with one flipped over and placed on top of the other.

Assume that the parties begin at point P_1, where A is on indifference curve I_{A1} and B is on indifference curve I_{B1}. This is not a stable equilibrium since the parties can make themselves better off by trades that bring them within the "bargaining lens" formed by the overlap of the two curves. Relative to P_1, any exchange within the lens makes one party better off without making the other worse off and represents a Pareto-superior transformation. As the parties begin to bargain, with both moving to higher indifference curves, the size of the lens will shrink until they reach the point of *Pareto-optimality* where the two indifference curves are tangent and no further Pareto-superior transformations remain to be made.

Figure 8.1 portrays three possible outcomes, where the parties bargain to a Pareto-optimal point that satisfies the Jevons requirement of tangency. At point P_2 the parties split the contractual surplus. However, points P_3 (where all the gains accrue to A) and P_4 (where all the gains accrue to B) are also possible results, since they lie within the bargaining lens and are points of tangency. Since one person is made better off and no one is made worse off, the move from P_1 to either P_3 or P_4 represents a Pareto improvement, just like the move from P_1 to P_2. As I have drawn the curves, the parties might end up at any point of tangency between P_3 and P_4, depending upon the mixture of alertness, sympathy, guile, intelligence and acumen that goes in to form bargaining ability. Economists define the locus of points of tangency, running from P_4 through P_2 to P_3, as the *Contract Curve*, which I have arbitrarily drawn in.

By the 1930s, the ordinalist revolution was complete, and cardinal utility was relegated to the dustbin of economics. What had made cardinal utility so unpalatable was the idea of interpersonal comparisons of utility. It is hard enough to measure one's own happiness in a felicific calculus. However, that task would seem to pale before the difficulty of comparing the utility gains of two different bargainers. I might have a rough sense of how much better off I would be with an additional unit of x_1, but how can I measure how much worse off you would be were I to gain and you to lose a unit of x_1?

Ironically, cardinal utility made a remarkable theoretical recovery through the work of game theorists such as John von Neumann and Oscar Morgenstern in the 1940s and John Nash in the 1950s.[2] For game theorists, the Contract Curve within the bargaining lens represents the core or *presolution* to the bargaining game. This is the set of feasible, Pareto-optimal and individually rational outcomes to the bargain, where an outcome is feasible when it represents an outcome available through cooperation, Pareto-optimal when it is feasible and further cooperative gains are impossible for any coalition of players, and individually rational when no player is better off on his own than he is as a member of a bargaining coalition. Where game theorists departed from the ordinalists was in proffering not only a presolution but also a *solution* to the bargaining game: a unique outcome within the bargaining lens along the Contract Curve which satisfies certain axiomatic standards.

The game theorist's bargaining solution assumes a cardinal rather than a merely ordinal measure of utility. With cardinality, we can assign a measure of utility for each party at every point on the Contract Curve. This need not entail a measure of total utility for each tradeoff of goods. Instead, we might normalize the game by assigning a value of zero to the disagreement point where the bargaining surplus disappears, and a value of 100 to the solution that assigns all of the surplus to only one party.[3] In doing so, we can disregard overall measures of happiness and focus on how the bargain affects utility levels of the two parties.

We can think of the move from presolution to solution by imagining how business parties might negotiate a contract. They begin, let us say, by bargaining over the terms of the contract that assign the risk of loss to one party or the other. If the risks are assigned to the wrong party, he might have to incur wasteful harm prevention costs, with the result that further negotiations and a reassignment of risks might produce a more efficient agreement. When the parties have arrived at the optimal set of terms they have reached a presolution to the bargaining game. What remains to be negotiated is the price, which might be any figure between the highest price the buyer will pay and the lowest price the seller will accept. Each price will offer the parties a different division of the bargaining gains, and each is a solution to the bargaining problem.

Figure 8.2 maps the bargaining game of Figure 8.1 onto cardinal utility space. In Figure 8.1 the two axes represented different quantities of goods (e.g. apples and oranges), and the indifference curves reflected ordinal differences in utility from possession of these goods; in Figure 8.2 the two axes measure different values of cardinal utility associated with possession of different quantities of these goods. The point of origin is point P_1 from Figure 8.1, and the concave curve from P_3 to P_4 represents Figure 8.1's Contract Curve as seen in utility space. Once again, the Contract Curve represents the presolution, and what bargaining theorists seek to do is arrive at a particular point on the Contract Curve as the solution to the game.

The best-known solution to the bargaining game is the *Nash solution*, which maximizes the parties' utility gains. This is a two-step operation: first, normalize the utility levels of the parties as we saw above (e.g. 0 to 100), from the worst to the best payoff on the Contract Curve; and second, multiply the utility levels of the parties at various points on the Contract Curve to find the point with the highest joint product. For example, a solution that gives both parties 50 would have a joint product of 2,500 and would be superior to a solution which gives 25 to one party and 75 to the other (for a joint product of 1,875). I assume that P_2 satisfies this test, which would make it the game's unique solution on Nash standards. But there are other tests, which on abstract principles seem no less plausible. For example, David Gauthier has argued for the universal appeal of a principle of minimax relative concession.[4] In Gauthier's model each bargainer begins by claiming the entire bargaining surplus and then

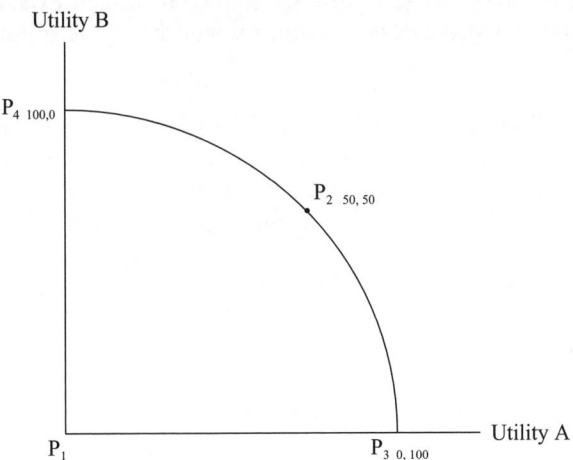

Figure 8.2 The Nash solution

concedes a portion of it in order to reach an agreement. The size of his relative concession is measured by what he is willing to give up, relative to what he had asked for. Each party wants to make the smallest possible concession, but the party who makes the greater relative concession will expect the other party to make a concession in turn. Minimizing the maximum relative concession gives a party the most he can expect to get, according to Gauthier, and represents the only solution to the bargaining problem acceptable to parties with equal rationality.

Game theoretic solutions to the bargaining problem won a great many converts in the 1950s and 1960s. Might they also supply a standard for substantive fairness screening by courts? To do so, courts would have to measure the parties' cardinal utility levels, and this has been thought an impossible task. However, the epistemological objection to measuring cardinal utility is likely overstated. We do make common sense comparisons of utility all the time, when we divide up presents among children, when we agree to wealth transfer schemes that transfer tax revenues from rich to poor, and when we pass on the fairness of contracts. Our notions of bargaining fairness often rest on a rough approximation of the parties' utility gains. But this might be all we need, where the goal is merely to identify the corner solutions of extreme unfairness where we might want to set aside a contract.

This suggests that game theoretic bargaining solutions might assist in providing the content of substantive fairness norms. With the arrival of experimental economics in the 1970s, however, it soon became clear that game theoretic solutions had poor predictive power. In experimental tests, bargainers did not bargain for the Nash solution, as we shall see. Nor is the Nash solution an attractive normative standard for a judge who reviews a contract for substantive unfairness. Many game theoretic solutions depart markedly from our common sense intuitions about fairness in exchange. Consider, for example, what the Nash solution would be in the following bargain:

> *The Starving Millionaire* – Anthony is an adventurous millionaire whose travels have taken him to a remote desert. There his car breaks down, and he finds himself alone and very hungry. After a few days of wandering on foot, he comes across Conrad, a mercenary innkeeper. After questioning Anthony about his wealth, Conrad agrees to give Anthony food and lodging, and to help him return to civilization. In return, he demands all of Anthony's wealth. "Think about it for a few days," he tells Anthony.

Such bargains are not enforced at common law, since innkeepers are obliged to offer their guests food and shelter on reasonable terms.[5] This result accords with our ethical intuitions and, as we shall see, also serves efficiency goals. But this solution departs markedly from the Nash and

Gautier solutions, which might have asked Anthony to give up something like half his wealth. Since Anthony gains his life from the bargain, the common law solution assigns nearly all of the bargaining surplus to him, and this would be substantively unfair on Nash and Gauthier standards.

Game theoretic solutions to the bargaining problem are prized for their "elegance," which is usually a synonym for their simplicity. It turns out, however, that our fairness instincts are a good deal more complex than the Nash outcome or other axiomatic solutions. Most people would regard Conrad's threat as deeply offensive, but this is left out of the game theoretic model. Similarly, our fairness intuitions sharply diverge from the Nash solution in a bargain taken from a Graham Greene novel:

> *The Tenth Man* – Ten hostages are held by terrorists and are told that one of them will be executed tomorrow. The choice of who is to die is left to the prisoners, and they pick straws. The fatal short straw goes to the wealthier prisoner, who offers $1,000,000 to the other nine if one of them will take his place before the firing squad. One of the prisoners accepts, since his family desperately needs the money.

Most of us would regard this contract as egregiously unfair. The wealthy prisoner has taken advantage of his fellow prisoner's poverty to escape death. However, the sense of unfairness is not captured by the Nash solution, which would divide the bargaining surplus down the middle, possibly by giving the volunteer $500,000, if $1,000,000 is all the wealthy prisoner has.

Axiomatic theories achieve their elegance by abstracting the bargaining problem from the circumstances of the case. However, what matters most in gauging the fairness of the outcome are the circumstances. They provide the atmosphere in which one bargainer oppresses a second or steals a march on a third. In *The Starving Millionaire*, it is the threat advantage that is unfair and which makes the division of the bargaining gains inequitable. And in *The Tenth Man*, it is the willingness to exploit the penniless victim's desire to provide for his family that produces the troubling outcome.

Apart from threat advantages, the skills that favor a bargainer might seem less than amiable. The unskilled bargainer might be one of painter Georges de la Tour's callow fops, bedecked with ribbons and rings and surrounded by confidence men and tricksters with aces up their sleeves. Should they employ actual fraud, the common law will afford a remedy for the victim. But there might also be come-ons, puffs and other strategic devices that do not ascend to the level of fraud but which seem to offer an unfair advantage, and for this the common law might offer relief under the doctrine of unconscionability.

When courts impeach a substantively unfair contract they sacrifice bargaining gains, which are lost when the contract is not enforced. After all, even in substantively unfair contracts, both parties may be made better off. Nevertheless, a substantive fairness review might serve efficiency goals in three ways. (1) On *cooperation* theories, the fairness review increases the level of contracting by reducing the probability of bargaining break-downs that result from hard bargaining. Where unfair bargains are set aside, the parties are more likely to moderate their demands and come to agreement. (2) *Incentive* explanations of fairness norms suggest that the parties might make wasteful investments in care when substantively unfair contracts are upheld.[6] (3) Finally, setting aside unfair contracts may promote *screening* efficiencies by reducing the costs of producing informa-tion about the bargain. While there are few cases where a contract will be set aside under any one of these theories, the threat of unenforceability might usefully deter overreaching by bargainers.

Cooperation theories

For the Church Fathers, the only kind of value was an objective one that is the same for every party. So viewed, bargaining is a non-cooperative, zero-sum game, where one party's gain is the other one's loss. The Edgeworth Box Function usefully explodes this view. Where values are subjectively determined, bargaining is a cooperative, non-zero-sum game, and both parties might be made better off. Within the cooperative game, however, there is a non-cooperative game where the parties bargain along Figure 8.2's Contract Curve for their share of the contractual surplus, and here one party's gain is, indeed, the other one's loss. A dollar more for the seller means a dollar less for the buyer.

Contract negotiations perform two functions: they identify the set of efficient terms that constitute the contract; and they determine each party's share of the bargaining gains. The first function establishes the amount of joint gains and the second divides them up. At times, the two functions work at cross-purposes. Each party will want as large a share of the surplus as possible, and so has an incentive to adopt a "hard" bargaining strategy.[7] However, a claim for disproportionate individual gains might result in a breakdown of negotiations and the loss of joint gains as the parties dig their heels in.[8] The negotiating strategy must therefore strike a balance between excessive and inadequate cooperation. While the former strategy concedes too much of the bargaining surplus to the other party, the latter risks its destruction.

To the extent that bargaining is a non-cooperative division of the contractual surplus, the unamiable traits of guile and strategic behavior might seem to advantage a bargainer. But one can be too clever by half, and a reputation for sharpness will mean the loss of future bargains. At the extreme, in Banfield's Montegrano, the most grasping and suspicious society is the pre-capitalist one where long traditions of mistrust prevent the parties from reaching agreement. Max Weber was under no illusions about primitive societies, and his universal reign of absolute unscrupulousness was a "specific characteristic of precisely those countries whose bourgeois-capitalistic development, measured according to Occidental standards, has remained backward."[9]

In a less grasping society, by contrast, habits of compromise will encourage the formation of contracts. For this reason, social norms that constrain hard bargaining may serve efficiency goals. For example, Ian Macneil has identified norms of fair-dealing that facilitate bargaining.[10] Popular negotiation books also stress that bargainers should treat opposite parties as collaborators rather than adversaries. The more the other party gains of the surplus, the easier it is to close the deal, and a sense of sympathy for fellow bargainers is a better bargaining strategy than the appearance of slickness or guile.

Norms that constrain hard bargaining might thus serve efficiency goals. Such norms are in part social, with non-cooperative strategies viewed with disfavor and fair dealing prized as a commercial virtue. But courts might also enforce cooperative norms by leaning against the enforcement of hard bargains. Setting aside a bargain on substantive fairness norms will result in an immediate efficiency loss, since the parties will forego the gains from that agreement. However, future bargainers will react to the imposition of fairness norms by scaling back extreme claims in the course of negotiations, and the net result might be a significant increase in the number of contracts and a wealthier society.

On cooperation theories, what matters is whether a bargain is reached and not the way the gains are divided. So viewed, substantive fairness is seen as a coordination problem. In a coordination game, all parties seek to adopt the same strategy without much caring what it is. For example, the choice of which side of the road to drive on is a coordination problem, since all that matters is that everyone sticks to the same side. Cooperation theories also see bargaining as a coordination game, since what matters is the creation and not the division of the bargaining surplus.

This assumes that substantive fairness norms should promote bargaining, not mandate a particular payoff. If so, courts should mimic how bargainers divide up the pie. The judicial standard of fairness should be the same as the solutions selected by most bargainers, whatever these might be. In practice, bargainers cluster around a division of gains that most people would recognize as fair. What they do not bargain for are the Nash and Gautier solutions.[11]

In bargaining experiments parties were asked to divide a set of lottery tickets, with different monetary values assigned to the tickets.[12] The Nash and Gauthier theories would have predicted an even split of the tickets, whether or not they had the same cash value. That is, they would have treated a ticket with an expected value of $10 the same as one with an expected value of $100. However, parties bargained for an equal split of tickets only where the cash payoffs were the same or where they were not informed of the other's monetary payoff. Where the cash values were different, and where they knew the other's payoff, many parties bargained for an "equal expected value" solution in which they divided the tickets unequally so as to produce the same expected value for each bargainer.[13]

There are at least two possible explanations for this result. First, an equal split of the bargaining surplus might accord with intuitive ideas about *fairness*. Second, the parties might not have any preferences about a fair split of the surplus, but might select equal payoff solutions because they serve as a *focal point* of agreement. A focal point is a solution to a coordination game that the parties recognize and select when they have no prior knowledge about the other party's ideas about a suitable outcome. In a famous experiment, Thomas Schelling asked participants to imagine that they were to meet another person in New York City, with the hitch that neither of them knew where or when they were to do so. While communication was banned, most people nevertheless agreed to meet under the clock at Grand Central Station at noon on January 1.[14] That was simply where and when they thought that the other person would choose to meet. Similarly, bargainers might choose to split it down the middle because that is where most of them would expect to meet each other, and not because it seems like a just result.

Neither explanation seems able to account for all our bargaining behavior. Focal point theories poorly predict the outcome in ultimatum games, where bargainers are willing to bear a personal loss to punish another party for unfairness. In ultimatum games, one party (the "sender") divides up a fixed amount of money and the other (the "receiver") must accept or reject his share. If he rejects it, neither party receives anything. In the focal point (and Nash) solution, the sender claims most of the pie for himself and offers the smaller share to the receiver ($99 for sender, $1 for receiver); who accepts it since the alternative is to receive nothing at all ($1 if the receiver accepts, 0 if he rejects). This is the focal point of agreement, since it is the only possible division of gains available to the receiver once the sender has made up his mind. However, this is not how parties bargain. Most receivers reject sharply unequal splits even when this means giving up fairly large offers.[15] This result is consistent with fairness explanations of bargaining but inconsistent with focal point theories. So strong are fairness norms that in one experiment many senders offered equal payoffs (50–50) when they would have received a higher amount (e.g. 60) when receivers reject the offer, with the sender's preference for fairness trumping his individual rationality and the gain of 10 from disagreement.[16]

However, fairness theories cannot explain all bargaining behavior. Fairness concerns might explain ultimatum but not "dictator" games. In a dictator game, the receiver cannot reject the sender's offer (and make both of them receive zero). The sender proposes a split, and whatever he says goes. Not surprisingly, bargainers are more generous to the other party in ultimatum than in dictator games, where they can get what they want.[17] Evidently, something more than a taste for fairness is at work.

Fairness concerns might also mask self-interested behavior. In the ultimatum game, receivers are more likely to be offered a favorable division of the surplus if they can signal their intention to reject unfair offers. This explains why the surplus is more likely to be split down the middle when the parties can talk to each other or when the game is repeated through several iterations.[18] In addition, when fairness norms are internalized, as suggested in Chapter 3, the receiver's emotional signals might also communicate to senders that an unfair split will be rejected. A sense of justice that visibly bristles in the face of deviousness or overreaching may deter unfairness from strangers. Like the trustworthy, the fair-minded need not wait for the next world for their reward.

However, this is not to deny the salience of fairness constraints in bargaining. Even if bargaining behavior is partly self-interested, or wholly self-interested at some deep internalized level, the concern for fairness does shape bargaining solutions and, indeed, explains anomalous market behavior. When demand for a good increases we would expect to see prices go up. Nevertheless, stores often refuse to mark-up shovels during snowstorms or flashlights during power outages. Instead, the merchant sacrifices the profits and rations the goods, one to a customer. What seems to be behind the apparent generosity are fairness norms and the risk that a "price-gouging" merchant will be punished by outraged consumers once the emergency is over.[19] Similarly, Robert Frank reports that firms with higher profits pay higher wages. This violates the economic principle that workers are paid the value of what they produce, regardless of the firm's profitability. However, this result is consistent with the notion that fairness dictates that profits should be shared with workers.[20]

Whether a court should police unfair bargains on cooperation theories depends not only on how the bargaining gains are split, but also on the circumstances surrounding the negotiations. Fairness norms are most plausibly imposed when transaction costs are high and there are barriers to bargaining. Where there is little opportunity for lengthy negotiations, one-sided initial offers are more likely to result in a bargaining breakdown.[21] The likelihood of disagreement also increases where parties are distant and do not deal on a face-to-face basis.[22] Cooperation theories might therefore explain why the rescue contracts described in the next section are set aside, where the ship is about to go under and where neither party has much time or ability to discuss terms. Rather than haggle until the ship goes down, the parties might be better off if they let a court settle on the price.

In sum, cooperation theories argue for a substantive fairness review of egregiously one-sided bargains. Some bargains, and some bargaining gains, will be lost when unfair contracts are set aside; but such losses might be dwarfed by the greater number of bargains that are reached because fewer negotiations break down as a result of hard bargaining.

Incentive theories

The second explanation of judicial fairness norms sees them as addressing an incentive problem. Where one party has an extreme threat advantage over the other, both parties might be led to make inefficient investments in anticipation of a one-sided bargain. We shall consider two such cases, blackmail and rescue contracts, but the list of extortionate contracts is not closed. By policing them, common law courts usefully weaken the parties' misincentives to overinvest in the bargain.

Courts set aside extortionate contracts under the doctrine of *duress*. Contracts induced by the threat of an illegal act are tainted by duress and presumptively value-decreasing and unenforceable.[23] Where the promisee has threatened physical harm, the promisor's consent to a contract is not a badge of efficiency and the resulting contract will be void. The highwayman's "Your money or your life" does give the victim a choice but the consent does not bind him. As Justice Holmes remarked: "[i]t always is for the interest of a party under duress to choose the lesser of two evils. But the fact that a choice was made according to interest does not exclude duress."[24]

Not every threat will constitute duress. Where the threat is legally permissible, the contract will ordinarily be enforceable even if the promisor has no real alternative but to submit.[25] The seller may insist on his price, the landlord on his rent and the lawyer on his fee, even if the other party thinks them steep. However, in exceptional cases such as rescue contracts, a defense of duress will lie even if the threatened act is lawful. Absent a remedy, both rescuer and victim might react to the possibility of a one-sided contract by taking excessive pre-bargain care. Potential rescuers will look for rescue opportunities and potential victims will take extra care to minimize the need for a rescue. Such costs are socially wasteful when the costs of the precautions exceed their gains, and a court's substantive fairness review will reduce incentives to take wasteful precautions. Winners will have less to gain from the contract, and losers less to lose. In this way, the doctrine of duress might serve both efficiency and fairness goals.

Blackmail

The paradox of blackmail is that it criminalizes a threat to perform an act which, if performed without the threat, would be legal. The blackmailer threatens to reveal a secret unless the victim pays hush money. But where truth is a defense to an action for libel, the blackmailer could not be prosecuted if he released the information to the public without attempting to profit from it. This anomalous result is justified on incentive theories. Were blackmail contracts enforced (and were blackmail not a crime), both parties would incur wasteful expenses: blackmailers would incur costs to seek out information about their victims, who in turn would either reduce their level of deviant behavior or invest in efforts to keep it confidential.

The costs of blackmail might not be excessive if it served a social purpose. The information that the victim seeks to keep confidential will usually concern his deviance from social norms, and if these are valuable an argument might be made for enforcing blackmail contracts. Enforcement would give blackmailers a greater incentive to ferret out damaging information about their victims, and with a greater probability of blackmail the costs of deviance will increase and its level will decline. This might be no bad thing where the deviant act is a criminal wrong. Even where the offence does not rise to the level of illegality, the threat of blackmail might usefully deter lying, cheating and a variety of lesser wrongs.

However, blackmail should be suppressed if the norms it enforces are vicious. Not every social norm is benign. Some are rooted in feelings of envy or prejudice and pander to base instincts. Even if there is some value to the norm, this might be slight compared to the humiliation deviants experience on exposure. Few people, apart from the hypocrite, would ever express a wish to bind themselves to virtue by making public their most private moments. There are also things, not discreditable in themselves, that we would not want to see spread over the Internet. Few of us would wish to be observed by a 24-hour spy-cam. In all such cases, blackmail may over-deter by imposing a stifling and dull conformity or by leading potential victims to hide their sins behind a mask of Puritan rectitude. In addition to these costs, the costs incurred by blackmailers in producing the information would be entirely wasteful in such cases.

Incentive theories would therefore justify a ban on blackmail contracts. However, contractual remedies will not assist victims, who would have to disclose the secret information to pursue the remedy. And since victims would not sue, blackmailers would not be deterred. This explains why blackmail is not merely a civil wrong but also a crime.

Contracts of rescue

In a rescue contract, victims bargain with salvors after a hazard, with payment contingent on a successful rescue. Not infrequently, the salvor has the victim over a barrel and can extract an exorbitant price for a rescue that costs the salvor relatively little. Because of this, both salvors and victims have an increased incentive to take precautions in anticipation of a contract of rescue. The rescuer will seek to increase the likelihood of a rescue, while the victim will try to reduce the likelihood of accident. When these precautions are excessive, the imposition of substantive fairness norms might serve incentive efficiencies.

From an economic perspective, the victim's need for a rescue is an accident against which both parties might take care. Like Goldilocks, we want not too much and not too little care. We want it just right, which in this context means minimizing all of the costs associated with the rescue. These costs include each party's pre-accident costs to avoid the harm, the cost of the rescue, and the loss incurred if the rescue fails. The victim's pre-rescue costs include the special precautions he takes before visiting remote places, as well as the cost of entirely avoiding still more dangerous places. Rescuers will bear the actual costs of the rescue and the costs of pre-rescue care taken in anticipation of a possible rescue. In *The Starving Millionaire*, for example, the rescuer's costs include the cost of the food given to Anthony, as well as the pre-rescue costs of opening and maintaining an inn in the desert to the extent that it was built and operated to take advantage of gains from rescues.

When the rescue contract is enforced, the parties will divide up a bargaining surplus (the gains associated with avoiding the loss that would have resulted if there had been no rescue, less the actual costs of the rescue). How this is divided will affect the incentives of both parties to invest in pre-rescue care, and an efficient duress rule would lead the parties to invest in optimal pre-rescue harm prevention. In some cases, this will mean that the court will strike down and reduce the bargained-for price of the rescue.

When any pre-rescue care by the rescuer would have been wasteful, the optimal duress rule will permit rescuers to recover only the actual costs of the rescue and not the costs of any pre-rescue care. If they receive less than this they will not have an adequate incentive to undertake the rescue; and if they receive more than this both rescuers and victims might take excessive care. As incentive theories predict, courts are more likely to police unfair bargains in such cases, and rescue contracts might then be set aside even if there is little evidence of extortionate bargaining. In *Post v. Jones*,[26] the master of the shipwrecked vessel might have chosen between three possible rescuers, all of whom bid for the cargo in an auction. In these circumstances, the finding of duress by the Supreme Court against the winning bidder might appear strained.[27] However, the rescue took place off the Bering Straits of Czarist Alaska by whalers who (with the other two bidders) were "the only civilized visitors of the territory,"[28] and it is difficult to imagine what pre-rescue care the rescuers might efficiently have taken. It would not have made sense to wait around for a ship to founder. In such cases, the rescuer has an adequate incentive to undertake a rescue if he is compensated for the cost of the actual rescue.

Incentive theories suggest an explanation for the greater readiness of courts to enforce contracts of rescue made on land rather than at sea. In the case of sea rescues like *Post v. Jones*, there may be little that the rescuer can do before happening upon the victim to increase the probability of the rescue. But this is less likely to be the case when the rescue is on land. For example, highway towing companies incur substantial pre-rescue care costs in maintaining a fleet of tow trucks, and the imposition of substantive fairness norms would drive them out of business. Moreover, victims usually have a choice between a number of towing companies and are in a better position to bargain over prices. It is not as though they are about to sink into the sea.

However, there is no sharp distinction between sea and land rescues, and some sea rescuers might take efficient pre-rescue care. In the busy sea lanes, professional salvors have rescue ships at the ready, and rescue agreements are more likely to be enforced in such cases.[29] In addition, professional rescuers at sea are granted higher awards by courts through the principle of salvage. In *The Lamington*, for example, the court noted that the skill attained from long experience, coupled with more powerful machinery,

> are of more service to an imperiled vessel than is the aid which may be expected from a chance rescuer. To provide such skill, machinery, and appliances, and to keep them always ready for instant service, though they may be called for but occasionally, is now regarded as a meritorious act, calling for a liberal award.[30]

Moreover, some pre-rescue care might be inefficient in the case of land rescues. In *The Starving Millionaire*, for example, Conrad could not have anticipated many guests like Anthony, and setting aside the rescue contract between Conrad and Anthony would not greatly affect the number of inns that are built in deserts. Incentive theories therefore suggest an explanation for the "status" obligation of innkeepers to offer their guests food and shelter on reasonable and not extortionate terms.[31] Though ostensibly motivated by non-economic fairness considerations, such laws serve efficiency goals; and though they seem designed to protect guests, such laws benefit innkeepers by increasing the incentives of guests to travel. Were the rescue contract enforced, people like Anthony would be afraid to travel, even as tourists avoid countries where they expect to be gouged.

Screening theories

Screening theories might also explain why courts strike down unfair bargains. As we saw in Chapter 5, screening refers to the production of information by the parties about a bargain. Even reading a contract gives rise to screening costs, and consumers frequently avoid such costs by signing agreements without reading them. While reading a maze of fine print reduces the likelihood of oppressive provisions, the costs may exceed the gains and rational consumers might prefer to take the risk of one-sided, inefficient terms by signing the contract without reading. When such terms may be identified more easily by a court *ex post* than by consumers *ex ante*, a substantive fairness review might usefully economize on screening costs.

However, screening theories are unpersuasive unless courts are able to identify the set of efficient terms more accurately than consumers. A review of cases where contract terms have been set aside does not inspire great confidence in the ability of courts to rewrite contracts. Courts have set aside exemption clauses, security interests and termination provisions without evidencing any great understanding of economic issues.[32] In the process, they have likely mandated inefficient terms.

Consumers might also have stronger screening skills than proponents of screening efficiencies suppose. An agreement may be efficient as to its terms even if not all consumers screen. Non-screening consumers might be adequately protected if some consumers screen and it is impracticable for the seller to discriminate by offering one kind of contract to screeners and another to non-screeners.[33] Non-screeners can then free ride on the screening activities of more meticulous consumers. In addition, an increase in judicial screening will come at the expense of a decline in consumer screening, since screening consumers have less reason to review contract terms when courts are more ready to do so. The result would be a smaller number of extremely unfair terms, but a greater number of slightly unfair ones. This will not always benefit non-screening consumers.

However, the possibility of harsh terms remains. Perhaps there will simply be too few screening consumers. Or the contract might be offered to only one buyer, who chooses not to screen. In such cases the fairness review should be restricted to terms that cannot be said to serve efficiency purposes, and which few or no consumers would have understood. While these are substantial hurdles, there is no reason to assume that they can never be surmounted. For example, a fairness review was warranted in the old chestnuts of *Thornborow* v. *Whitacre*[34] and *James* v. *Morgan*.[35] In *Thornborow*, the defendant borrowed £5 and in return promised to give the plaintiff two grains of rye-corn in the first week, four grains in the second, eight grains in the third, and so on for a year. At trial the defendant argued that if the promise were enforced, there would not be enough grain in the world to satisfy it. In *James*, the defendant bought a horse in return for a barley-corn for the horse's first shoe nail, two for the second nail, four for the third, and so on. The price came to over six tons of barley. Both contracts were set aside. The price was extortionate, and this was too difficult for the mathematically unsophisticated defendants to work out. Special terms as to the method of payment sometimes serve efficiency purposes, but clearly did not do so in these cases. As a strategy of last resort, then, a substantive fairness review might usefully reduce screening costs.

Fairness and efficiency norms are commonly thought antithetical. This perception is not wholly inaccurate, for a concession to fairness will often come at the expense of efficiency gains. However, where fairness efficiencies obtain, it is misleading to think of one norm being traded off against another. Instead, greater fairness may be accompanied by greater wealth.

Standard form contracts

Our intuitions about substantive fairness are not always consistent with efficiency norms. In particular, courts that impeached contracts under the doctrine of unconscionability in the last half of the twentieth century had little regard for efficiency. Instead, they invoked fairness intuitions which, being intuitions, seemed not to require much further analysis. In particular, courts set aside pre-printed "standard form" contracts because of the perceived unfairness of take-it-or-leave-it terms. The modern reader, for whom pre-printed consumer contracts are simply a fact of life, will find this odd, but the idea that they posed a threat to liberty had a powerful hold on the legal academy as recently as 30 years ago and these suspicions have not been wholly erased from the jurisprudence.

Following the legal antipathy to standard form contracts to its roots leads to two false and inconsistent ideas, both German in origin. The first, associated with the will theory of contracts, is that consent requires mutual mental acts. The requisite meeting of the minds takes place when woodsman and homeowner dicker over a cord of firewood, but not when a standard form contract is signed without being read. This romantic view of bargaining did not inform the second objection to standard form contracts, which rested on Marxist theories about monopoly capitalism brought to America by Friedrich Kessler shortly before the Second World War. Kessler thought that, in moving from Nazi Germany to the US, he had simply traded off one form of tyranny for another – the tyranny of advanced capitalism in which a few corporations dominated all economic activity and deprived consumers of real choices. If the naive American consumer failed to identify this form of home-grown fascism, the Marxist concept of false consciousness might account for the self-deception. "[A]pparently the realization of the deepgoing antinomies in the structure of our system of contracts is too painful an experience to be permitted to rise to the full level of our consciousness."[36]

The mixture of German idealism and vulgar Marxism was a heady cocktail, and if few academics swallowed Kessler's politics they shared his concern about standard form contracts. But the link between pre-printed contracts and monopolization was never made clear. Even supposing that monopolies dominated the economy (and few enough of Kessler's 1939 behemoths still survive), there is no reason to think that they would exploit their bargaining power through an inefficient, one-sided set of terms. Instead, the monopolist would bargain to the Contract Curve by exploiting all opportunities for Paretian improvements in his choice of terms, since failing to do so would be like leaving money on the table. The monopolist would then exert his market power in his pricing decision. Standard form contract terms would be efficient, but the price would be set above a competitive level so that the seller could extract monopolistic profits. Nor did courts that frowned on standard form contracts pay much attention to factual questions about market share, or enquire whether problems of monopoly might better be left for standard antitrust remedies. Instead, Kessler and his followers simply inferred that industries were monopolistic from the fact that standard form consumer contracts tend to look alike. But this has it backwards. If anything, similar terms are more likely to be associated with competitive markets, even as prices that hover at the same level are found in price-taking, competitive markets. A disparity in terms, like a disparity in prices, more plausibly suggests the presence of price-making firms with market power seeking to extract monopolistic profits.[37]

The more likely explanation for standard form contracts is that they economize on the firm's bargaining costs. Pre-printed consumer contracts make it easier for a firm to bargain and prove the content of a contract in court. The firm that abandons these economies and insists on negotiating each term separately would have to charge consumers higher prices to make up the difference, and there must be very few consumers who would stand in a queue for the privilege of taking the time to purchase the higher-priced goods in a dickered contract. In addition, standard form contracts usefully address the conflict of interest between the seller and its agents or employees. Salesmen whose compensation depends on the number of goods sold have an incentive to offer sweetheart warranties to consumers in order to boost sales and commissions. As such warranties are inefficient they will impose costs, but the costs are borne by the firm and not the salesman, who might not be around when the consumers come to collect on the warranties. Standard form contracts which specify that they contain the whole contract, eliminate this agency cost problem. The judicial controversy surrounding standard form agreements is an object lesson in the dangers of ascribing improper motives to imperfectly understood benign transactions.

Substantive fairness norms that specify how bargaining gains are to be divided are generally thought inefficient, and a relic of scholastic philosophy. Where a substantive fairness review is defended, it is usually on fairness grounds. However, a better defense of judicial intervention may be made from the perspective of cooperation, incentive and screening efficiencies.

Appendix: optimal duress standards

Assume that victims react to the possibility of an oppressive rescue contract by incurring harm avoidance costs x. Rescuers react to the possibility of a rescue by incurring pre-rescue salvor costs y in addition to the actual costs of the rescue R. The social costs of the accident also include the loss L that arises when victims are not rescued. (We assume that $L > R$, since the rescue would otherwise not be attempted.) The expected value of such losses will depend on P_V, the probability that the victim will require a rescue, as well as $(1 - P_R)$, the probability that he will not be rescued. For the victims, $P_V(x)$ is the probability of an accident given x; and for the rescuers, $P_R(y)$ is the probability of a successful rescue given y, conditional upon an accident occurring. Increases in x and y will decrease the probability of an accident and increase the probability of a rescue, respectively, but at a declining rate.[38]

An efficient legal regime will seek to minimize the social cost of the accident:

$$C(x,y) = P_V(1 - P_R)L + P_V P_R R + x + y \qquad (1)$$

Minimizing C with respect to x and y yields:

$$E^x = -P_V{}^x[(1 - P_R)L + P_R R] \qquad (2)$$

$$E^y = P_R{}^y P_V(L - R) \qquad (3)$$

where E^x and E^y are the marginal costs of pre-rescue care for victim and rescuer, respectively.[39] In equations (2) and (3), these costs are seen to equal the marginal benefits of harm reduction. Let x^* and y^* be the socially optimal values of x and y that satisfy (2) and (3), and assume that these are unique.

When the rescue contract is enforced, the parties will divide up a bargaining surplus of $L - R$. How this is divided will affect the incentives of the parties to invest in pre-rescue care of x and y, and an efficient duress rule will lead the parties to invest x^* and y^* in harm prevention. What kind of duress rule serves efficiency goals depends crucially on the assumptions we make about x^* and y^*.

Assume first that rescuers fortuitously happen upon victims, and that any pre-rescue care by the rescuer is wasteful, so that $y^* = 0$. The social cost of the accident will then be:

$$C(x) = P_V[(1 - P_R)L + P_R R] + x$$

and the uniquely optimal duress rule will permit rescuers to recover R and no more than R. To see this, note that rescuers have adequate incentives to carry out a rescue if given R,[40] and that victims will then select x according to (2). To see that any other division of the bargaining surplus would be inefficient, note that giving rescuers less than R will lead them to abandon all rescues; and that giving rescuers more than R will lead victims to take excessive care. If rescuers are permitted to extract the entire bargaining surplus, the victim loses L whether or not he is rescued, and will set:

$$E^x = -P_V^x L \qquad (4)$$

On comparing (4) with (2), it is seen that victims will then take excessive care.

See further F.H. Buckley, "Three Theories of Substantive Fairness, "*Hofstra L. Rev.*19: 33 (1991); William M. Landes and Richard A. Posner,

"Salvors, Finders, Good Samaritans and Other Rescuers: An Economic Study of Law and Altruism," *J. Legal Stud.* 7: 83 (1978).

Liability rules in accident law cannot be constructed to lead the parties to take efficient care. If liability rules imposed the entire cost of the harm (less the actual costs of the rescue) on the rescuer when the victim has taken efficient care, then the rescuer would have adequate incentives to take pre-rescue care. See William M. Landes and Richard A. Posner, *The Economic Structure of Tort Law*, 73–80 (Cambridge, MA: Harvard University Press, 1987); Steven Shavell, *Economic Analysis of Accident Law*, 36–40 (Cambridge, MA: Harvard University Press, 1987). However, imposing a duty to rescue would be self-defeating where the rescue is costly, since potential rescuers would shun those places where the duty is likely to be triggered. The result would be fewer, not more, rescues. For that reason, the law does not impose a duty to rescue except in circumstances where the duty would not reduce the level of rescuing. For example, when two ships collide, the master of each is required to render assistance to individuals of both vessels. See 46 U.S.C. § 2303(a)(1) (Supp. 2004). A duty triggered by a collision will not lead potential rescuers to avoid the scene of a rescue since they are already there.

9　Contractarian virtue

What's so good about happiness? It can't buy you money.

Henny Youngman

In the previous eight chapters I have argued that contract law rules, including those that limit our bargaining freedom, are best understood through the prism of law-and-economics. Other explanations of contract law, which ignore the incentive effects of legal rules and the benefits and costs of legal institutions, fail to offer a persuasive account of contracting. Yet, it does not follow that contract law is benign from a broader consequentialist perspective that considers the effects of free bargaining on society as a whole, and in this chapter I examine two objections to the social consequences of contract law.

The first objection is associated with the names of two prominent twentieth-century intellectuals, economist Joseph Schumpeter and sociologist Daniel Bell.[1] Schumpeter and Bell argued that free bargaining regimes are self-defeating because the virtues that allow trust to flourish and wealth to be created are then subverted by that wealth. Commercial societies become regimes of greed and spiritual torpor, "where virtue loses all her loveliness,"[2] and where everyone selfishly looks after number one. Free bargaining might thus undermine the virtues that sustain it and sow the seeds of its own destruction. This might happen because commercial societies are peace-loving and their citizens make poor soldiers. If so, a commercial society might lack the courage and loyalty to defend itself and its contractarian institutions from external attack by totalitarian regimes. Free bargaining has also been thought to promote unscrupulousness and sap the virtue of fidelity that induces bargainers to rely upon each other. Finally, the wealth of commercial societies might turn prudent producers into hedonistic consumers, like the family firm built up by a hardscrabble, industrious sire and passed on to a sophisticated, spendthrift heir.

The second objection, associated with the nineteenth-century Romantic tradition, is that contractual institutions will succeed all too well. In the process, however, they will dry up other sources of joy. Getting and spending, we will lose the power to appreciate beauty and the bonds of solidarity that unite us to each other. Believers might fear that the spirit of commerce will deaden our hearts to religious impulses. We might also lose touch with the world of solemnity and grandiloquence found in Racine's tragic drama, which offers "an image of what life might be like if it were lived at all times on a plane of high decorum and if it were at all instants fully responsive to the obligations of nobility."[3]

The cultural contradictions of contract law

We shape our institutions and then our institutions shape us. Every age has had its own forms of economic production, which in turn elicited a different set of virtues. The virtues of a pre-capitalist society, where advancement came from war and conquest, were those of the soldier. In a commercial age, however, the heroic virtues are less prized than the bourgeois virtues, which Montesquieu described as the spirit of "frugality, economy, moderation, work, wisdom, tranquility, order and regularity."[4] The two sets of virtues shared a common goal, said Benjamin Constant, but the means are different.

> War and commerce are merely two means of arriving at the same end: that of possessing what we desire. ... One who would always be the strongest has no need of commerce. It is the experience that ... the use of force ... is exposed to resistance and possible failure which brings him to resort to commerce, that is to a softer and surer method of persuading another that it is in his interest to promote one's interest ... . It is clear that the more the commercial spirit dominates the weaker the warrior spirit becomes.[5]

Enlightenment thinkers celebrated the pacific virtues of Montesquieu's *doux commerce*. "It is almost a general rule that wherever the ways of man are gentle there is commerce," he said; "and wherever there is commerce, there the ways of man are gentle."[6] Similarly, Adam Smith noted that "commerce and manufactures gradually introduced order and good government, and with them, the liberty and security of individuals ... who had before lived almost in a continual state of war with their neighbours, and of servile dependency upon their superiors."[7] Kant even thought that the rise of commercial virtue would make war obsolete. In our time, this has given us the "McDonalds" rule: no two countries with a McDonalds in each have ever gone to war with each other.[8]

However much they fit us for business, the pacific virtues might seem to unfit us for war, as Constant thought; and not a few dictators have underestimated the military prowess of commercial states. "A nation of shopkeepers" was what Napoleon called the British – but that was before Waterloo. In the last century, Nazi sympathizers such as Werner Sombart and Carl Schmitt said much the same thing, contrasting the prowess of heroic nations with the lassitude of trading nations. More than anyone, Joseph Schumpeter argued that bourgeois virtue is self-defeating in his *Capitalism, Socialism, and Democracy*. Unlike Sombart and Schmitt, Schumpeter allied himself with America and free markets. However, he was a declinist who thought that capitalism's destructive energies would sweep away the heroic virtues that built it and the institutions that sustain it.

Schumpeter's pessimism is curious, since *Capitalism, Socialism, and Democracy* is best-known for its trenchant rejection of the Marxist argument that capitalism is self-defeating. Marx thought that free markets would result in monopoly capitalism, with greater and greater industrial concentration, until big corporations dominated our lives and we lost our freedom. Nonsense, said Shumpeter. Look at the world of business, and what one notices is not monopolization but the "creative destruction" of capitalism. Old firms die and new firms replace them. But Schumpeter's capitalism is self-defeating in another way. The book was written in the middle of the Second World War, and Schumpeter predicted that capitalist societies would be unable to resist military threats from authoritarian societies. The nineteenth-century military successes of the West, said Schumpeter, were attributable to the "aristocratic element." But the bourgeois is rationalist and unheroic, and "can only use rationalist and unheroic means to defend his position or to bend a nation to his will."[9]

With the benefit of hindsight, these fears now seem greatly exaggerated. The Second World War and the Cold War have proven that capitalist societies can resist foreign threats. In part, this is because of the technological edge of the military in wealthy, free market societies. In addition, a nation of shopkeepers may possess pluck and courage in abundance, and the argument that the heroic virtues are displaced by commercial virtues seems very dated after 9-11. The most successful military states, as it turns out, are precisely those in which Montesquieu's *doux commerce* has most strongly taken hold. This is especially true since 1991, when communism collapsed under the weight of its own inefficiencies. Since then, we have lived in a unipolar world, where the chief commercial society enjoys a military dominance without parallel in world history. Schumpeter's declinist predictions could not have been more wrong.

A second way in which free markets might be self-defeating was suggested in Daniel Bell's 1976 *Cultural Contradictions of Capitalism*.[10] Bell argued that free markets depend for their survival on the general acceptance of bourgeois cultural norms such as fortitude, prudence and solidarity that free markets tend to dissolve. These virtues flourished in a pre-capitalist era, and promoted its growth, but capitalism perversely weakens them. Market societies produce self-absorbed hedonists who squander their inheritance of bourgeois virtue, and like prodigal sons burn through the wealth accumulated by their doting, Puritan forebears. These attacks on free bargaining turned the Marxist analysis of capitalism on its head. Marx had predicted that capitalism would be destroyed by its economic failure; but Schumpeter and Bell predicted it would be destroyed by its success.

Many of Bell's concerns, like those of Schumpeter, now seem dated. The 1970s were an era of pessimism and malaise, where inflation, environmental degradation and energy shortages led some to think that the end was nigh. The apocalyptic predictions of material decay have since been falsified, but these issues have been replaced with a very different set of problems, which Bell anticipated. For Bell, the real danger was a moral more than a material collapse, and during the last decade many fin-de-siècle social conservatives shared these concerns. America is manifestly able to produce the material capital of a wealthy society, but to many it seemed less able to produce the social capital of cooperative behavior and stable families; and, if Bell was right, the decline in social capital might in time threaten material capital as well.

The contrast between material and social capital recalls Sallust's complaint about Imperial Rome's "private wealth and public poverty." That tag was formerly employed by liberals such as John Kenneth Galbraith to argue for increased government spending. Now, however, the concern for public poverty is voiced by conservatives such as Robert Bork and William Bennett to describe a spiritual deficit. Similarly, it was formerly the liberal who asked us to look at the "root causes of crime," back when these were thought to be economic. But now that the root causes seem social, and attributable to the decline in traditional family structures and the weakening of moral norms, we might more profitably seek advice on the causes of crime from social conservatives such as Myron Magnet and James Q. Wilson.

The Bell thesis is nevertheless vague on how free market institutions might have contributed to a social capital deficit. How did contract law ever get in the way? As Stephen Holmes trenchantly puts it: "Antiliberals endlessly berate their enemies for 'instrumental thinking.' But they do not clearly explain the evil of producing better goods at lower cost."[11] Yet free markets do depend on a set of shared social norms, and in what follows I identify three of the virtues – fortitude, prudence and solidarity – on which Bell thought free markets depend, and ask how they fare in commercial societies. If free bargaining weakened foundational commercial virtues, there might be something to the Bell thesis.

First, a want of *fortitude* or the ability to endure discomfort exposes a commercial society to internal decline as well as external attack. Bargains for future performance assign risks, and with risk comes the possibility of regret. From an *ex ante* perspective, the contracts to which parties of full capacity have agreed should be presumed mutually beneficial: otherwise they would not have entered into them. From an *ex post* perspective, however, there may be winners and losers. For example, a supply contract for a commodity might turn out to be very costly for one of the parties if prices fluctuate greatly. If such contracts are unenforceable on some overgenerous doctrine of excuse or impossibility, then society is the poorer, as the efficiency gains of joint projects may be lost. A court that, lacking fortitude, sympathizes too closely with *ex post* losers and excuses their breaches will reduce the scope of free contracting and weaken the economy.

In the past, common law systems were more concerned to promote fortitude and to frown on self-pity. Nineteenth-century common law courts were skeptical of claims for emotional distress, unless it was a foreseeable consequence of negligent physical harm.[12] Back then, courts were also more likely to enforce contracts and to disregard pleas that changed circumstances argued against enforcement. The link between emotional distress in tort law and the doctrine of excuses in contract law may also be observed today in the private law regimes of different countries. For example, English and Canadian courts, which remain less ready to compensate for bruised feelings, are also more prepared to enforce contract terms strictly than American courts. The list of events that might excuse performance, through a mistake or a change in circumstances, are drawn more narrowly in England and Canada than in the US.

Emotional distress sometimes results from consumer contracts that go bad, but this does not provide a justification for second-guessing consumer choices. Rather, it argues for stricter enforcement of contracts, where the consumer chooses the damages regime he wants. If given the choice, notes Paul Rubin, consumers would waive the right to sue for emotional distress, for the same reason that they never buy insurance for emotional distress.[13] First, the transaction costs of the litigation system, with lawyer's fees, court costs and delay, consume much of the recovery and make the tort system a poor insurance device. Most consumers will prefer to waive such claims in return for a lower purchase price. Second, insurance for emotional distress makes little sense when the accident reduces the ability to enjoy the damages award. The question is not whether the loss is painful, but whether today's healthy person would wish to transfer present wealth (in the form of an insurance premium) to a future person who would enjoy the money less. That is why no one would wish to purchase insurance for emotional distress for the loss of a child, even though the distress is very real. Better to keep the insurance premium and apply it to the live child's education. With a stronger adherence to free bargaining norms, and enforceable waivers of tort remedies, we would have fewer, not more, claims for emotional distress.

Nor is there much evidence that free markets subvert fortitude, as Bell suggests. If American courts welcome claims for emotional distress, this might more plausibly be attributed to a litigation regime that favors plaintiffs and to populist traditions of civil juries and elected judges. Moreover, American civil remedies substitute for the kinds of state intervention that other countries employ to remedy bad luck. Europe lacks forgiving American-style bankruptcy laws but offers state subsidies to failing businesses; and Britain limits civil recovery for physical and emotional injuries but provides broader Medicare coverage. It would be highly speculative to say that one legal regime more than another promotes fortitude.

The second contractarian virtue is *prudence*, defined as the willingness to defer present consumption and invest in profitable opportunities for future gain. Both Schumpeter and Bell thought that free markets subverted prudence by encouraging profligacy. What Schumpeter had in mind was a generational betrayal, in which one generation inherits a patrimony from its ancestors but leaves nothing for its descendants. We are all members of a social contract in which our parents provide for us in consideration for a return promise that we provide for their grandchildren. So long as the promises are kept, the bargain is constantly renewed and persists indefinitely over time. But when one generation is taught to think of itself only, it may break the bargain. A generation of vipers might rebel against its parents and then, when it has children, sedate them with addictive drugs when they show the slightest signs of disobedience. It might profess abstract principles of justice and send its children to broken schools. It might refuse to save for the future and leave its children bankrupt.

Schumpeter considered the family a fundamental mainstay of capitalism. Look at capitalism's creative destruction, he said, and what you see are entrepreneurs driving new, emerging firms. And behind each entrepreneur is a wife and child for whom the entrepreneur seeks to provide. Emerging firms are often family businesses that solve problems of bargaining misbehavior at the same time that they strengthen the incentive to produce. Take away the bequest motive and you have a different kind of *homo economicus*.[14]

Bell had similar worries. Following Max Weber, Bell thought that capitalism flourished in the arid garden of Puritan virtue. "Sobriety, frugality, sexual restraint and a forbidding attitude to life" might not seem quite the recipe for a joyous life,[15] but Bell, nevertheless, thought them a good career move for the rising capitalist. In Weber's day the Protestant virtues seemed firmly entrenched; in 1976 the world looked very different to Bell, who drew what he thought a logical conclusion about capitalism's impending decline.

Bell thought the moral decay was hastened by a new device, which had arisen to corrupt the prudent saver: installment sales. Easy sales credit persuaded people to buy goods they could ill afford, mortgaging their future earnings in the process. What this gave us, said Bell, was hedonism, a "world of fashion, photography, advertising, television, travel. ... A world of make-believe in which one lives for expectations, for what will come rather than what is. And it must come without effort."[16] All this from a Land's End catalogue. Heaven knows what Bell would have said about the weekly credit card in the mail.

Several kinds of mistakes seem to be going on here. First, the pursuit of pleasure does not threaten free markets. Indeed, no one needs markets more than the hedonist, for they supply him with his pleasures. The point is so obvious that Bell must have had something else in mind, likely the competition with the Soviet Union. In 1976 one did not know just how feeble the Soviet economy was, and many of Bell's contemporaries feared that the cause of freedom would be endangered if the Soviets overtook the West in material production. As it turned out, they need not have worried. Second, the hedonist might have a robust incentive to save to fund his future consumption. The true modernist is not a surfer but a litigator who dockets 3,000 hours a year and whose spouse works similar hours as a tax lawyer. As an empirical prediction, Bell had it exactly wrong. On average, people in First World countries work harder than those in backward countries, and people in the US work hardest of all.[17] Third, if personal debt loads threaten virtue or free markets in the way that Bell (and Ezra Pound) thought, one might have thought that the fresh start policies in the American Bankruptcy Code would fix things nicely. Through liberal bankruptcy discharge, discussed in Chapter 7, personal debts can be scaled back to zero. Indeed, the fresh start of Chapter 7, the world's most forgiving personal bankruptcy law, explains why debt levels are so high in America. Since the overcommitted American debtor can walk away from his creditors with relative ease, it is not surprising that he borrows more heavily than consumers in other countries.

The third contractarian virtue is *solidarity*, which is the virtue of individuals bound together in a strong community. Solidarity is not a virtue itself so much as a font of virtue, for we learn to be moral through our dealings with others. We are not born virtuous and then corrupted by civilization, as Rousseau thought. Instead, we need others to flourish and attain moral responsibility.

Recently, scholars have bemoaned the loss in solidarity in America. Robert Putnam's *Bowling Alone* described an America in which people have stopped participating in clubs and associations, and Alan Ehrenhalt's *Lost City* mourned a similar decline in civic participation.[18] Putnam's findings have been doubted,[19] and after the civic revival that followed 9-11 the general air of declinism now seems a little dated. Nevertheless, crime levels remain high in this country, as do illegitimacy rates. America is also a highly mobile country, and migration weakens social norms. The high divorce rates in the Bible Belt and the high personal bankruptcy rates in the economically dynamic Sunbelt would be puzzling but for the fact that these are high migration states.[20] Where one does not know the neighbors, the social stigma of promise-breaking is weak.

Assume, therefore, that fears about the loss of solidarity are well-founded. Even so, it does not follow that free markets or contract law have contributed to the weakening of communitarian bonds, which plausibly are stronger in a commercial society than in pre-capitalist Montegrano. By any objective measure, including club memberships, attendance at religious services and charitable giving, America is a profoundly communitarian society, and more so than the traditional societies to which it is compared. There is a simple reason for this. Interpersonal bonds are more valuable and thus more prevalent in free market societies, where they permit the parties to exploit a broader range of bargain opportunities. In a hierarchical society, the relationships that count are non-contractual and vertical: lord and vassal, priest and layman. But commercial societies are more egalitarian, and the contractual, horizontal relationships of joint bargainers are more important.

Tocqueville noted that, more than Europeans, Americans were joiners: they appeared to have a penchant to form clubs around the most trivial causes.[21] A naive explanation is that Americans are simply more gregarious than other people. A more plausible explanation is that, as members of a highly commercial society, Americans have a greater need for self-protection through club membership than people in a more hierarchical society. Within a hierarchy, a person can appeal to higher authorities for protection against forms of misbehavior that do not ascend to the level of crimes; but in a more egalitarian and transient society, such as the US, a person must make his own self-protective networks. He cannot appeal to his lord or mayor, but might seek an informal redress through a professional association or private club. We would, therefore, expect more, not fewer, private communities in a commercial society such as the US; and that is just how things have turned out.

Within a commercial society contract law strengthens bonds of solidarity by permitting the parties to formalize their relationships. Contract law superimposes a remedy in damages on top of the reputational sanction for breach and, as we saw in Chapter 3, this promotes trust between the parties. What threatens solidarity is not enforcement but, rather, the excuses for non-performance that may be found in no-fault divorce law, bankruptcy discharges and over-broad contract law remedies for the defaulting party. A legal system that better respected communitarian values would jealously guard the stock of enforceable promises by narrowing excuses from performance and by permitting bargainers to waive them *ex ante* in their agreements. It would permit the parties to opt out of no-fault divorce regimes and fresh start policies in bankruptcy, and would refuse to set aside a contract for changed circumstances when the parties had made clear that they intended to remain bound however things turned out.

History has not been kind to the argument that free markets are self-defeating. *Capitalism, Socialism and Democracy* and *The Cultural Contradictions of Capitalism* read like period pieces, since the economic problems that alarmed Schumpeter and Bell seem much less troubling today. The prediction that free market systems would fall prey to foreign enemies or internal cultural contradictions has proven false. America did not fall into an economic decline. Social conservatives might possibly be right about the general decline in moral norms, but as for the economic virtues that support business, there's no arguing with success.

The Romantic objection

The second objection to contractual institutions is that they deaden the heart to the confusing mixture of inner experience, nostalgia for the past, communitarian sentiment, religious mystery and aesthetic joy that constitutes the Romantic tradition.[22] Eighteenth-century Enlightenment figures such as Hume, Voltaire and Smith had celebrated contractarian virtue, material progress and the triumph of reason over superstition. What followed was a Romantic reaction, led by such nineteenth-century figures as Wordsworth, Chateaubriand and Schiller who rejected the Enlightenment's orderliness, materialism and rationalism. The tension between the two traditions continues to this day, and many modern thinkers can fairly be placed within one camp or the other. We have not finished with the nineteenth century, or with the eighteenth either.

The Romantic tradition transcends political boundaries. Oliver Goldsmith's nostalgic evocation of a more primitive past in *The Deserted Village* was an early example of Romantic nostalgia that was echoed by the authors of *The Communist Manifesto*. "All that is holy is profaned," wrote Marx and Engels. "All that is solid melts into air." In the last century, Jean-Paul Sartre's left-wing anti-liberalism and Leo Strauss' right-wing anti-liberalism were both strongly influenced by the views of Nazi sympathizer Martin Heidegger. In our time, anti-liberals left and right join hands to oppose free markets. On the left, political scientist Benjamin Barber decries a "McWorld," which has sunk to a tawdry common cultural denominator; while on the right, conservative philosopher John Gray expresses the same concerns about the corrosive effects of free trade.[23] Both extremes nudge each other, often with little show of recognition.

Merely reading the list of the anti-liberal enemies of free markets and modernity can induce an ideological vertigo: Herbert Marcuse and Roberto Unger on the left; Maurice Barrès and Alexander Solzhenitsyn on the right; as well as Alasdair Macintyre and Christopher Lasch who straddle both camps. The nineteenth-century aesthetes, with their contempt for bourgeois morality and their nostalgia for a hierarchical pre-capitalist Europe, also defy categorization, except as anti-liberals. Théophile Gautier and Oscar Wilde both saw markets as a poison that deadens the soul to deeper virtues and joys and, as an antidote, proposed an aesthetic sensibility where play, art and prayer might flourish.

Disputes over markets and free bargaining are as fundamental as almost any political issue. However, this raises the question how a consensual, capitalist act might be divisive. The Romantic's answer is moral and aesthetic externalities. The social perfectionist, introduced in Chapter 7, argued that immoral contracts harm third parties by corrupting them. The Romantic takes this a further step and argues that all contracts, moral and immoral, impose negative externalities by coarsening a society and obscuring our sense of the sacred. In what follows we examine two ways in which this might be thought to happen.

The Romantic's first objection is that free markets weaken religious impulses by diverting attention from spiritual to material matters.[24] Christianity always saw a nexus between material wealth and spiritual poverty. The rich young man of St Matthew's Gospel did not murder, steal, commit adultery, or bear false witness, and still his heart was troubled. "What lack I yet?" he asked. "If thou wilt be perfect," Christ answered, "go and sell all thou hast, and give to the poor . . . and come and follow me." The young man turned sadly away, since he was very rich, and as he left Christ told his disciples the eye-of-the-needle parable (Matthew 19:16–24). St Paul summed up the message from the Gospels by observing that the love of money is the root of all evil (I Timothy 6:10).

The Enlightenment's religious skeptics saw a similar link between spiritual wealth and material poverty, and drew the opposite conclusion. In his *Philosophical Letters* Voltaire praised English commercial virtues, which diverted men from sectarian, religious battles.

> Go into the London Stock Exchange, that place more respectable than a good many courts, and there you'll see representatives from all nations assembled for the utility of mankind. There the Jew, the Mohammedan, and the Christian deal with one another as if they were of the same religion, and give the name of infidel only to those who go bankrupt.[25]

Before the temple of Mammon, every enthusiasm that might have inflamed the passions had dissolved into benign indifference. There was an established religion, of course, but what delighted Voltaire was that no one seemed to take it seriously.

Voltaire had seen the future, and it worked. Another notable Enlightenment skeptic, Benjamin Franklin, recounted an anecdote to show his indifference to religion. In the midst of the First Great Awakening, the great evangelist George Whitefield passed through Philadelphia, where he preached for several days running. Much of the city turned out to hear him, and the sermons were greeted with extraordinary scenes of religious enthusiasm. Franklin went too, but not to be converted. Instead, he was fascinated by how loudly Whitefield could preach. Franklin walked a few blocks away, and he could still hear Whitefield plainly. Further out the sermon could still be understood. With a few quick calculations, Franklin concluded that stories about Roman generals haranguing a whole army were plausible. That is, if the generals could bawl as loudly as Whitefield.[26]

Many of the leading Enlightenment figures subscribed to a Deism that denounced organized religion while professing a personal belief in God. But even this went too far for some. David Hume rejected the Deist's belief in God as entirely speculative, and others dismissed the question of God's existence as a piece of unnecessary baggage. The French mathematician Laplace, whose model of perfect rationality we saw in Chapter 5, was one of these. When Napoleon asked him what place his system left for God, Laplace coolly replied: "Sire, I have no need for that hypothesis."

The Romantic reaction to the Enlightenment was marked by an openness to much that the skeptics had discarded, and for Chateaubriand, Coleridge and Hugo this included the medieval and religious. While some Romantic figures (notably Shelley) were atheists, the prevailing sentiment was an anti-anti-religious fascination with the hidden, the mysterious and the sacred. The Romantics saw commercial societies and modernism as a world of immanence, of the here-and-now. The intuition that a transcendent reality underlies ordinary experience, which Christians express through the Incarnation and Romantics through their awe of nature, is lost when the spirit is no longer made flesh and the world is no longer sacred or magical. The world of wonders recedes and Max Weber's world of disenchantment (*entzauberung*) takes its place.

All this amounts to a prediction that a society will become less religious as it becomes more commercial. If so, the US will seem a curious counterexample, since it is both the most commercial and the most religious country in the developed world. By any measure, including church attendance rates and opinion polls, religious sentiments are far weaker in European countries, which pride themselves on their difference from a materialist America. If the objection from religion amounts to a prediction about how people behave, it is unpersuasive; and if it does not, there is little reason to pay much attention to it, since the inner experience of religion is veiled to human eyes.

Weber famously saw an affinity between American commercial virtues and its Puritan heritage. The Puritan had seen business as a quasi-religious calling, and his religious asceticism was transformed into the frugal virtues of the American businessman. In time, thought Weber, American commerce would cast off its religious anchor.

> Victorious capitalism, since it rests on mechanical foundations, needs [religion's] support no longer. The rosy blush of its laughing heir, the Enlightenment, seems also to be irretrievably failing, and the idea of duty in one's calling prowls about in our lives like the ghost of dead religious beliefs.[27]

What Weber had in mind was the second Romantic objection to commercial society: commercial virtues transform us into utilitarian calculators, who barter sentiment for efficiency and joy for wealth. The complaint was strikingly made by D.H. Lawrence, in a comment on that paragon of commercial virtue, Benjamin Franklin. "Rarely use venery," advised Franklin. But the point, said Lawrence, is that one should never *use* venery. The commerçant is wonderfully able to extract a contractual surplus; he is "calculating and daring at the same time, above all temperate and reliable, shrewd and devoted to [his] business." But withal something still is lacking, said Weber, if successful businessmen are "specialists without spirit" and "sensualists without heart."[28]

Weber's contemporary, Werner Sombart, offered an even more pessimistic view of what he described as the spirit of capitalism, which he thought was dominated by acquisition, competition and rationality. The pre-capitalist economy had been centered on the idea of human nature, which defined consumer needs and assigned fixed roles to suppliers. "Goods were produced and traded in order adequately to meet the consumers' needs and to provide an ample livelihood for producers and merchants; the standards and the expectations of both consumers and producers were fixed by long established usage."[29] By contrast, in capitalist economies that are dominated by the principle of acquisition, the aim of economic activity does not relate back to a living person.

Sombart's analysis of the demand side of economics is puzzling, since he did not explain why satisfying consumer demands is unrelated to a living person. His analysis of the supply side and the corrupting influence of markets on suppliers was less opaque, if no less contentious. The acquisitive instinct is intrinsically dehumanizing, he said, and there are no limits to the rapacity of suppliers in a capitalist society. The "psychological compulsion to boundless extension" detaches the actor from his needs and leads him to sacrifice his happiness for a self-defeating pursuit of greater and greater wealth.[30] The grasping pursuit of wealth will lead to unscrupulous and ruthless competition, with every moral inhibition abandoned.

Sombart's assertion that commercial societies are more devious than pre-commercial ones is an empirical claim, without much evidence to back it up. For where would we expect to find our trust repaid by honest dealing – in a successful commercial society, where bargainers have strong private incentives to maintain a reputation of probity, or in Banfield's pre-commercial Montegrano? Would our property be more at risk in Constant's commercial society or in his warrior one? As we saw, Max Weber thought that economically primitive societies were far more unscrupulous than advanced ones. "The *auri sacra fames* [greed for gold] of a Neapolitan cab-driver . . . is, as anyone can find out for himself, very much more intense, and especially more unscrupulous than that of, say, an Englishman in similar circumstances."[31] At best, there is little reason to think that the vice of overreaching, which Aristotle called *pleonexia* and which economists call opportunism, is more prevalent today than in the past, human nature having changed little.

While Sombart became a National Socialist (the original "third way" between capitalism and communism), his criticism of market economies would not seem out of place today in an anti-liberal Internet blog.[32] The tool employed by capitalists in the pursuit of wealth is economic rationality, which Sombart identified with long-range planning, the strict application of means to ends and exact calculation. People who view life from an economic perspective (Weber's Puritans, Sombart's Jews and the blogger's Americans) find themselves turning every experience into a calculation of profits and losses that squeezes out non-commercial pleasures.

> All untamed natural growth disappears and, where it proves disturbing, even the aesthetically-pleasing individual is mercilessly weeded-out. The idea of strict adaptation of means to ends, one of the essential ideological props of capitalism, permeates the totality of the culture and leads in the course of time to a purely utilitarian valuation of human beings.[33]

The same objection was more poetically expressed by Wordsworth. "Getting and spending, we lay waste our powers / Little we see in nature that is ours." The utilitarian who is insensible to aesthetic joys is Charles Dickens' Gradgrind in *Hard Times*, or the philistine who opens a novel or book of poems to search for social utility in Théophile Gautier's Preface to *Mademoiselle de Maupin*.

> "What! Not a word on the needs of society, nothing civilizing or progressive!" … No, imbeciles and cretins, a book will not make a thin soup, a novel is not a plain pair of boots, a sonnet is not a syringe, a drama is not a railway … The real utility of novels is that, when reading them one sleeps and does not read useful, virtuous and progressive newspapers.[34]

Martin Heidegger's analysis of technology was similar, if less accessible. Heidegger's enemies were the rationalist who distinguishes between man as a subject and the objects of this world, and the technologist who, in turn, asks how objects can be made to serve man. What both forget, said Heidegger, is that we lack direct access to the self and discover ourselves not through self-reflection but only as part of the world. The pre-moderns saw man in this way, as being-in-the-world (*dasein*), and therefore had a more reverential attitude to the world: it expressed different possibilities of being and was pregnant with life. The rooted man inhabits a world alive with meaning, association and wonder. The way back to the earlier sense of a sanctified nature was language, the language of poets and not of philosophes, for poetic language magically transmits ineffable values that rootless metaphysics has abandoned. Through poetry we recognize that modernism had left us stranded, like the stranger in the poem of Hölderlin with which Heidegger ended his essay on "The Question Concerning Technology." "You linger on the cold shore / Among your own and know them not."[35]

The poetic view of life is admittedly not captured by free bargaining. Contract law permits us to achieve happiness by satisfying our preferences.

But happiness might seem an unworthy goal, when compared to Hölderlin's ecstatic sense of a god-filled world, or the solemnity and formality of Racine's tragic drama. Happiness is a suitable goal for those who are content with a quotidian life, slouched before the television set. But that is not a prescription for a joyful life. The quest for happiness might even seem a little banal, when compared to the other goods of this world, and, like Paul-Jean Toulet, we might wish to guard against an easeful contentment.

> Quand l'ombre est rouge, sous les roses,
>   Et clair le temps,
> Prends garde à la douceur des choses.

> When the shadows are red, underneath the roses,
>   And the sky is clear,
> Beware of the sweetness of things.[36]

I feel sorry for you, wrote Baudelaire to a critic, that you are so easily made happy.[37]

Does this amount to a telling criticism of free bargaining? Not unless the pursuit of happiness closes off avenues of joy. But how might that happen? No one ever suggested that, because bargaining permits us to satisfy our preferences, we should bargain till we drop. No time for friendship, music, poetry – just bargain, bargain, bargain. That would be every bit as foolish as a ceaseless search for joyous experience, like Walter Pater's invocation in The Renaissance "to burn always with this hard, gem-like flame, to maintain this ecstasy." Joy is too ephemeral to be grasped in that manner.

Our experience with states that sought to define themselves through joy or beauty is not one many of us would like to see repeated. The first self-conscious attempt to transcend liberal democracy with a "politics of beauty" was Gabriele D'Annunzio's city of Fiume, which became the model for the aestheticized politics of Fascism and Nazism. The idea that the arts declined under capitalism, which was the theme of Ezra Pound's "usura" canto, led to a search for an authentic art, rooted in the soil and promoted by a totalitarian state which saw itself as a work of art and expressed its political vision through highly stylized mass meetings and monumental architecture. Racial hatred was, itself, aestheticized, through portraits of heroic Aryan males and caricatures of racial enemies. What the Fascist state offered, said one of its admirers, was an experience of joy entirely missing from the old parliamentary democracies it supplanted. "The young fascist in his camp, amongst his peace comrades (who could be his war comrades), the young fascist who sings, who marches, who works, who dreams, is first of all a joyous being."[38] This from Robert Brasillach in 1939, six years before he was executed for collaboration with the Germans.

Had Sombart, Heidegger and Brasillach been right, life in the National Socialist Germany would have been more joyful than life in America today. Such views belong in a political bestiary, or in Mel Brooks' *The Producers*. Nor is there much reason to think that happiness and joy are substitutes, and that choosing one excludes the other. While the lot of Soviet citizens under communism was distinctly unhappy, it was not for that reason joyful. Joy cannot be measured, any more than happiness, but there is much more reason to think them complements that are found together than substitutes that exclude each other.

Bentham thought that the goal of all legislation should be the maximization of everyone's happiness or utility. While that might be a proper aim for the legislator, it is less than satisfactory for the individual as a goal for a successful life. Asking too much of each of us, utilitarianism would make us all less happy. We should be left in the unhappy position of the young John Stuart Mill, who had learned Greek at five and algebra at nine, but was exposed to no religion and little poetry. He had absorbed all of the proper utilitarian views on democracy and economics, but had lost the capacity to enjoy life and wished for death. Then one day he read a pathetic story by a now-forgotten writer and was moved to tears. He realized that he was capable of emotion and with this his recovery began. In questions of public policy he remained a utilitarian and, as we have seen, became the foremost champion of liberty. But his utilitarianism was of a different order from Bentham's, who thought one pleasure as good as another, and observed that poetry was no better than the child's game of pincushion. Mill's utilitarianism was qualitative, and not simply quantitative, since he thought some pleasures superior to others. The experience of the transforming joy of great poetry is superior to that of pincushion, even if people report themselves equally pleased by the two. Yet the choice of pleasures must rest with the individual, Mill thought, and *On Liberty* remains the best defense of personal liberty. As we saw, the gossip about his relationship with Mrs Taylor might have helped to shape his fierce anti-perfectionism. But it is equally plausible to suppose that his defense of diversity, of the many different ways in which people might flourish, was a reaction against the appallingly single-minded rationalism in which he was reared.

Like Mill, we are called on to maintain a private space for the personal experiences of love and beauty and all of the numberless occasions of happiness and laughter that delight us and harm no one else. We must make room in our lives for private joys along with public policies. We are not required to subscribe to a moral or political theory that makes us personally miserable. Instead, like Mill, we are asked to seek a fusion between rationalism and romanticism, between the public realm of sensible rules and institutions and the private realm of joy that alone makes life worthwhile. It is mischievous and silly to suggest that in choosing one we must reject the other.

Even the anti-liberal critics of free bargaining admit that we may pursue multiple goals, for they portray capitalist man as seeking both too much and too little pleasure. Sometimes it is hard to keep it all straight. Is capitalist man Sombart's joyless drudge or Bell's giddy hedonist? Is he a thin-lipped Puritan or a leering sensualist, an efficient planner or a debt-ridden consumer, a calculating miser or a compulsive spender? He cannot be all of these things; and if one is as plausible as the other then none are plausible. The anti-liberal's complaints are long on rhetoric but short on analysis or evidence.

Moreover, the Sombart-Heidegger view of capitalism is incomplete if it cannot explain why people would choose to live a joyless life. Why couldn't they move, or (like the 1970s' drop-out) stop to smell the flowers? That was what Franklin did, after all. After he made his bundle, he retired from business to devote himself to the things in which he took delight: intellectual conversation, literature, science and the service of his country.

Neil Kinnock mocked the view that people failed to exploit opportunities for pleasure by asking "Were they simply thick?" But that was just what many New Left people thought 40 years ago, after reading Herbert Marcuse's account of false consciousness in commercial societies. Marcuse was a student of Heidegger who attained a cult following among students at Western universities in the 1960s. What he sought to explain is why Marxism failed to take hold in the West, and in *One-Dimensional Man* he offered his answer: consumer tastes and political opinions are controlled by a mass media which, in turn, is controlled by big business.[39] People are made to buy useless consumer goods and are not exposed to progressive thought. The result is a form of "repressive tolerance," which keeps people entertained but excludes any subversive thoughts. For Marcuse, liberal democracies were totalitarian, and like Friedrich Kessler he thought they resembled Nazi Germany.

Forty years on, the contempt for liberal democracy wears ill. The truly totalitarian regimes in the Soviet bloc that Marcuse admired find few supporters, and those only at the extreme fringes. Moreover, most of us will find the implications of the argument from false consciousness deeply troubling. If individual choices deserve no respect in the market-place, they deserve no greater respect in elections. We should, then, have no reason to prefer democracy to any other form of government. All this for a theory of consciousness that is neither verified nor verifiable, and which asks us to assume that admirers of totalitarianism, alone, possess true consciousness.

With less arrogance, we might then find less to condemn in commercial societies. The dull commerçant might be a faithful husband and honest friend, and these virtues, though grudged by the aesthete, are reverenced the while. The salesman is also an adventurer, who in a day might navigate past dangerous shoals and experience his own epiphanies, the epiphanies of everyday life, like *Ulysses'* Leopold Bloom. Even Benjamin

Franklin was a vastly more interesting man than D.H. Lawrence made him out to be. Franklin's *Autobiography* is a record of an extraordinary life, packed with incident, which culminated in a diplomatic career that sealed the success of the American Revolution. He was anything but a Puritan, and his ability to savor the Ancien Régime's *douceur de vie* shocked the prim John Adams. If Franklin's rules for life were sensible, they were wise for that reason, and after all not very different from those of Leon Battista Alberti, the Renaissance architect and humanist.[40]

It is foolish to suppose that artists are indifferent to monetary rewards. Alberti moved from one rich patron to another, as did most Renaissance artists. For their part, the patrons, from Abbott Suger in the twelfth century to J.P. Morgan in the twentieth, found that the desire to collect gave them an incentive to accumulate yet more wealth. With commerce, said Alberti, buyers can afford art, and the prospect of a price for their skills will attract the architect, sculptor, painter and musician. So it has always been. Abundance is the mother of the arts, as Voltaire noted in *Le mondain*.[41] The great art centers, whether in Alberti's Florence, Voltaire's Paris, or today's New York and Sante Fe, are, above all, cities with disposable income.[42] And if America has great art museums today, it is only because the paintings were first purchased by private collectors with names like Barnes, Carnegie, Freer, Frick, Guggenheim, Mellon, Morgan and Rockefeller.

In sum, the cultural objections to free contracting regimes are unpersuasive. Commercial societies are much more robust than critics such as Joseph Schumpeter and Daniel Bell gave them credit for. Schumpeter and Bell correctly noted that the strength of free markets depends on a general acceptance of underlying social norms. Where they went wrong was in thinking that these norms are subverted by free markets. All of the evidence points in the other direction. Nor is the Romantic objection much stronger. This is not to minimize the concern for the wounds of modernism or the need for a revival of humanist traditions. Yet, when one considers how free bargaining permits individuals to flourish, how it promotes virtue, and how it maintains the arts, it is not too much to claim that contract law is a humanism too.

Notes

Preface

1 If the crucial insight of law-and-economics is that private law rules should be designed with incentive effects in mind, then the honor of founding law-and-economics must go to Bentham.

2 R.M. Hare, *Moral Thinking: Its Levels, Methods, and Point* (Oxford: Oxford University Press, 1981); Derek Parfit, *Reasons and Persons* (Oxford: Oxford University Press, 1984). For an overview, see J.J.C. Smart, "An Outline of a System of Utilitarian Ethics," in J.J.C. Smart and Bernard Williams, *Utilitarianism: For and Against*, 1 (Cambridge: Cambridge University Press, 1973).

3 4 Co. 92 (1602). Going back further, the purely executory stipulatio was enforceable in Roman law in the second century AD. Barry Nicholas, *An Introduction to Roman Law*, 162 (Oxford: Clarendon, 1962).

1 The promising game

1 John R. Searle, *The Construction of Social Reality* (New York: Free Press, 1995).

2 1478 Y.B. Pasc. 17 Edw. IV, fo. 1, pl. 2 per Brian C.J.

3 *Edgington* v. *Fitzmaurice*, 29 Ch. D. 459, 483 (1885) per Bowen L.J.

4 F.A. Hayek, "The Use of Knowledge in Society," *Am. Econ. Rev.* 35: 519 (1945).

5 Searle, *Construction of Social Reality*, 103.

6 *Joyce* v. *D.P.P.*, [1946] A.C. 347 (H.L.).

7 Blaise Pascal, *II Œuvres complètes, Pensée*, 47 (Paris: Pléiade, 2000).

8 John R. Searle, *Speech Acts*, 33–42 (Cambridge: Cambridge University Press, 1969). See also John Rawls, *A Theory of Justice*, 344–46 (Cambridge: Harvard University Press, 1971). In addition, H.L.A. Hart's power-conferring rules are constitutive rules. Hart rejected John Austin's definition of rules as commands backed by a sovereign. That might do for some kinds of rules, said Hart, but not for the rules that create institutions such as contract law and marriage, under which individuals have the power to create binding obligations. H.L.A. Hart, *The Concept of Law*, 27–32 (Oxford: Clarendon, 1961).

9 Frederick Hayek, *The Fatal Conceit: The Errors of Socialism* (University of Chicago Press, 1998).

10 Alan D. Sokal, "Transgressing the Boundaries: Toward a Transformative Hermeneutics of Quantum Gravity," *Social Text* 46/47: 217 (1996). See Alan D. Sokal (ed.), *The Sokal Hoax: The Sham that Shook the Academy* (New York: Bison, 2000).

11 David Hume, *A Treatise on Human Nature*, 516, III.ii.V (Oxford: Oxford University Press, 1967).

12 Searle's analysis of promissory institutions owes much to Hume, as does John Rawls' account of the institution. John Rawls, "Two Concepts of Rules," *Phil. Rev.* 64: 3 (1955). Rawls distinguished between regulative rules and the conventional rules of promising, where the latter necessarily depend on a linguistic convention.

13 Fred Korn and Shulamit Korn, "Where People Don't Promise," *Ethics* 93: 445 (1983). See further Sione Lâtûkefu, *Church and State in Tonga* (Honolulu: University Press of Hawaii, 1974); K.L. Morton, *Kinship, Economics, and Exchange in a Tongan Village* (University of Oregon Ph.D., Sept. 1972).

14 Sir Henry Maine, *Ancient Law*, 303 (Boston: Beacon, 1963).

15 *Laver v. Fielder*, 32 Beav. 1, 13; 55 Eng. Rep. 1, 5 (1862).

16 J.L. Austin, *How To Do Things with Words*, 10 (New York: Oxford University Press, 1965) (emphasis in original).

17 Joseph Raz, "Promises and Obligations," in P. Hacker and J. Raz (eds) *Law, Morality, and Society*, 210, 214–15 (Oxford: Clarendon, 1977).

18 *Webb v. McGowan*, 168 So. 196, aff'd, 168 So. 199 (Ala. Sup. Ct., 1936).

19 Patrick Atiyah, *Promises, Morals and Law* (Oxford: Oxford University Press, 1983). Since then, Atiyah has retreated from these views, and acknowledged the role of law-and-economics in providing an intellectual defense of contract law. Patrick S. Atiyah, *An Introduction to the Law of Contract* (Oxford: Clarendon, 1995).

20 H.L.A. Hart, "Legal and Moral Obligation," in A.I. Melden (ed.) *Essays in Moral Philosophy* 82, 102 (Seattle: University of Washington Press, 1958); Joseph Raz, "Voluntary Obligations and Normative Powers (2)," *Proc. Aristotelian Soc.* 46: 79, 95–98 (Supp. 1972). In the exceptional cases seen in Chapters 6–7, a contract is unenforceable because its content is immoral.

21 "We need a principle of political obligation which binds the citizen to one *particular* state above all others." A. John Simmons, *Moral Principles and Political Obligation*, 31–32 (Princeton: Princeton University Press, 1979).

22 The term is taken from Rawls, *A Theory of Justice*, 344–46.

23 John Searle, "How to Derive an 'Ought' from an 'Is'," *Phil. Rev.* 73: 43 (1964); Searle, *Speech Acts*, 177.

24 See Haig Khatchadourian, "Institutions, Practices and Moral Rules," 86 *Mind* 479 (1977). Searle himself noted that his argument concerned the philosophy of language and not ethics, or "oughts" and not "moral oughts." Searle, *Speech Acts*, 176–77.

25 "The question was, why ought I to keep my promise? For that I ought to keep it everyone grasps. But it is absolutely impossible to furnish a proof of this categorical imperative, just as it is impossible for a geometer to prove ... that to make a triangle he must take three lines .... That I ought to keep a promise is a postulate of pure reason." Immanuel Kant, *The Metaphysics of Morals*, 58–59, § 19 (trans. Mary Gregor) (Cambridge: Cambridge University Press, 1996).

26 John Stuart Mill, "Utilitarianism," in *10 Collected Works of John Stuart Mill*, 203, 207 (Toronto: University of Toronto, 1969).

27 R.M. Hare, "The Promising Game," *Rev. Int'l de Phil.* 18: 398, 408–12 (1964).

28 In upholding choice-of-law clauses, the Privy Counsel importantly expanded freedom of contract. *Vita Food Products Inc.* v. *Unus Shipping Co.* [1939] A.C. 277.

2 Rival theories of contract law

1 This is Scanlon's principle of Loss Prevention. See T.M. Scanlon, *What We Owe to Each Other*, 300–01 (Cambridge: Harvard University Press, 1998).

2 Charles Fried, *Contract as Promise: A Theory of Contractual Obligation*, 10 (Cambridge: Harvard University Press, 1981).

3 Consideration is defined in Restatement (Second) of Contracts § 71 (1981) as the promisee's bargained-for performance or return promise, and is ordinarily a necessary element of his action against the promisor for breach of contract.

4 On reliance as a requirement for promissory estoppel, see Robert A. Hillman, "Questioning the 'New Consensus' on Promissory Estoppel: An Empirical and Theoretical Study," *Colum. L. Rev.* 98: 580 (1998) (reliance is a crucial element in promissory estoppel liability); Sidney W. DeLong, "The New Requirement of Enforcement Reliance in Commercial Promissory Estoppel: Section 90 as Catch 22," *Wisc. L. Rev.*: 943 (1997) (same). These articles cast doubt on earlier studies, which reported that detrimental reliance was not required when the promise had been made seriously. Edward Yorio and Steve Thel, "The Promissory Basis of Section 90," *Yale L. J.* 101: 111 (1991).

5 Grant Gilmore, *The Death of Contract*, 64 (Columbus: Ohio State, 1974).

6 The circularity problem was noted by L. Fuller and W. Perdue, "The Reliance Interest in Contract Damages: 1," *Yale L. J.* 46: 52, 59–60 (1936).

7 Reliance damages might equal expectation damages when the economist's opportunity costs are taken into account. That is, by relying on a promisor, a promisee might have had to forsake an alternative contract, which in competitive markets would offer him a like gain. However, courts will not award an expectation measure as reliance damages unless the promisee can provide clear evidence about the foregone contract.

8 The initial doubts raised about the expectation measure of damages were not tinged with a political agenda. In their study of the reliance measure, Fuller and Perdue described the expectation interest as "a queer kind of compensation," but concluded that it usefully facilitated business arrangements. Fuller and Perdue, *Reliance Interest*, 53. By the 1970s, however, the attack on the expectation measure was bound up with an ideological opposition to free bargaining.

9 Patrick Atiyah, *The Rise and Fall of Freedom of Contract* (Oxford: Oxford University Press, 1976).

10 168 So. 196, aff'd, 168 So. 199 (Ala. Sup. Ct., 1936).

11 As we saw in Chapter 1, promises may serve the evidentiary goal of placing a value on the benefit, and this is what happened in *Webb* v. *McGowan*, where the benefit was the value of the employer's life and not the pension that was the content of the employer's promise. However, the pension was easier to value than the life, and by making the promise the employer showed that he regarded his life as worth at least as much as the pension.

12 See Samuel Williston, "Freedom of Contract," *Cornell L. Q.* 6: 365, 366–67 (1921).

13 Louis Menand, *The Metaphysical Club*, 243–50, 261–67 (New York: Farrar, Straus and Giroux, 2001).

14 *Hegel's Philosophy of Right*, 33 (trans. T.M. Knox) (Oxford: Oxford University Press, 1967).

15 Ibid., 41.

16 "[D]ans sa mystique, l'autonomie de la volonté consacrerait la liberté pour les parties, de contracté *à leur guise*, et sur *tout qui leurs intéresse*, puisque le Code civil les assimile au législateur." Réné Savatier, *La théorie des obligations*, s. 91, 142 (Paris: Dalloz, 1967) (emphasis in original). The reference to the self-legislating contractor was to art. 1134 of the Civil Code: "les conventions légalement formées tiennent lieu de loi à ceux qui les ont faites." ("agreements legally made take the form of a law for those who have made them"). The origin of this idea can be traced as far back as Aquinas. *Summa theologica*, II-II, q. 88, a. 10. In James Gordley's revisionist account of

contracting, will theories were a late scholastic invention from which the Thomistic foundation was burned away in the nineteenth century. James Gordley, *The Philosophical Origins of Modern Contract Doctrine*, 162, 214–29 (Oxford: Clarendon, 1991).

17 "On doit finalement constater que le principe politique de l'autonomie en matière de contrats repose sur une conception individualiste ou libérale de la vie." Hans Kelsen, *La théorie juridique de la convention*, [1940] Archives de philosophie de droit 48.

18 Fried, *Contract as Promise*, 13.

19 Randy Barnett, "A Consent Theory of Contract," *Colum. L. Rev.* 86: 269 (1986).

20 Atiyah, *Rise and Fall of Freedom of Contract*, 6.

21 This kind of positive liberty is to be distinguished from that of Isaiah Berlin's "Two Concepts of Liberty." Isaiah Berlin, *Four Essays on Liberty* (Oxford: Oxford University Press, 1969). Berlin's positive freedom is rational self-direction, and resembles Benjamin Constant's "liberty of the ancients," which refers to the rights of citizens to participate in the political process.

22 Murray Rothbard, *The Ethics of Liberty*, 133–48 (New York: New York University Press, 2002).

23 David Hume, "Of the Original Contract," in Ernest Barker (ed.) *Social Contract*, 145, 160–61 (Oxford: Oxford University Press, 1970).

24 John Rawls, *A Theory of Justice*, 112 (Cambridge: Harvard University Press, 1971). For an argument that fair play obligations do not arise unless the recipient has voluntarily agreed to the receipt, see A. John Simmons, *Moral Principles and Political Obligation*, ch. 5 (Princeton: Princeton University Press, 1979).

25 Hegel, *Philosophy of Right*, 63.

26 Hugo Grotius, *II De Jure Belli et Pacis*, 330–31, XI.iv (F.W. Kelsey trans.) (Oxford: Clarendon, 1925).

27 Immanuel Kant, *The Metaphysics of Morals*, 59, § 20 (trans. Mary Gregor) (Cambridge: Cambridge University Press, 1996).

28 Ibid., 56.

29 Richard Craswell, "Contract Law, Default Rules, and the Philosophy of Promising," *Mich. L. Rev.* 88: 489, 514–15 (1989).

3 The economic theory of contract law

1 Rawls, "Two Concepts of Rules," 64.

2 Hume, *Treatise of Human Nature*, 514, III.ii.IV. In Smith's encomium to specialization, the day-laborer's woolen coat could not have been bought without the joint labor of "the shepherd, the sorter of the wool, the wool-comber or carder, the dyer, the scribbler, the spinner, the weaver, the fuller, the dresser," to say nothing of the delivery-men, wholesalers and retailers. Adam Smith, *The Wealth of Nations Books I-III*, I.i, 116 (London: Penguin, 1999).

3 Hume, *Treatise of Human Nature*, 520–21, III.ii.V.

4 In the original Prisoners' Dilemma game, the parties have been arrested and charged with burglary. The prosecutor has evidence to convict on a lesser charge, but unless he can get a confession they will be acquitted of burglary. Accordingly, the prosecutor keeps the parties apart and offers each a deal: if you confess to burglary and the other party doesn't, you'll get a break at sentencing. Defection means confessing, but this is what each party does, since each fears the sucker's payoff where he keeps silent and the other implicates him in return for sweetheart treatment by the prosecutor. The parties would be better off if they could adhere to a code of "honor among thieves" and cooperate by keeping silent.

5 To simplify, we assume a world without interest rates or time-value of money.
6 Charles Goetz and Robert Scott, "Enforcing Promises: An Examination of the Basis of Contract," *Yale L. J.* 89: 1261 (1980).
7 Thomas Hobbes, *Leviathan*, 231 (London: Penguin, 1968) [1651].
8 George Akerlof, "The Market for 'Lemons': Quality Uncertainty and the Market Mechanism," *Quarterly Journal of Economics* 84: 488 (1970).
9 Even in those states a party might exit a no-exit "covenant" marriage through an out-of-state no-fault divorce.
10 Margaret F. Bring and F.H. Buckley, "No-Fault Laws and At-Fault People," *Int'l Rev. Law and Econ.* 18: 325 (1998).
11 Michael A. Spence, "Job Market Signaling," *Q. J. Econ.* 87: 355 (1973). See, generally, Eric Rasmusen, *Games and Information: An Introduction to Game Theory*, 205–11 (Cambridge: Blackwell, 2nd edn, 1994).
12 See, generally, Daniel B. Klein, *Reputation: Studies in the Voluntary Elicitation of Good Conduct* (Ann Arbor: Michigan, 1997). The success of E-Bay owes something to its ability to replicate reputational signaling on the Internet. After a sale, buyers are invited to rate the seller's performance, and these ratings are posted for future buyers. This gives sellers a stronger incentive to perform in good faith. Even where a game is not repeated, as in E-Bay, there is experimental evidence that parties approach a bargain with an instinct to cooperate rather than to defect. Andres Ortmann, John Fitzgerald and Carl Boeing, "Trust, Reciprocity, and Social History: A Re-Examination," *Exp. Econ.* 3: 81 (2000).
13 Robert Trivers, "The Evolution of Reciprocal Altruism," *Quart. Rev. Biology* 46: 35–57 (1971).
14 Robert Axelrod, *The Evolution of Cooperation* (New York: Basic, 1984).
15 In the Axelrod round-robin, a colleague of mine submitted the ALL-D strategy, which defeated TFT and was not defeated by any other strategy. However, TFT did a great deal better than ALL-D when played against more cooperative strategies, and did considerably better than ALL-D overall.
16 Lester G. Telser, "A Theory of Self-enforcing Agreements," *J. Bus.* 22: 1 (1980); Benjamin Klein and Keith Leffler, "The Role of Market Forces in Assuring Contractual Performance," *J. Pol. Econ.* 89: 615 (1981).
17 Janet Tai Landa, *Trust, Ethnicity, and Identity: Beyond the New Institutional Economics of Ethnic Trading Networks, Contract Law, and Gift Exchange* (Ann Arbor: University of Michigan Press, 1994).
18 For a biological explanation of kinship preferences on theories of "inclusive fitness," see Martin Daly and Margo Wilson, *Sex, Evolution, and Behavior*, 279, 281 (Boston: Willard Grant, 2nd edn, 1983); W.D. Hamilton, "The Genetical Evolution of Social Behaviour I," *J. Theoretical Biology* 7: 1, 8 (1964); W.D. Hamilton, "The Genetical Evolution of Social Behaviour II," *J. Theoretical Biology* 7: 17 (1964).
19 Deut. 23:19–20. See also Deut. 28:12 and Lev. 25:35–37; and see, generally, Marc Shell, *Money, Language, and Thought*, ch. 3 (Berkeley: California, 1982); Lewis Hyde, *The Gift: Imagination and the Erotic Life of Property* (New York: Vintage, 1979). The Biblical distinction sensibly permitted Jewish lenders to levy interest on gentile borrowers, since gentile lenders were not under an obligation to lend on an interest-free basis to Jewish borrowers.
20 Ruth Benedict, *The Chrysanthemum and the Sword: Patterns of Japanese Culture* (New York: Mariner Books, 1989).
21 Psychologist Michael Lewis identifies an interior sense of shame in the emotional pain felt by those who are shamed. Michael Lewis, *Shame: The Exposed Self*, 75–77 (New York: Free Press, 1992). For Lewis, guilt is a less intensive emotion than shame, and one more easily dissipated through

corrective action. But even here shame assumes a reputational loss and guilt does not.

22 Richard Wollheim, *On the Emotions*, 190–92 (New Haven: Yale University Press, 1999).
23 Ronit Bodner and Drazen Prelec, "Self-Signaling and Diagnostic Utility in Everyday Decision Making" (unpublished paper, 2001).
24 Robert H. Frank, "If *Homo Economicus* Could Choose his own Utility Function, Would He Want One with a Conscience?," *Am. Econ. Rev.* 77:593 (1987). See, further, Robert H. Frank, *Passions within Reason: The Strategic Role of the Emotions* (New York: Norton, 1988); Jack Hirshleifer, "The Emotions as Guarantors of Threats and Promises," in John Dupré (ed.) *The Latest on the Best*, 307 (Cambridge: MIT Press, 1987). From an evolutionary perspective, our emotional responses to particular environments might have been selected for survival because they serve us in social competition. This suggestion has been labeled the "Machiavellian Emotion Hypothesis" by Paul Griffiths in "Basic Emotions, Complex Emotions, Machiavellian Emotions," in Anthony Hatzimoysis (ed.) *Philosophy and the Emotions*, 39 (Cambridge: Cambridge University Press, 2003).
25 Individuals seem to possess a remarkable ability to identify defectors. Leda Cosmides and John Tooby, "Cognitive Adaptation for Social Exchange," in Jerome H. Barkow, Leda Cosmides and John Tooby, *The Adapted Mind: Evolutionary Psychology and the Generation of Culture*, 163 (New York: Oxford, 1992).
26 "Si l'homme savait rougir de soi, quels crimes, non seulement cachés, mais publics et connus, ne s'épargnerait-it pas!" Jean de La Bruyère, *Les characters*, xi, 151, 276 (Paris: Bookking, 1993).
27 Patricia Meyer Spacks, *Gossip*, 29 (New York: Knopf, 1985).
28 Charles Darwin, *The Expression of the Emotions in Man and Animals*, 202 (New York: Oxford, 1998) [1872]; Paul Ekman, Wallace V. Friesen and Maureen O'Sullivan, "Smiles when Lying," in Paul Ekman and Erika L. Rosenberg, *What the Face Reveals*, 201 (New York: Oxford, 1997); Paul Ekman, *Telling Lies: Clues to Deceit in the Marketplace, Politics, and Marriage* (New York: Norton, 1985). On laughter as a signaling mechanism, see F.H. Buckley, *The Morality of Laughter*, 180–84 (Ann Arbor: University of Michigan Press, 2003).
29 Benjamin Klein, B.R. Crawford and A. Alchian, "Vertical Integration, Appropriable Rents and the Competitive Contracting Process," *J. L. & Econ.* 21: 297, 308–10 (1978).
30 This conflates three different bonding strategies discussed by Anthony Kronman: hostages, collateral and hands-tying. Anthony Kronman, "Contract Law in the State of Nature," *J. L. Econ. & Org.* 1: 1 (1985). What is common to all three strategies is that the promisor makes his promise more credible by a deliberate choice to make defection more painful. On bonding strategies, see, generally, Jon Elster, *Ulysses Unbound*, 64–77 (Cambridge: Cambridge University Press, 2000).
31 Jon Elster, *Ulysses and the Sirens: Studies in Rationality and Irrationality* (New York: Cambridge, 1984).
32 See also Oliver E. Williamson, "Credible Commitments: Using Hostages To Support Exchange," *Am. Econ. Rev.* 73: 519 (1983).
33 Stewart Macaulay, "Non-contractual Relations in Business: A Preliminary Study," *Am. Soc. Rev.* 28: 55 (1963); Ian R. MacNeil, "The Many Futures of Contracts," *S. Cal. L. Rev.* 47: 691 (1974).
34 Edward C. Banfield, *The Moral Basis of a Backward Society*, 116 (Glencoe, IL: Free Press, 1958).

4 Fidelity to promising

1 Respect requirements are similar to Scanlon's Principle of Due Care, in *What We Owe to Each Other*, 300, with the difference that Scanlon believes they might account for the institution of promising. This suffers from the same circularity problem we saw in Chapter 2 when considering reliance theories: promisee reliance cannot explain why promisees are entitled to rely. The Respect requirement I propose avoids this problem by assuming that the institution already exists. Scanlon has since come to adopt something close to the natural duties of support we discuss in the next section, "as rules that are morally obligatory in virtue of their general acceptance and social usefulness." T.M. Scanlon, "Reason, Responsibility, and Reliance: Replies to Wallace, Dworkin, and Deigh," *Ethics* 112: 507, 523 (2002).

2 A. John Simmons, *Moral Principles and Political Obligations*, 166–67 (Princeton: Princeton University Press, 1979).

3 A. John Simmons, *On the Edge of Anarchy: Locke, Consent, and the Limits of Society*, 257 n. 84 (Princeton: Princeton University Press, 1993). Political obligations might be different. While gratitude theories cannot explain why we are bound to perform our promises, we might owe a debt of gratitude to a state. The patriot is not self-interested, and his countrymen who benefit from his sacrifice might owe a debt of gratitude to him. Whether this grounds political obligations depends on whether duties owed to the patriot are somehow passed up through him to the state.

4 John Rawls, *A Theory of Justice*, 343 (Cambridge: Harvard University Press, 1971). Earlier versions of the principle of fairness, then called the principle of fair play, may be found in John Rawls, "Justice as Fairness," *Phil. Rev.* 67: 164, 180–84 (1958). See also H.L.A. Hart, "Are There any Natural Rights?," *Phil. Rev.* 64: 175, 185 (1955). The earliest version is found in Plato's *Crito*.

5 See Robert Nozick, *Anarchy, State, and Utopia*, 93–94 (Cambridge: Harvard University Press, 1974).

6 Hume, "Of the Original Contract," 145 at 156.

7 Simmons, *On the Edge of Anarchy*, 254–57.

8 Oswald Hanfling, "Promises, Games, and Institutions," *Proc. Aristotelian Soc.* 75: 13, 22 (1974–75) (non-rejectable institutions like promising must be distinguished from rejectable institutions like games).

9 For a similar reading of Locke's tacit consent, see Hanna Pitkin, "Obligation and Consent-I," *Am. Pol. Sc. Rev.* 60: 39 (1966).

10 This was the basis of Dworkin's argument against Richard Posner's contractarian defense of wealth maximization norms. Ronald Dworkin, "Why Efficiency?," *Hofstra L. Rev.* 8: 563, 574–79 (1980). David Gauthier's contractarian defense of constrained maximization norms also must be thought to assume that such norms are valuable whether or not one consents to them. David Gauthier, *Morals by Agreement*, 167–70 (1986).

11 Something like a natural duty of support is suggested in Niko Kolodny and R. Jay Wallace, "Promises and Practices Revisited," *Phil. & Pub. Aff.* 31: 119, 150 (2003).

12 Edmund Burke, "Appeal from the New to the Old Whigs," in Edmund Burke, *Further Reflections on the Revolution in France*, 73, 159–60 (Indianapolis: Liberty Fund, 1992).

13 Sir Robert Filmer, "The Anarchy of a Limited or Mixed Monarchy," in *Patriarcha and Other Writings*, 157 (Cambridge: Cambridge University Press, 1991).

14 Edmund Burke, *Reflections on the Revolution in France*, 161–62 (Oxford: Oxford, 1993). For other defenses of positional fidelity requirements, see

F.H. Bradley, "My Station and its Duties," in *Ethical Studies* (Indianapolis: Bobbs-Merrill, 1951); Alasdair MacIntyre, *After Virtue*, 199 (Notre Dame: Notre Dame Press, 1981).

15 Simmons, *Moral Principles and Political Obligations*, 18–19.

16 Corresponding to these two propositions are two kinds of anarchism. The political anarchist argues that states are unjust and that as a consequence we need not obey their rules. The philosophical anarchist does not take a position on the morality or immorality of states; instead, he argues that the principle of fidelity that links the individual to a state can never be satisfied, so that no one ever owes allegiance duties. In either case, no state could ever command the political allegiance of an individual. In rejecting positional allegiance requirements, Simmons is a philosophical but not a political anarchist.

17 As is argued, wrongly in my view, by T.M. Scanlon, *What We Owe to Each Other*, 316 (Cambridge: Harvard University Press, 1998).

18 This argument is made in Kolodny and Wallace, "Promises and Practices Revisited," 123.

5 Soft paternalism

1 Parfit, *Reasons and Persons*, 46.

2 See Gerald Dworkin, "Paternalism: Some Second Thoughts," in Rolf Sartorius (ed.), *Paternalism* 105, 107 (Minneapolis: University of Minnesota Press, 1983).

3 This is not a term of art, and is sometimes taken to refer to theories of ethics that define the good as the fulfillment of a common human nature. See Rawls, *A Theory of Justice*, 25; Thomas Hunka, *Perfectionism* (New York: Oxford University Press, 1993). However, I take perfectionism to mean the anti-neutralist belief that the state is entitled to promote its view of the good, which is how the term is used in George Sher, *Beyond Neutrality: Perfectionism and Politics* (Cambridge: Cambridge University Press, 1997).

4 Restatement (Second) of Contracts § 14.

5 The economic need for security of contracting explains one of the exceptions to the birthday standard. Where the minor presents a fake I.D. to the adult merchant, the minor is normally barred from asserting the defense of incapacity. Otherwise, the benefits of the bright-line rule would be impaired and the risk of unenforceability would increase. However, this assumes that the minor actually presented an I.D. A simple representation that "I am eighteen" would not suffice, as this would permit merchants to do an end-run around the law of capacity through boilerplate language in the contract. *Kiefer* v. *Fred Howe Motors, Inc.*, 158 N.W. 288 (Wisc. Sup. Ct., 1968).

6 *Aldrich* v. *Bailey*, 132 N.Y. 85, 87–88 (1892).

7 *Faber* v. *Sweet Style Mfg. Corp.*, 242 N.Y.S.2d 763 (Sup. Ct., Trial Term, 1963).

8 *Williamson* v. *Matthews*, 379 So.2d 1245 (Ala. Sup. Ct., 1980).

9 242 N.Y.S.2d 765.

10 David E. Bernstein, *Only One Place of Redress: African Americans, Labor Regulations, and the Courts from Reconstruction to the New Deal* (Durham, NC: Duke University Press, 2001).

11 *Williams* v. *Fears*, 179 U.S. 270 (1900), aff'g, 35 S.E. 699 (Ga.).

12 John Stuart Mill, *On Liberty*, 9 (Indianapolis: Hackett, 1978).

13 David M. Levy, *How the Dismal Science Got its Name: Classical Economics and the Ur-Text of Racial Politics*, 19–20 (Ann Arbor: University of Michigan Press, 2001).

14 Wendy McElroy, *Individualist Feminism of the Nineteenth Century: Collected Writings and Biographical Profiles* (New York: McFarland, 2001); Wendy

McElroy, *Freedom, Feminism and the State* (Oakland: Independent Institute, 2nd edn, 1991).

15 Alison M. Jagger, *Feminist Politics and Human Nature*, 148 (Totowa, NJ: Rowman and Littlefield, 1988). See also Frances Olsen, "From False Paternalism to False Equality: Judicial Assaults on Feminist Community, Illinois 1869–1895," *Mich. L. Rev.* 84: 1518, 1522, 1531–34 (1986); Ann Scales, "The Emergence of a Feminist Jurisprudence: An Essay," *Yale L. J.* 95: 1373 (1986).

16 John C. Calhoun, *Union and Liberty: The Political Philosophy of John C. Calhoun*, 467 (Indianapolis: Liberty Fund, 1992); Margaret L. Coit, *John C. Calhoun: American Patriot*, 300–02 (Boston: Houghton Mifflin, 1950). The affinities between Marxist and reactionary anti-market views are perfectly illustrated in the scholarship of Eugene Genovese. See Eugene D. Genovese, *The World the Slaveholders Made*, 124–27 (Middletown, CT: Wesleyan, 1988).

17 Arthur Leff, "Unconscionability and the Code – The Emperors' New Clause," *U. Pa. L. Rev.* 115: 485, 557 (1967).

18 Ironically, the revival of paternalism in contract law took place at the same time that the concept of incapacity was narrowed in mental health law, as seen in the deinstitutionalization movement, which emptied mental hospitals in the 1980s. See Sally Satel, *P.C.M.D: How Political Correctness Is Corrupting Medicine* (Basic Books: New York, 2000). When non-discrimination is the highest value, we are all a little off and we are none of us off; crucially, we are all the same.

19 Steven Pinker, *How the Mind Works*, ch. 4 (New York: Norton, 1997).

20 Paul Slovic, Melissa Finucane, Ellen Peters and Donald G. MacGregor, "The Affect Heuristic," in Thomas Gilovich, Dale Griffin and Daniel Kahneman, *Heuristics and Biases: The Psychology of Intuitive Judgment*, 397 (Cambridge: Cambridge University Press, 2002); Norbert Schwarz, "Feelings as Information: Moods Influence Judgments and Processing Strategies," ibid., 534. For an evolutionary account of emotional prompts, see John Tooby and Leda Cosmides, "The Past Explains the Present: Emotional Adaptation and the Structure of Ancestral Environments," *Ethol. Sociobiol.* 11: 375 (1990).

21 Robert B. Zajonc, "Feeling and Thinking: Preferences Need No Inferences," *Am. Psychol.* 35: 151, 154 (1980).

22 Robert Boyd and Peter J. Richerson, "Norms and Bounded Rationality," in Gerd Gigerenzer and Reinhard Selten (eds), *Bounded Rationality: The Adaptive Toolbox*, 281 (Cambridge: MIT Press, 2001).

23 Anthony Damasio, *Descartes' Error*, 193–94 (New York: Putnam, 1994).

24 Ibid., 169. See also Paul Slovic *et al.*, "The Affect Heuristic," in Gilovich, Griffin and Kahneman, *Heuristics and Biases*, 397.

25 Steven Mithen, *The Prehistory of the Mind: A Search for the Origins of Art, Religion, and Science*, 11 (London: Thames and Hudson, 1996).

26 Paul M. Churchland, *Matter and Consciousness: A Contemporary Introduction to the Philosophy of Mind*, 36–37 (Cambridge: MIT Press, 1986).

27 Institutions and culture also economize on mental calculation and information search. The introduction of money in an economy permits the development of market prices that contain information about the preferences of thousands of anonymous buyers and sellers. Contract law, with its stock of implied terms, also economizes on bargaining by making it unnecessary for the parties to settle all of their terms. For example, when a contract of sale is silent about quality, a term that the goods are fit is implied by sales law. We also operate in a culture in which winks, nods, grimaces and sighs all have a special meaning, and this reduces the costs of intra-cultural negotiations.

28 G.E. Hinton, "Mapping Part-whole Hierarchies into Connectionist Networks," *Artificial Intelligence* 46: 47 (1990).

29 For a useful overview, see Matthew Rabin, "Psychology and Economics," *J. Econ. Litt.* 36: 11 (1998).

30 Amos Tversky and Daniel Kahneman, "Availability: A Heuristic for Judging Frequency and Probability," in Daniel Kahneman, Paul Slovic and Amos Tversky (eds), *Judgment Under Uncertainty: Heuristics and Biases*, 163 (Cambridge: Cambridge University Press, 1982).

31 Amos Tversky and Daniel Kahneman, "Introduction," in Kahneman, Slovic and Tversky, *Judgment Under Uncertainty*, 14.

32 Daniel Kahneman and Amos Tversky, "Subjective Probability: A Judgment of Representativeness," in Kahneman, Slovik and Tversky, *Judgment Under Uncertainty*, 32.

33 See, e.g. Daniel Kahneman and Shane Frederick, "Representativeness Revisted: Attribute Substitution in Intuitive Judgment," in Gilovich, Griffin and Kahneman, *Heuristics and Biases*, 49, 51.

34 See, generally, Helmut Jungermann, "The Two Camps on Rationality," in R.W. Scholz, *Decision Making Under Uncertainty*, 63 (Amsterdam: Elsevier, 1983), reprinted in Terry Connolly, Hal R. Arkes and Kenneth R. Hammond, *Judgment and Decision Making: An Interdisciplinary Reader*, 575 (Cambridge: Cambridge University Press, 2nd edn, 2000).

35 P.S. Laplace, *A Philosophical Essay on Probabilities* (F.W. Truscott and F.L. Emory, trans.) (New York: Dover, 1951) [1814].

36 See Gerd Gigerenzer, *Adaptive Thinking: Rationality in the Real World*, 60–63 (Oxford; Oxford University Press, 2000); Peter Sedlmeier and Gerd Gigerenzer, "Teaching Bayesian Reasoning in Less Than Two Hours," *J. Exp. Psych.* 130: 380 (2001); Jonathan J. Koehler, "The Base Rate Fallacy Reconsidered: Descriptive, Normative and Methodological Challenges," *Behavioral and Brain Sc.* 19: 1 (1996).

37 This is not to suggest that people always turn into rational calculators when problems are presented in the form of frequencies. For a review of the psychological evidence, see Thomas Gilovich and Dale Griffin, "Introduction – Heuristics and Biases, Then and Now," in Gilovich, Griffin and Kahneman, *Heuristics and Biases*, 1, 14–15.

38 Cass R. Sunstein, "Introduction," in Cass R. Sunstein (ed.) *Behavioral Law and Economics*, 4 (Cambridge: Cambridge University Press, 2000). See Roger Buehler, Dale Griffin and Michael Ross, "Inside the Planning Fallacy: The Causes and Consequences of Optimism Time Predictions," in Gilovich, Griffin and Kahneman, *Heuristics and Biases*, 250.

39 Daniel Kahneman and Amos Tversky, "Choices, Values, and Frames," in Daniel Kahneman and Amos Tversky, *Choices, Values, and Frames*, 1, 2–4 (Cambridge: Cambridge University Press, 2000). For small probabilities of gains and losses the shape of the curves are reversed. For example, we seem to be risk-seeking for lotteries with a very small probability of a high payoff. Ibid., 54.

40 Daniel Kahneman and Amos Tversky, "Prospect Theory: An Analysis of Decision Under Risk," *Econometrica* 47: 263 (1979).

41 David A. Armor and Shelley E. Taylor, "When Predictions Fail: The Dilemma of Unrealistic Optimism," in Gilovich, Griffin and Kahneman, *Heuristics and Biases*, 334, 341.

42 Daniel Kahneman and Dale T. Miller, "Norm Theory: Comparing Reality to its Alternatives," *Psychol. Rev.* 93: 136 (1986). See also Dale T. Miller and Brian R. Taylor, "Counterfactual Thought, Regret, and Superstition: How to Avoid Kicking Yourself," in Gilovich, Griffin and Kahneman, *Heuristics and Biases*, 367.

43 Richard Thaler, "Toward a Positive Theory of Consumer Choice," *J. Econ. Beh. & Org.* 1: 39 (1980); Daniel Kahneman, Jack L. Knetch and Richard

H. Thaler, "Experimental Tests of the Endowment Effect and the Coase Theorem," *J. Pol. Econ.* 98: 1325 (1990). The endowment effect can be seen as an example of the loss aversion shown in Figure 5.1.

44 Richard A. Posner, *Frontiers of Legal Theory*, 273–74 (Cambridge: Harvard University Press, 2001). A study that found that selling price equaled buying price when the mugs were awarded to low scorers in a skills test is consistent with Posner's explanation. George Lowenstein and Samuel Issacharoff, "Source Dependence in the Valuation of Objects," *J. Behavioral Decision Making* 7: 157 (1994). There was no status loss when the low scorer sold his booby prize.

45 R.M. Hogarth, "Beyond Discrete Biases: Functional and Dysfunctional Aspects of Judgmental Heuristics," *Psychol. Bul.* 90: 197 (1981).

46 Maya Bar-Hillel, "On the Subjective Probability of Compound Events," *Org. Behav. and Hum. Performance* 9: 396 (1973).

47 Daniel Kahneman and Amos Tversky, "On the Study of Statistical Intuitions," in Kahneman, Sloviç and Tversky, *Judgment Under Uncertainty*, 493, 496.

48 For evidence of underweighing new evidence that conflicts with settled beliefs, see Ward Edwards, "Conservatism in Human Information Processing," in B. Kleinmuntz (ed.) *Formal Representation of Human Judgment*, 17 (New York: Wiley, 1968).

49 For evidence of learning in repeated experiments, see David S. Brookshire and Don L. Coursey, "Measuring the Value of a Public Good: An Empirical Comparison of Elicitation Procedure," *Am. Econ. Rev.* 77: 554 (1987); Colin F. Camerer, "Progress in Behavioral Game Theory," *J. Econ. Persp.* 11: 167 (1997).

50 On the real world persistence of overconfidence, see Hillel J. Einhorn and Robin M. Hogarth, "Confidence in Judgment: Persistence of the Illusion of Validity," *Psych. Rev.* 85: 395 (1978).

51 See Vernon L. Smith, Gerry L. Suchanek and A.W. Williams, "Bubbles, Crashes, and Endogenous Expectations in Experimental Spot Asset Markets," *Econometrica* 56: 1119 (1988); Nejat H. Seyhun, "Why Does Aggregate Insider Trading Predict Future Stock Returns?," *Q. J. Econ.* 107: 1303 (1992); Andrei Shleifer, *Inefficient Markets: An Introduction to Behavioral Finance*, 112–53 (Oxford: Clarendon, 2000).

52 Vernon L. Smith, "Theory, Experiment and Economics," *J. Econ. Persp.* 3: 151 (1989); Vernon L. Smith, "Rational Choice: The Contrast Between Economics and Psychology," *J. Pol. Econ.* 90: 877 (1991). In one experiment, subjects were less affected by the endowment effect when they were told they were acting as agents for another. Jennifer Arlen, Matthew Spitzer and Eric Talley, "Endowment Effects within Corporate Agency Relationships," *J. Legal Stud.* 31: 1 (2002). However, cognitive errors among investors have been found to survive in market settings. David Hirshleifer, "Investor Psychology and Asset Pricing," *J. Fin.* 56: 1533 (2001).

53 Jack L. Knetsch, *Property Rights and Compensation: Compulsory Acquisition and Other Losses* (Toronto: Butterworths, 1983).

54 Russell Korobkin, "The Endowment Effect and Legal Analysis," *Nw. U. L. Rev.* 97: 1227, 1228 (2003).

55 Samuel Issacharoff, "Contracting for Employment: The Limited Return of the Common Law," *Tex. L. Rev.* 74: 1783 (1996).

56 Deborah M. Weiss, "Paternalistic Pension Policy: Psychological Evidence and Economic Theory," *U. Chi. L. Rev.* 58: 1275 (1991).

57 Thomas H. Jackson, *The Logic and Limits of Bankruptcy Law*, 238–39 (Cambridge: Harvard University Press, 1986).

58 Ulrich Hoffrage, Ralph Hertwig and Gerd Gigerenzer, "Hindsight Bias: A By-Product of Knowledge Updating?," *J. Exp. Psych: Learning, Memory, and Cognition* 26: 566 (2000).

59 *Cotton* v. *Buckeye Gas Products*, 840 F.2d 935, 937–38 (D.C. Cir. 1988).
60 Christine Jolls, Cass S. Sunstein and Richard Thaler, "A Behavioral Approach to Law & Economics," *Stan. L. Rev.* 50: 1471, 1529–30 (1998); Donald C. Langevoort, "Behavioral Theories of Judgment and Decision Making in Legal Scholarship: A Literature Review," *Vand. L. Rev.* 51: 1499, 1508–10 (1998); Mark Kelman, Yuval Rottenstreich and Amos Tversky, "Context-Dependence in Legal Decision Making," *J. Legal Stud.* 25: 287 (1996).
61 Jeffrey J. Rachlinski, "A Positive Psychological Theory of Judging in Hindsight," *U. Chi. L. Rev.* 65: 571 (1998).
62 Hal R. Arkes and Cindy A. Schipani, "Medical Malpractice v. the Business Judgment Rule: Differences in Hindsight Bias," *Or. L. Rev.* 73: 587 (1994).
63 Jolls *et al.*, "A Behavioral Approach," *Stan. L. Rev.* 50: 1520–22.
64 See George Stigler, "The Economics of Information," *J. Pol. Econ.* 69: 213 (1961); John Conlisk, "Why Bounded Rationality?," *J. Econ. Persp.* 34: 669 (1996).
65 Herbert A. Simon, "Rational Choice and the Structure of Environments," *Psych. Rev.* 63: 129 (1956).
66 For a useful survey, see Eldar Shafir and Robyn A. LeBoeuf, "Rationality," *Ann. Rev. Psychol.* 53: 491 (2002).
67 Colin F. Camerer and Robin M. Hogarth, "The Effect of Financial Incentives in Experiments: A Review and Capital-Labor-Production Framework," *J. Risk and Uncertainty* 19: 7, 33 (1999).
68 Donald A. Redelmeir and Eldar Shafir, "Medical Decision Making in Situations that Offer Multiple Alternatives," *JAMA* 273: 302 (1995).
69 For examples of a more sophisticated understanding of cognitive paternalism's limits, see Jeffrey J. Rachlinski, "The Uncertain Psychological Case for Paternalism," *Nw. U. L. Rev.* 97: 1165 (2003); Jolls *et al.*, "A Behavioral Approach," 1471.
70 On weakness of the will, see, generally, Jon Elster, *Ulysses and the Sirens* (Cambridge: Cambridge University Press, rev. edn, 1984); Alfred R. Mele, *Autonomous Agents: From Self-Control to Autonomy* (Oxford: Oxford University Press, 2001); Alfred R. Mele, *Irrationality: An Essay on Akrasia, Self-deception, and Self-control* (New York: Oxford University Press, 1987).
71 "Son crime est plutôt une punition des Dieux, qu'un movement de sa volonté." Jean Racine, Phèdre, Préface, in *I Œuvres complètes Théâtre-Poésie*, 815, 817 (Paris: Pléiade, 1999).
72 On Jansenism's righteous sinner, see Blaise Pascal, *II Œuvres complètes, Pensée*, 220 (Paris: Pléiade, 2000); Leszek Kolakowski, *God Owes Us Nothing: A Brief Remark on Pascal's Religion and on the Spirit of Jansenism*, 9–14 (Chicago: University of Chicago Press, 1995).
73 "Si nous résistons à nos passions, c'est plus par leur faiblesse que par notre force." François de La Rochefoucauld, *Maximes et réflexions diverses*, n. 122 (Paris: Gallimard, 1976).
74 Douglas Glen Whitmas, "Meta-Preferences and Multiple Selves," mimeo, November 3, 2003.
75 "Il l'aborda en disant: 'Salut, comte Tolstoi.' Et l'autre lui dit: 'Vous vous trompez, je ne suis celui que vous croyez. Que voulez-vous de Tolstoi?' 'Je viens saluer l'auteur d'*Anna Karénine* et de *la Guerre et la paix*.' 'Celui-là est mort.' 'Alors, je viens saluer l'auteur de *Rédemption*, de … .' 'Celui-là, c'est moi.'" Maurice Barrès, *Mes cahiers 1896–1923*, 718 (Paris: Plon, 1994).
76 537 A.2d 1227 (N.J. Sup. Ct., 1987).
77 Alfred R. Mele, *Self-deception Unmasked* (Princeton: Princeton University Press, 2001). See also Alfred R. Mele, *Motivation and Agency* (New York: Oxford

University Press, 2003); Annette Barnes, *Seeing Through Self-deception* (Cambridge: Cambridge University Press, 1997).

78 Robert Trivers, "The Elements of a Scientific Theory of Self-deception," mimeo, 2003; Wiliam von Hippel, Richard J. Shakarchi and Jessica L. Larkin,"Self-serving Bias and Self-deception," mimeo, 2003.

79 Raphael Demos, "Lying to Oneself," *J. Phil.* 57: 588 (1960); Donald Davidson, "Deception and Division," in Jon Elster (ed.) *The Multiple Self*, 79 (Cambridge: Cambridge University Press, 1986).

80 Alfred R. Mele, *Irrationality*, 123 (New York: Oxford University Press, 1987).

81 Blaise Pascal, *II Œuvres complètes, Pensée*, 43 (Paris: Pléiade, 2000). Psychologists report that patients may exhibit the physical symptoms of depression before they realize they are depressed. Michael Lewis, *Shame*, 15–16 (New York: Free Press, 1992). Jon Elster's *Alchemies of the Mind*, 107–31 (Cambridge: Cambridge University Press, 1999) provides a fascinating study of how self-deception has been portrayed in literature.

82 See George Ainslie, *Picoeconomics: The Strategic Interaction of Successive Motivational States within the Person* (New York: Cambridge University Press, 1992).

83 Reinhart Selten, "What is Bounded Rationality?," in Gigerenzer and Selten, *Bounded Rationality*, 13, 32–33.

84 Richard H. Thaler, *The Winner's Curse: Paradoxes and Anomalies of Economic Life*, 99–100 (Princeton: Princeton University Press, 1992).

85 The manner in which hyperbolic discounting tests are framed might also determine the results, with people simply preferring the most salient outcomes. Ariel Rubenstein, "'Economics and Psychology'? The Case of Hyperbolic Discounting," *International Economic Review* 44: 1207 (2003).

86 Aristotle, *Nicomachean Ethics*, VII.3. (trans. Roger Crisp) (Cambridge: Cambridge University Press, 2000). See also Donald Davidson, "How Is Weakness of the Will Possible?," in Joel Feinberg (ed.) *Moral Concepts*, 93 (Oxford: Clarendon Press, 1970).

87 Amelie O. Rorty, "Akrasia and Conflict," *Inquiry* 22: 193 (1980); Amelie Rorty, "Self-deception, Akrasia and Irrationality," *Soc. Sc. Information* 19: 905 (1980), reprinted in Jon Elster (ed.) *The Multiple Self*, 115 (Cambridge: Cambridge University Press, 1986).

88 Elster, *Ulysses and the Sirens*, 65–66.

89 George Orwell, *4 Collected Essays, Journalism, and Letters*, 527 (Harmondsworth: Penguin, 1970).

90 Friedrich Nietzsche, *Thus Spoke Zarathustra*, 46–47 (London: Penguin, 1961) [1885].

91 "La société demande autre chose encore. Il ne lui suffit pas de vivre; elle tient à vivre *bien*." Henri Bergson, *Le rire*, 14 (Paris: P.U.F., 1940). See also Tyler Cowen, "Self-Constraint and Self-Liberation," *Ethics* 101: 360 (1991).

92 Gary S. Becker and Kevin Murphy, "A Theory of Rational Addiction," *J. Pol. Econ.* 96: 675–700 (1988). Another, more intuitive, definition of addiction focuses on the price elasticity of addictive goods. Prices are elastic when a small change in price is associated with a large change in consumption. The popular conception of addiction is a psychological craving that cannot be denied. Were this so, the demand for tobacco and hard drugs would be highly inelastic: the addict would willingly pay the higher price to maintain his level of consumption. In fact, smokers and heavy drinkers are sensitive to price changes of tobacco and alcohol. See Gary S. Becker, "An Empirical Analysis of Cigarette Addiction," *Am. Econ. Rev.* 84: 396–418 (1994), reprinted in Gary S. Becker (ed.) *Accounting for Tastes*, 85 (Cambridge: Harvard University Press, 1996); Philip J. Cook and George Tauchen, "The Effect of Liquor Taxes

on Heavy Drinking," *Bell J. Econ.* 13: 379–90 (1982). For a review of the psychologist's understanding of addiction, see Jon Elster, *Strong Feeling*, chs 3, 5 (Cambridge: MIT Press, 1999).

93 Becker's definition of addiction adds a further condition of tolerance: the more the addict has consumed the addictive good in the past, the less pleasure he gets from a given present consumption level. In my examples, this would be true of heroin but not coffee or classical music.

94 Other explanations are suggested in Jon Elster, *Strong Feelings*, 171–73 (Cambridge: MIT Press, 1999). In addition, addiction might result from a calculated gamble by inexperienced individuals who do not know that they are prone to addiction, where the good is pleasant for most people and the probability of addiction is low. Athanasios Orphanides and David Zervos, "Rational Addiction with Learning and Regret," *J. Pol. Econ.* 103: 739 (1995).

95 Thomas H. Jackson, *The Logic and Limits of Bankruptcy Law*, 234–37 (Cambridge: Harvard University Press, 1986).

96 Michael Jensen, "The Agency Costs of Free Cash Flow, Corporate Finance, and Takeovers," *Am. Econ. Rev.* 76: 323 (1986).

97 Steven F. Venti and David A. Wise, "Aging and the Income Value of Housing Wealth," *J. Pol. Econ.* 44: 371 (1991).

98 More accurately, the tax subsidy comes from the fact that homeowners are not required to report the value of their use of their home as income. Apartment owners can also deduct mortgage interest as a business expense, but must report rent they receive from tenants as income.

99 Richard H. Thaler, "Mental Accounting Matters," in Kahneman and Tversky, *Choices, Values, and Frames*, 241, 242.

100 George Ainslie, "The Dangers of Willpower," in Jon Elster and Ole-Jørgen Skog (eds) *Getting Hooked: Rationality and Addiction*, 65, 74 (Cambridge: Cambridge University Press, 1999).

101 Ibid., 70.

102 Robert Nozick, *Anarchy, State, and Utopia*, 42–43 (New York: Basic Books, 1974).

103 Screening costs are to be distinguished from signaling costs. Screening is the production of information by a promisee about a promisor; signaling refers to the promisor's efforts to persuade the promisee of the promisor's trustworthiness. Various signaling explanations for restrictions on free bargaining have been suggested, but these are technical and highly speculative. See Charles Wilson, "A Model of Insurance Markets with Incomplete Information," *J. Econ. Theory* 16: 167 (1977); Samuel A. Rea, "Arm-breaking, Consumer Credit and Personal Bankruptcy," *Econ. Inquiry* 22: 188 (1984); Philippe Aghion and Benjamin Hermalin, "Legal Restrictions of Private Contracts Can Enhance Efficiency," *J. Law Econ. & Org.* 6: 381 (1990).

104 Richard Hare, "What Is Wrong with Slavery?," *Phil. & Pub. Aff.* 8: 103 (1979).

6 Private perfectionism

1 For recent statements of perfectionism, see Robert P. George, *Making Men Moral* (Oxford: Clarendon, 1993); George Sher, *Beyond Neutrality: Perfectionism and Politics* (Cambridge: Cambridge University Press, 1997).

2 The most prominent modern neutralists are John Rawls and Ronald Dworkin. See John Rawls, *A Theory of Justice*, 94 (Cambridge: Harvard University Press, 1971); "Liberalism," in Ronald Dworkin, *A Matter of Principle*, 181 (Cambridge: Harvard University Press, 1985). Rawls appears to have retreated

from his earlier neutralism in his more recent *Political Liberalism*, 235 (New York: Columbia University Press, 1993). Yet even here Rawls writes that "the government can no more act ... to advance human excellence, or the values of perfection ... than it can act to advance Catholicism or Protestantism, or any other religion." Ibid., 179–80.

3 See, for example, Bruce Ackerman, *Social Justice in the Liberal State*, 368–69 (New Haven: Yale University Press, 1980).

4 Joel Feinberg, *Harmless Wrongdoing*, 305 (New York: Oxford University Press, 1990).

5 Steven Wall, *Liberalism, Perfectionism and Restraint*, ch. 4 (Cambridge: Cambridge University Press, 1998); Steven Wall, "The Structure of Perfectionist Toleration," in Steven Wall and George Klosko (eds) *Perfectionism and Neutrality* (Lanham, MD: Rowman and Littlefield, 2003).

6 For an argument that a Kantian theory of rights is inconsistent with perfectionism, see Thaddeus Metz, "Respect for Persons and Perfectionist Politics," *Phil. & Pub. Aff.* 30: 417 (2002).

7 See David E. Bernstein, *You Can't Say That: The Growing Threat to Civil Liberties from Antidiscrimination Laws*, 85, 104–05, 129–30, 145–53 (Washington: Cato Institute, 2003).

8 Aristotle, *Politics*, iii.5.1280^b (trans. Stephen Everson) (Cambridge: Cambridge University Press, 1996).

9 Sher, *Beyond Neutrality*, 153.

10 Mill, *On Liberty*, 74.

11 Ibid., 81.

12 The idea that perfectionism is compatible with a diversity of goods can be seen in recent scholarship on Aristotle's perfectionist ethics. For a neo-Aristotelian argument that perfectionism might respect agent-relative flourishing requirements, see Douglas B. Rasmussen, "Human Flourishing and the Appeal to Human Nature," in Ellen Paul, Fred D. Miller and Jeffrey Paul (eds) *Human Flourishing*, 1 (Cambridge: Cambridge University Press, 1999).

13 Charles Taylor, "The Diversity of Goods," in Charles Taylor 2 *Philosophy and the Human Sciences: Philosophical Papers*, 230 (Cambridge: Cambridge University Press, 1985).

14 There is an enormous literature on incommensurability, for which Ruth Chang (ed.) *Incommensurability, Incomparability and Practical Reason* (Cambridge: Harvard University Press, 1997) provides a useful introduction. Goods might be incommensurable because they are at the margin and it is difficult to say which lot is better without wasteful mental calculation. Other kinds of goods are incommensurable because of the psychic costs associated with "tragic choices," where we are asked to choose between two things dear to us. Julian Sorel's choice between the red and the black is an example of both kinds of incommensurability.

15 Isaiah Berlin, "John Stuart Mill and the Ends of Life," in *Four Essays on Liberty*, 173, 188 (Oxford: Oxford University Press, 1969). Berlin's value pluralism is ably defended in John Gray, *Two Faces of Liberalism*, ch. 2 (New York: New Press, 2000).

16 Quote reprinted with permission of *THE ONION*. Copyright 2003, by ONION, INC. www.theonion.com.

17 Robert B. Strassler (ed.) *The Landmark Thucydides*, 112 at 2.37.2 (New York: Touchstone, 1996).

18 George, *Making Men Moral*, 37.

19 Cass R. Sunstein, "Preferences and Politics," *Phil. & Pub. Aff.* 20: 3 (1991).

20 Cass R. Sunstein, "On the Expressive Function of Law," *U. Pa. L. Rev.* 144: 2021 (1996).

21 Richard Herrnstein and Drazen Prelec, "A Theory of Addiction," in George Lowenstein and Jon Elster (eds) *Choice over Time*, 331 (New York: Russell Sage Foundation, 1992).
22 In his indifference to morality, David Lurie is so very much a symbol of modernity than many moderns will fail to recognize his moral disintegration and find the book puzzling. In fiction, Lurie most closely resembles Camus' Meursault in L'Étranger, another novel that confuses the modern reader.
23 Aristotle, *Nicomachean Ethics*, 1125a.
24 Joseph Conrad, *Heart of Darkness*, 24 (New York: Everyman's, 1993).
25 Joseph Raz, *The Morality of Freedom*, 420–23 (Oxford: Clarendon, 1986).
26 In addition, the last people who can complain about the perfectionism implicit in the law of illegality are anarchists like Murray Rothbard who regard legal enforceability of licit contracts as an improper exercise of state power. For them the problem is the legal contracts that are enforced, not the illegal ones that are not. In their world, all contracts would be treated as illegal.
27 See e.g. John Finnis, *Natural Law and Natural Rights*, chs 3 and 4 (Oxford: Oxford University Press, 1980).
28 About 40 percent of Americans were born in another state than the one they live in. Kristin A. Hansen, *1990 Selected Place of Birth and Migration Statistics for States*, Bureau of the Census CPH-L-121, Table 1. Another 10 percent are foreign-born.
29 Charles M. Tiebout, "A Pure Theory of Local Expenditures," *J. Pol. Econ.* 64: 416 (1956).
30 *Gregory v. Ashcroft*, 111 S. Ct. 2395, 2399 (1991). See further Albert Breton, *The Economic Theory of Representative Government*, 114 (Chicago: Aldine, 1974).
31 Mill himself would likely have favored such zoning restrictions, as he accepted similar arguments for mandatory employment laws. Here, as elsewhere, Mill was something less than a thoroughgoing libertarian.
32 *Boy Scouts of America v. Dale*, 120 S. Ct. 2446 (2000).
33 Gregory S. Alexander, *Commodity and Propriety: Competing Visions of Property in Early American Legal Thought 1776–1970* (Chicago: Chicago, 1997).

7 Social perfectionism

1 Ronald Coase, "The Problem of Social Cost," *J. Law & Econ.* 3: 1 (1960).
2 Charles Taylor, "Atomism," in Charles Taylor, *Philosophy and the Human Sciences: Philosophical Papers*, 207 (Cambridge: Cambridge University Press, 1985).
3 Richard Arneson, "The Principle of Fairness and Free-Rider Problems," *Ethics* 92: 616, 621 (1982).
4 More technically, the efficient amount of public goods is produced when the (marginal) cost of one more unit of good would exceed the additional (marginal) benefit, and this might happen where the costs of production are entirely borne by one person and the benefits are shared with the public. David D. Haddock, "Irrelevant Internalities, Irrelevant Externalities, and Irrelevant Anxieties," Northwestern University School of Law Research Paper 03–16 (August 14, 2003).
5 If envy is defined more broadly as a concern for relative preferences, for how we compare with the neighbors, it might have a positive side. As a spur to competition, to "keeping up with the Joneses," it combats a natural indolence. For a debate over whether status competitions of this kind might nevertheless reduce happiness levels and justify luxury or consumption taxes,

see Robert H. Frank, *Luxury Fever: Money and Happiness in an Era of Excess* (Princeton: Princeton University Press, 1999) and Richard A. Epstein, *Skepticism and Freedom: A Modern Case for Classical Liberalism*, ch. 7 (Chicago: University of Chicago Press, 2003).

6 Max Weber, *The Protestant Ethic and the Spirit of Capitalism*, 57 (trans. Talcott Parsons) (New York: Scribner's, 1958).

7 Jules Coleman, "Efficiency, Utility, and Wealth Maximization," *Hofstra L. Rev.* 8: 509 (1980).

8 *Allen* v. *Rescous*, 2 Lev. 174 (1676) (contract to assault a third party).

9 2 M. & W. 149 (1836).

10 *Archbolds (Freightage), Ltd.* v. *Spanglett, Ltd.* [1961] 1 Q.B. 374 (C.A.).

11 *Vita Food Products* v. *Unus Shipping Co.* [1939] A.C. 277, 293.

12 108 N.Y.S.2d 597 (Sup. Ct., 1951).

13 *Shaw* v. *D.P.P*, [1962] A.C. 220, 268 (creating a new criminal offence of a conspiracy to corrupt public morals).

14 *Garforth* v. *Fearon*, 1 Hy. Bl. 328 (1787).

15 *Porter* v. *Freudenberg*, [1915] 1 K.B. 857.

16 In re Baby M, 537 A.2d 1227, 1249 (N.J. Sup. Ct., 1987). The contract was in implicit violation of New Jersey's adoption statutes, but the court dealt with it under the broader purview of public policy. Not much turned on this, however. In awarding custody, the court took into account the difference in status between the parties and gave the baby to the yuppy buyers.

17 Elisabeth M. Landes and Richard A. Posner, "The Economics of the Baby Shortage," *J. Legal Stud.* 7: 323, 343 (1978). Judge Posner returned to the fray in "The Regulation of the Market in Adoptions," *B.U. L. Rev.* 67: 59 (1987).

18 L.R. 1 Ex. 213 (1866).

19 *Hewitt* v. *Hewitt*, 394 N.E.2d 1204 (Ill. Sup. Ct., 1979).

20 *Marvin* v. *Marvin*, 134 Cal. Rptr.815 (1976) (awarding "palimony").

21 Walter Berns, "Pornography vs. Democracy: The Case for Censorship," *The Public Interest* 22: 19–20 (1971).

22 Mill, *On Liberty*, 79.

23 Ibid., 87.

24 Ibid., 80.

25 Ibid., 67, 58, 56.

26 Francis Fukuyama, *The Great Disruption*, 42–46 (New York: Free Press, 1999).

28 Patrick Devlin, *The Enforcement of Morals* (London: Oxford University Press, 1965); H.L.A. Hart, *Law, Liberty, and Morality* (London, Oxford University Press, 1962).

29 Devlin, *Enforcement of Morals*, 111.

30 Ibid., 110.

31 Hart, *Law, Liberty, and Morality*, 17, 29, 50, 51, 52.

32 Benedict Anderson, *Imagined Communities* (London: Verso, 1991).

33 "L'oubli, et je dirai même l'erreur historique, sont un facteur essentiel de la creation d'une nation." Ernest Renan, *Que'est-ce que une nation?* 13 (Paris: Mille et un nuits, 1997).

33 Devlin, *Enforcement of Morals*, at 17.

34 The term is Joel Feinberg's, though he used it in a different way, to designate evils that really do not hurt anyone else, such as evil thoughts. Joel Feinberg, *Harmless Wrongdoing*, 79 (Oxford: Oxford University Press, 1990).

35 George, *Making Men Moral*, 65–71.

36 Alan Wolfe, *One Nation After All* (East Rutherford, NJ: Penguin USA, 1999).

37 James Fitzjames Stephen, *Liberty, Equality, Fraternity*, 13 (Indianapolis: Liberty Fund, 1993).

38 See Robert C. Solomon, "The Virtues of a Passionate Life: Erotic Love and 'The Will to Power,'" in Ellen Frankel Paul, Fred D. Miller and Jeffrey Paul, *Virtue and Vice*, 91 (Cambridge: Cambridge, 1998); Robert C. Solomon, *The Joy of Philosophy: Thinking Thin* versus *the Passionate Life*, 65 ff. (New York: Oxford University Press, 1999).

39 Dire d'un homme colère, inégal, querelleux, chagrin, pointilleux, capricieux: 'c'est son humeur' n'est pas l'excuser, comme on le croit, mais avouer sans y penser que de si grands défauts sont irrémédiables." Jean de La Bruyère, *Les characters*, 232 (L'homme 9) (Paris: Gallimard, 1975).

40 Edmund Burke, *Reflections on the Revolution in France*, 87, 81 (Oxford: Oxford, 1993).

41 Leon Kass, "The Wisdom of Repugnance," *The New Republic*, June 2, 1997, reprinted in Leon R. Kass and James Q. Wilson, *The Ethics of Human Cloning*, 19 (Washington: AEI, 1998).

42 For the view that the emotions can be seen as a form of thought, see Robert C. Solomon, *The Passions: Emotions and the Meaning of Life* (Indianapolis: Hackett, 1993); Martha C. Nussbaum, *The Therapy of Desire* (Princeton: Princeton University Press, 1994); Martha C. Nussbaum, *The Fragility of Goodness: Luck and Ethics in Greek Tragedy and Philosophy* (Cambridge: Cambridge, 1986). A mildly dissenting view is offered in Richard Wollheim, *On the Emotions*, 116 (New Haven: Yale University Press, 1999).

43 François Truffaut, *Jules et Jim*, 108 (Paris: Seuil, 1971).

44 The evidence is reviewed in David Popenoe, *Life Without Father*, 52–78 (Cambridge: Harvard University Press, 1999).

45 Mavis Hetherington, Martha Cox and Roger Cox, "Long-term Effects of Divorce and Remarriage on the Adjustment of Children," *J. Amer. Academy of Child Psychiatry* 24: 518 (1985).

46 See Sara McLanahan and Irwin Garfinkel, "Single Mothers, the Underclass, and Social Policy," 501 Annals, AAPSS 92, 98–99 (1989) (reporting that 18 percent of single mothers in 1987 had been dependent on welfare for ten or more years); Irwin Garfinkel and Sara S. McLanahan, *Single Mothers and Their Children: A New American Dilemma*, (Washington: Urban Institute, 1986).

47 See Barbara Dafoe Whitehead, *The Divorce Culture* (New York: Alfred Knopf, 1997), reprising her earlier article, "Dan Quayle Was Right: Harmful Effects of Divorce on Children," *Atlantic* 271: 47 (1993). For a summary of the literature, see David Blankenhorn, *Fatherless America* (New York: Basic Books, 1995).

48 765 F. Supp. 181, 183 (D. N.J.), rev'd, 958 F.2d 1242 (3d Cir. 1992).

49 Wesley R. Smith, "Don't Stand So Close to Me: Judges Are Giving Neighborhoods a Bum Rap," *Policy Rev.* 70: 48 (Fall 1994).

50 765 F. Supp. at 183.

51 Ronald Dworkin, "Liberalism," in *A Matter of Principle*, 181 (Cambridge: Harvard University Press, 1985).

52 David Hume, "Idea of a Perfect Commonwealth," in Eugene F. Miller (ed.) *Essays, Moral, Political, and Literary*, 512, 514 (Indianapolis: Liberty Fund, 1987).

53 Sigmund Freud, *Civilization and its Discontents*, 69–70 (trans. J. Strachey) (New York: Norton, 1961).

54 Harold Demsetz, "Information and Efficiency: Another Viewpoint," *J. L. & Econ.* 12: 1 (1969).

55 Hart, *Law, Liberty, and Morality*, 12.

56 *Shaw* v. *D.P.P*, [1962] A.C. 220. Nor does it follow that political speech rights are better protected when pornographers are free to do their thing.

Recent American constitutional experience shows that political speech may be curbed in the name of campaign finance reform even where courts display a deep solicitude for the pornographer's free speech rights.

57 Devlin, *Enforcement of Morals*, 19, 16.

58 On slippery slopes, see Eugene Volokh, "The Mechanisms of the Slippery Slope," *Harv. L. Rev.* 116: 1026 (2003); Mario J. Rizzo and Douglas G. Whitman, "The Camel's Nose Is in the Tent: Rules, Theories, and Slippery Slopes," *UCLA L. Rev.* 51: 539 (2003).

8 Substantive fairness

1 William Jevons, *The Theory of Political Economy* (5th edn, 1957) [1871]. More technically, for parties A and B and any two goods x_1 and x_2, then in equilibrium:

$$MU_1A/MU_2A = -dx_2/dx_1 = MU_1B/MU_2B$$

where MU_NP is the marginal utility of good x_N to party P; dx_1 is the amount of good x_1 given by A to B; and dx_2 is the amount of good x_2 given by B to A.

2 John von Neumann and Oscar Morgenstern, *Theory of Games and Economic Behavior*, 240–42 (1944); John Nash, "The Bargaining Problem," *Econometrica* 18: 155 (1950); John Nash, "Two-Person Cooperative Games," *Econometrica* 21: 128 (1953).

3 More technically, cardinality means that bargaining solutions are invariant under positive, linear transformations of the form

$$V(A) = aU(A) + b, \qquad a > 0$$

where $V(A)$ is the value of the game to A, $U(A)$ is the value of his utility, and a and b are constants. Transformation-invariance need not entail interpersonal comparability. On some bargaining theories, each party decides whether to claim or concede an outcome solely by reference to his own utility level. Since he need not know the other party's utility, interpersonal utility comparisons are unnecessary. For adjudication or arbitration to work, however, the third party judge or arbitrator must know both parties' utility levels, and this assumes both cardinality and interpersonal comparability. See John Harsanyi, *Rational Behavior and Bargaining Equilibrium in Games and Social Situations*, 13–15, 191–93 (Cambridge: Cambridge University Press, 1977).

4 David Gautier, *Morals by Agreement*, 150–51 (Oxford: Oxford University Press, 1986). For two-person bargaining games, Gauthier's solution is identical to that suggested in Ehud Kalai and Meir Smorodinsky, "Other Solutions to Nash's Bargaining Problem," *Econometrica* 43: 513 (1975).

5 Innkeepers exercise a public or "common" calling, which imposes on them the status obligation to lodge and entertain guests for reasonable compensation. *Thompson* v. *Lacy*, 106 Eng. Rep. 667, 668 (1820).

6 William M. Landes and Richard A. Posner, "Salvors, Finders, Good Samaritans, and Other Rescuers: An Economic Study of Law and Altruism," *J. Legal Stud.* 7: 83 (1978).

7 Experimental studies report that hard bargainers outperform their rivals, at least for those agreements that are reached. Sidney Siegel and Lawrence E. Fouraker, *Bargaining and Group Decision Making Experiments in Bilateral Monopoly*, 60–69, 82–85, 99 (New York: McGraw Hill, 1960).

8 Alvin E. Roth, "Toward a Focal Point Theory of Bargaining," in Alvin E. Roth (ed.) *Game-Theoretic Models of Bargaining*, 259, 265–67 (Cambridge: Cambridge University Press, 1985).

9 Max Weber, *The Protestant Ethic and the Spirit of Capitalism*, 57 (New York: Scribner's, 1958).

10 Ian Macneil, *The New Social Contract: An Inquiry into Modern Contractual Relations*, 44–47 (New Haven: Yale University Press, 1980). See also Stewart Macaulay, "Non-contractual Relations in Business: A Preliminary Study," *Am. Soc. Rev.* 28: 55, 61 (1963).

11 For overviews, see Colin F. Camerer, *Behavioral Game Theory*, 154–55 (Princeton: Princeton University Press, 2003); John H. Hagel and Alvin E. Roth, *The Handbook of Experimental Economics*, 254–92 (Princeton: Princeton University Press, 1995); Alvin E. Roth, "Laboratory Experimentation in Economics: A Methodological Overview," *Econ. J.* 98: 974, 979–83 (1988).

12 Experimenters rely on lottery tickets in order to control for uncertainties over the bargainers' utility functions. Were the parties to negotiate for the prizes themselves and not for tickets for the prizes, the Gauthier and Nash solutions would both depend on how much each party valued the prize. The valuation problem would make it difficult to verify the solution, unless it were arbitrarily assumed that utilities are linear with money. When the players bargain for lottery tickets, on the other hand, outcomes are less sensitive to differences in utility functions, and the probability of receiving a prize might serve as a proxy for the utility gain.

13 Alvin E. Roth and Michael Malouf, "Game-theoretic Models and the Role of Information in Bargaining," *Psych. Rev.* 86: 574 (1979). Bargainers who were informed about their opponents' monetary payoffs were found to react differently than bargainers whose information was limited to artificial commodities (with the lottery tickets paid off in "chips"). Alvin E. Roth, Michael Malouf and J. Keith Murnighan, "Sociological Versus Strategic Factors in Bargaining," *J. Econ. Behav. & Org.* 2: 153, 174 (1981).

14 Thomas Schelling, *The Strategy of Conflict* (Cambridge: Harvard University Press, 1960).

15 Daniel Kahneman, Jack L. Knetsch and Richard Thaler, "Fairness and the Assumptions of Economics," *J. Bus.* 59: S285 (1986); Werner Guth, Rolf Schmittberger and Bernd Schwarze, "An Experimental Analysis of Ultimatum Bargaining," *J. Econ. Behav. & Org.* 3: 367 (1982).

16 Elizabeth Hoffman and Matthew Spitzer, "The Coase Theorem: Some Experimental Tests," *J. L. & Econ.* 25: 73 (1982).

17 Robert Forsythe, Joel L. Horowitz, N.E. Savin and Martin Sefton, "Fairness in Simple Bargaining Experiments," *Games and Econ. Beh.* 6: 347 (1994).

18 Alvin Roth, "Bargaining Experiments," in Hagel and Roth, *Handbook*, 253, 294–98 (face-to-face negotiations); Werner Guth and Reinhard Teitz, "Ultimatum Bargaining for a Shrinking Cake – An Experimental Analysis," in R. Teitz, W. Albers and R. Selten, (eds) *Bounded Rational Behavior in Experimental Games and Markets* (Berlin: Springer, 1988) (repeated ultimatum game).

19 See Alan L. Olmstead and Paul W. Rhode, "Rationing Without Government: The West Coast Gas Famine of 1920," *Am. Econ. Rev.* 75: 1044, 1052–53 (1985) (describing the West Coast gasoline shortage of 1920, where oil companies refrained from raising prices because they were concerned with a public outcry over price increases that were not caused by increased costs). See also Daniel Kahneman, Jack L. Knetsch and Richard H. Thaler, "Fairness as a Constraint on Profit Seeking: Entitlements in the Market," in Kahneman and Tversky, *Choices, Values, and Frames*, 317 (Cambridge: Cambridge University Press, 2000).

20 Robert Frank, *Passions Within Reason: The Strategic Role of the Emotions*, 177–78 (New York: Norton, 1988).

21 Don L. Coursey, "Bilateral Bargaining, Pareto Optimality, and the Empirical Frequency of Impasse," *J. Econ. Behav. & Org.* 3: 243 (1982) (finding a greater number of disagreements when negotiation time was shortened).
22 Jack Ochs and Alvin E. Roth, "An Experimental Study of Sequential Bargaining," *Am. Econ. Rev.* 79: 355, 378–80 (1989).
23 Restatement (Second) of Contracts § 176(1)(a).
24 *Union Pacific Ry.* v. *Public Serv. Comm'n*, 248 U.S. 67, 70 (1918).
25 See Restatement (Second) of Contracts § 175 comment a.
26 60 U.S. (19 How.) 150 (1856).
27 The masters of the victim and one of the rescuers were brothers, and this might have led the court to suspect a side payment between them. In addition, counsel for the cargo owners suggested that the master of the victim was in shock at the time of the agreement. However, the court abstained from making any findings about these issues.
28 Ibid., 152.
29 See Grant Gilmore and Charles Black, *The Law of Admiralty*, 581 (Mineola, NY: Foundation Press, 2nd edn, 1975).
30 86 F. 675, 684 (2d Cir. 1898).
31 Supra note 5 of this chapter.
32 *Harbutt's "Plasticine" Ltd.* v. *Wayne Tank Co.*, [1970] 1 Q.B. 447 (C.A.); *Williams* v. *Walker-Thomas Furniture Co.*, 194 A.2d 914, 916 (D.C. 1964); *Mister Broadloom Corp. (1968) Ltd.* v. *Bank of Montreal*, 44 O.R. (2d) 368 (1983).
33 Alan Schwartz and Louis Wilde, "Intervening in Markets on the Basis of Imperfect Information: A Legal and Economic Analysis," *U. Pa. L. Rev.* 127: 630, 655 (1979).
34 92 Eng. Rep. 270 (1705).
35 83 Eng. Rep. 323 (1664).
36 Friedrich Kessler, "Contracts of Adhesion – Some Thoughts about Freedom of Contract," *Colum. L. Rev.* 43: 629, 633 (1943).
37 Michael J. Trebilcock, "The Doctrine of Inequality of Bargaining Power," *U. Toronto L.J.* 26: 359 (1976).
38 Thus $P_V(x) > 0$, $P_V^x < 0$, and $P_V^x > 0$; and $P_R(y) > 0$, $P_R^y > 0$, and $P_R^{yy} < 0$.
39 To minimize the function $C(x,y)$, the partial derivatives, $C[x]$ and $C[y]$, are set to zero. Further, it is assumed that $C^{xx} > 0$ and $C^{yy} > 0$, ensuring that the values which satisfy (2) and (3) are local minimas and not maximas.
40 For simplicity we assume that all attempted rescues succeed. Were it otherwise, and rescuers were unable to recover on a failed rescue, the salvage award for a successful rescue would have to be increased.

9 Contractarian virtue

1 Joseph Schumpeter, *Capitalism, Socialism and Democracy* (New York: Perennial, 1962) [1942]; Daniel Bell, *The Cultural Contradictions of Capitalism* (New York: Basic, 1976).
2 George Fitzhugh, "Sociology for the South," reprinted in David A. Hollinger and Charles Capper (eds), *I The American Intellectual Tradition: A Sourcebook*, 470, 473 (New York: Oxford University Press, 3rd edn, 2001). Fitzhugh's book was an apology for slavery.
3 George Steiner, *The Death of Tragedy*, 77 (New Haven: Yale, 1996) [1961].
4 Montesquieu, *II Œuvres complètes, Esprit des lois* V.6, 280 (Paris: Pléiade, 1951).
5 "La guerre et le commerce ne sont que deux moyens différents au meme but: celui de posséder ce que l'on désire. ... C'est l'expérience qui, en lui

prouvant que ... l'emploi de sa force ... est exposée a divers résistances et à divers échecs, le porte à recourir au commerce, c'est-à-dire à un moyen plus doux et plus sûr d'engager l'intérêt des autres à ce qui convient à son intérêt." Benjamin Constant, "De l'esprit de conquête," in *Écrits politiques*, 130 (Paris: Gallimard, 1997).

6 "C'est presque une règle générale, que partout où il y a des moeurs douces il y a du commerce; et que partout où il y a du commerce il y a des moeurs douce." Montesquieu, *Esprit des lois* XX.1, 585.

7 Adam Smith, *The Wealth of Nations Books I–III*, III.iv, 508 (London: Penguin, 1999).

8 Thomas L. Friedman, *The Lexus and the Olive Tree*, 248–49 (New York: Anchor, 2001).

9 Schumpeter, *Capitalism, Socialism, and Democracy*, 137.

10 Bell's complaints were echoed two years later in Irving Kristol's *Two Cheers for Capitalism* (New York: Basic Books, 1978).

11 Stephen Holmes, *The Anatomy of Antiliberalism*, 217 (Cambridge: Harvard University Press, 1993).

12 *Victorian Railways Comm.* v. *Coultas*, 13 App. Cas. 222 (P.C. 1888).

13 Paul H. Rubin, "Courts and the Tort-Contract Boundary in Products Liability," in F.H. Buckley, *The Fall and Rise of Freedom of Contract*, 119, 125 (Durham: Duke University Press, 1999); John E. Calfee and Paul H. Rubin, "Some Implications of Damage Payments for Nonpecuniary Losses," *J. Legal Stud.* 21: 371 (1992).

14 Burke also emphasized the importance of the bequest motive. "The power of perpetuating our property in our families is one of the most valuable and interesting circumstances belonging to it, and that which tends most to the perpetuation of society itself." Edmund Burke, 102 "Reflections on the Revolution in France," in 8 *The Writings and Speeches of Edmund Burke* (Oxford: Oxford University Press, 1989).

15 Bell, *Cultural Contradictions*, 55.

16 Ibid., 70.

17 "What on Earth?," *Washington Post*, September 11, 1999, A15.

18 Robert Putnam, *Bowling Alone* (New York: Simon and Schuster, 2001); Alan Ehrenhalt, *The Lost City: The Forgotten Virtues of Community in America* (New York: Basic Books, 1996).

19 Everett C. Ladd, *The Ladd Report* (New York: Free Press, 1999).

20 Margaret F. Brinig and F.H. Buckley, "No-Fault Laws and At-Fault People," *Int. Rev. Law & Econ.* 18: 325 (1998); F.H. Buckley and Margaret F. Brinig, "The Bankruptcy Puzzle," *J. Legal Stud.* 27: 187 (1998).

21 Alexis de Tocqueville, *II Democracy in America*, 114 (New York: Vintage, 1990).

22 The literature on the subject is vast. Particularly useful are: Stephen Holmes, *The Anatomy of Antiliberalism* (Cambridge: Harvard University Press, 1993); Jerry Z. Muller, *The Mind and the Market: Capitalism in Modern European Thought* (New York: Knopf, 2002). For a highly readable discussion of the many meanings of Romanticism, see Isaiah Berlin, *The Roots of Romanticism* (Princeton: Princeton University Press, 1999).

23 Benjamin Barber, *Jihad vs. McWorld: How Globalism and Tribalism Are Reshaping the World* (New York: Ballantine, 1996); John Gray, *False Dawn: The Delusion of Global Capitalism* (New York: New Press, 1998).

24 See Michael Novak, *The Spirit of Democratic Capitalism* (New York: Touchstone, 1982).

25 "Entrez dans la Bourse de Londres, cette place plus respectable que bien des cours; vous y vovez rassemblés les députés de toutes les nations pour utilité

des hommes. Là, le juif, le mahométan et le chrétien traitent l'un avec l'autre comme s'ils étaient de la même religion, et ne donnent le nom d'infidèles qu'à ceux qui font banqueroute." Voltaire, *Mélanges, Lettres philosophiques* 17–18 (sixth letter) (Paris: Pléiade, 1961).

26 Benjamin Franklin, *Autobiography*, 111 (Oxford: Oxford World's Classics, 1993).

27 Weber, *Protestant Ethic*, 181–82. Weber's identification of the commercial spirit with Puritanism was anticipated by Matthew Arnold, whose business-minded "Philistines" were religious dissenters in the Puritan tradition. Matthew Arnold, *Culture and Anarchy* (Cambridge: Cambridge University Press, 1993) [1869].

28 Weber, *Protestant Ethic*, 69, 182.

29 Werner Sombart, *Economic Life in the Modern Age*, 6 (New Brunswick: Transaction, 2001), originally published as "Capitalism," in Edwin R. Seligman and Alvin Johnson (eds) *Encyclopedia of the Social Sciences III*, 195 (New York: Macmillan, 1930).

30 Ibid., 7.

31 Weber, *Protestant Ethic*, 56–57. In a study of cooperation habits in West Germany and the former East Germany, it was found that eastern subjects behaved in a considerably more selfish manner than western subjects. Axel Ockenfels and J. Weinmann, "Types and Patterns – An Experimental East–West Comparison of Cooperation and Solidarity," *J. Pub. Econ.* 71: 275 (1999).

32 The teenage rebel who ridicules his parent's bourgeois values will find that he has been anticipated by Sombart's distinction between the aristocratic *homme ouvert* and the bourgeois *homme clos*. Sombart, *Economic Life*, 42 ("The Origins of the Capitalist Spirit"). Modern critics of liberalism, individualism and markets might profitably study the literature of fascism, which was at least as sophisticated as more recent attacks on modernity, and often a good deal more so. As Zeev Sternhell notes, a shared contempt for liberal democracy made it easier for the Germans to co-opt left-wing intellectuals such as Emmanuel Mounier in occupied France. Mounier woke up in 1940 and discovered that he and his new masters agreed on a surprising number of things. Zeev Sternhell, *Ni droite ni gauche: L'idéologie fasciste en France*, 437, 470–83 (Paris: Fayard, 3rd edn, 2000).

33 Sombart, *Economic Life*, 9.

34 " 'Quoi! Pas un mot des besoins de la société, rien de civilisant et de progressif!' ... Non, imbéciles, non crétins et goitreux que vous êtes, un livre ne fait pas de la soupe a la gélatine; un roman n'est pas une paire de bottes sans couture; un sonnet, une seringue à jet continu; un drame n'est pas un chemin de fer ... L'utilité spirituelle est que, pendant qu'on lit des romans, on dort, et on ne lit pas des journaux utiles, vertueux et progressifs . . . ." Théophile Gautier, *Mademoiselle de Maupin*, Préface 63–65 (Pairs: Livre de poche, 1994).

35 "Dann am kalten Gestade / Bei den Deinen und kennst sie nie."

36 Paul-Jean Toulet, *Les contrerimes*, 93 (Chansons: Romances sans musique I) (Paris: Gallimard, 1979).

37 "Je vous plains, monsieur, d'être si facilement heureux." Charles Baudelaire, *II Œuvres complètes* (Paris: Pléiade, 1976).

38 "Le jeune fasciste dans son camp, au milieu des camarades de la paix qui peuvent être les camarades de la guerre, le jeune fasciste qui chante, qui marche, qui travaille, qui rêve, il est tout d'abord un être joyeux." Robert Brasillach, *Les sept couleurs*, 207 (Paris: Livre de Poche, 1965) [1939]. On Fascism as an aesthetic movement, see George L. Mosse, *The Fascist Revolution: Toward a General Theory of Fascism*, ch. 2 (New York: Howard Fertig, 1999).

39 Herbert Marcuse, *One-Dimensional Man: Studies in the Ideology of Advanced Industrial Societies* (Boston: Beacon, 1964). Marcuse argued that conservative ideas should not be tolerated and that America would be more democratic if governed by progressive intellectuals. Herbert Marcuse, "Repressive Tolerance," in Robert P. Wolff, B. Moore and H. Marcuse, *A Critique of Pure Tolerance*, 81 (Boston: Beacon, 1969).

40 Leon Battista Alberti, *The Family in Renaissance Florence, Book Three* (trans. Renée New Watkins) (Prospect Heights, IL: Waveland, 1994).

41 "L'abondance à la ronde, Mère des arts et des heureux travaux." Voltaire, *Le mondain*, lines 14–15 (1736).

42 See Colin Platt, *Marks of Excellence: The Why, When and Where of Western Art 1100–1900 AD* (London: HarperCollins, 2004); Tyler Cowen, *In Praise of Commercial Culture*, ch. 3 (Cambridge: Harvard University Press, 1998).

Index